# FABRIC
# DYEING &
# PRINTING

Right: Georgina von Etzdorf's highly popular designs combine the qualities of colour and texture.

Previous page: Cressida Bell uses simple motifs with a screen printing technique for the dramatic effect on this scarf.

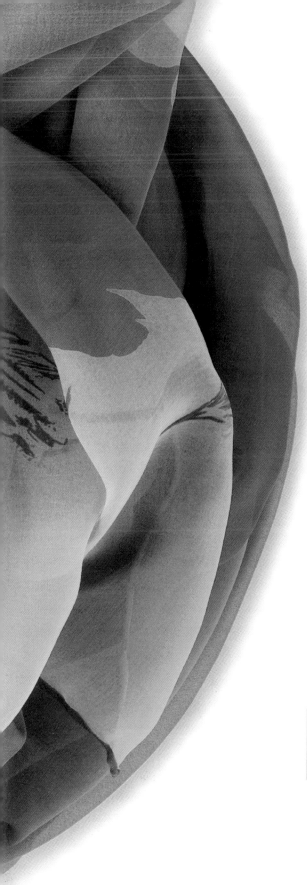

# FABRIC DYEING & PRINTING

## KATE WELLS

conran
OCTOPUS

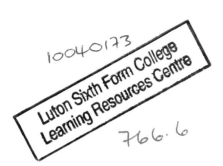

First published in 1997 by Conran Octopus Limited,
37 Shelton Street, London, WC2H 9HN

Reprinted in 1998

**Editorial Director:** Suzannah Gough

**Senior Editor:** Catriona Woodburn

**Editorial Assistant:** Paula Hardy

**Copy Editors:** Andrew Anderson,
Peter Bentley, Helen Wire

**Art Editor:** Paul Griffin

**Location and Step Photography:** Peter Kinnear

**Fabric Photography:** Mary-Rose Loyd

**Picture Researcher:** Jo Alexander

**Production Manager:** Julia Golding

Printed in Hong Kong

## SAFETY IN YOUR STUDIO

The art of patterning fabrics with dyes is a form of chemistry and this should always be remembered. Many textile dyes and auxiliaries are harmless when handled with care, but some are dangerous and I have indicated in the relevant text any extra precautions that should be taken. It is important to wear protective clothing, including gloves and an apron, and maintain good standards of working and cleanliness when handling and storing any of these products. Keep the studio area clean, tidy and free of obstructions on the floor and other surfaces. When weighing out and mixing dyes and patterning pastes, cover the work surface with paper that can be thrown away if dye powder is spilt.

Dye and chemical suppliers are required by law to issue safety sheets with all their products. These should be requested when buying a dye or chemical for the first time, as they will inform you of any hazards that should be protected against. Suppliers are legally bound to update this information and I would recommend checking about once a year. If in doubt contact the manufacturer for advice.

As a general guide, avoid any risk of ingestion, prohibit smoking, and do not consume or prepare food or drinks in the areas where dyes and chemicals are prepared or used. The reverse also applies. I do not recommend using a kitchen for the dyeing of cloth, or the mixing and use of patterning pastes. To prevent inhalation of any dust or fumes good ventilation is important. Wear an appropriate respirator when dealing with powders, dyes or solvents. If possible, buy your dyes in a granular or liquid state. Any dyes, auxiliaries or chemicals that come into contact with the skin should be washed off immediately with cold water. To prevent any liquid or dust getting into the eyes, wear protective goggles. In the event of an incident, wash the eye with clean cold water and seek medical attention immediately. Keep a well-stocked first-aid box in the studio area in case of small accidents.

Check with your doctor should any allergic reactions occur as a result of using dyes and chemicals. Some substances are potentially harmful and extra care should be taken during pregnancy.

# CONTENTS

Below: Simple motifs such as spots and stripes can be employed to great effect. Using delicate pastel shades, Sally Weatherill handpainted the pattern onto a silk base giving the design a luxurious finish.

# INTRODUCTION

*Decorating is a natural instinct. We have done it since time immemorial, both in our homes and to enhance our bodies in one way or another. Pattern-making is very rewarding and different cultures attempt it in very different ways, but one of the most common has been to use printing and dyeing methods. Some are very time-consuming whilst others are fast – but all achieve exciting and endlessly varied results.*

*Some of the more traditional techniques such as block, lino and potato printing are in danger of being lost whilst others such as batik, tie-and-dye, and screen printing are constantly being revived and revitalized with new results and applications. All, at one time or another, are being used somewhere around the world. It is a constant joy to see so many examples of techniques available everywhere. The processes are not always reliable: different climates and different weather conditions can affect the same technique. We can never cease to be surprised at the possibilities and changes that each process offers. The industry can often be daunted by trying to repeat a particular effect, whilst craftspeople may push for greater variety from piece to piece.*

*This book gives an introduction to all the processes – whether the user is a student at college or school, a knowledgeable printer or dyer starting a hobby, or a designer setting-up a more serious business. There is something in it for each of us.*

*In England, the 20th century has seen a number of highly enterprising people turn their interest into a living. Laura Ashley transferred her ideas from teacloths printed as a hobby on a kitchen table with the simplest of techniques into a multi-million pound business. Zandra Rhodes has taken her own personal style of decoration into fashion and the home. Helen David of English Eccentrics has made her many and varied approaches to design enhance not only the scarf, but also many fashion collections. Georgina von Etzdorf has made printing more tactile and exciting for accessories, whilst Tricia Guild at Designer's Guild has, through her management of colour, styling and pattern-making, revitalized our approach to furnishing and interior decoration. Timney Fowler is known for producing bold furnishings, using black and white as a basis for their work.*

*From earlier in the century, William Morris, Enid Marx, Barron and Larcher, and Fortuny, have all inspired us. They have given us not only a tremendous sense of pattern-making skills but have also, in the case of Fortuny, pointed a way forward to achieve very rich and sumptuous effects with velvets, silks and brocades.*

*All these designers have experimented, all have struggled with different ways of working. This book takes a look at printing and dyeing in all its forms – and the possibilities are infinite. Kate Wells has made it her ambition to explore these possibilities. Working with dyes has given her enormous satisfaction over the years and here she shares her tremendous knowledge and experience, to enable us either to explore fabric patterning as a hobby or take it further into a career. Perhaps this book will inspire and help to start many new business ventures, both big and small, in the future. She has certainly inspired me with her boundless enthusiasm, drive and determination.*

PROFESSOR JOHN MILES
Head of School of Fashion and Textiles,
Royal College of Art

Opposite: Jonathan Fuller's psychedelic
design on viscose rayon was created
using reactive dyes in a photoscreen
print combined with simple paper stencils.

# 1

# THE EVOLUTION OF PATTERN FABRICS

Man's desire to decorate his environment has been evident since the very earliest periods of civilization. Basic printing techniques and dyes were first applied in patterning directly onto the human body, but with the production of crude fabrics such colouring and patterning methods were soon transferred to cloth.

Traditionally, decorated textiles employed colorants that were applied using dyeing, painting or printing techniques. There were two main types of coloration. The first was the production of an image by the application of the colorants directly to the surface of the cloth. The second relied upon the production of designs through resist dyeing processes (see chapter 13), in which case the patterning occurred where the resist had been applied. Throughout the history of decorated textiles, the success of both methods relied upon the discovery of substances which were colour fast (i.e. where the colour would not wash out of the fabric). As a result, the evolution of dye and patterning techniques have tended to run in parallel, with many decorative techniques following close behind the discovery of a new dye, fibre or manufacturing process.

### The First Examples of Printing Techniques

Basic patterning techniques have been used for ornamentation since the Palaeolithic period, dating as far

back as 20,000 BC. Some of the first known examples of patterning date from this period, and include the images of human hands and drawings of animals which were found on the cave walls of El Castillo and Altamira in Spain and the Pech-Merle grotto in France. Many of the drawings of animals were created using a series of dots applied with a stick, while the images of hands were produced by blowing ochre around the hand. These images are probably the first known examples of stencil printing.

By the Neolithic Era (2,000 BC), small blocks made out of dried clay or terracotta were used for patterning the body. The blocks are known as pintaderas, from the Spanish *pintado*, meaning mottled, (itself from *pintar*, to paint). Pintaderas are generally made from terracotta, with one flat side incised with geometric patterns and the other formed into a handle of sorts. They are still used today among the primitive tribes of the Gran Chaco in central South America and the Dyaks of Borneo. These tribes stamp their skin with repeat designs using coloured pastes made from ochre and mud.

**Above: An Amazon woman painstakingly decorates a girl's body. Complex designs can take many hours to complete.**

### Early Dyes

As techniques in painting and printing cloth developed, the processes of dyeing also evolved. During the Neolithic age, certain minerals and plants were discovered that would produce limited coloured stains upon fabric. Creams, fawns and browns were then obtained from the tannic

**Left: This prehistoric cave painting shows a negative image, created by blowing ochre around a hand.**

**Right: Plant dyes, like the henna used in this Indian hand design, have been used for centuries to beautify the body.**

substances contained in the barks, seeds and stalks of plants, while yellows, oranges and reds were acquired from the leaves and flowers of plants such as henna, safflower and madder. Black dyes could be formed by combining tannic substances extracted from plants with iron present in mud or river water. The use of clays and mud to colour fabric is still practised by tribal peoples today as in the mud cloths of the Bamana peoples of Mali and the Maoris of New Zealand.

Approximately four thousand years ago, the Egyptians were extracting dyes from the leaves of plants. Blues and subsequently greens, produced by over-dyeing blues and yellows, were obtained from the leaves of plants such as *Indigofera tinctoria* (indigo), *Isatis tinctoria* (woad) and *Polygonium tinctoria* (Eastern knotweed). All these plants contain the blue colouring substance indigotin. This was extracted by fermenting the crushed leaves with an alkali – obtained from urine, plant ashes or lime water. Indigo is still extracted using similar methods today. The Yoruba of Nigeria, the Miao of China and some tribes in the Yemen all harvest indigo-bearing plants.

## The Spread of Cloth Patterning Techniques

The need for the human race to clothe itself for protection was at first satisfied by using animal skins, tree bark and leaves, and then by the more advanced techniques of twisting and weaving threads to produce fabric. In due course, the application and patterning principles that were employed to decorate the body were transferred onto cloth.

The continent of Asia has perhaps influenced the decoration of fabrics for the longest period of history. Printing blocks have been found that date back to around 3000 BC, and by the time Alexander the Great invaded India in 327 BC colourful printed and painted chintzes, together with brightly coloured tie-and-dye cottons, were a common sight on the subcontinent. Alexander's invasion led to the establishment of new trade routes and, as a consequence, the patterned fabrics of India spread throughout Asia, Egypt and Greece. Arab traders in the second century AD brought Indian fabrics to Europe, via the Red Sea, and extended trade routes into central and west Africa, ensuring the worldwide spread of Indian techniques and methods of patterning.

Above: Body painting patterns, such as the face paint worn by this Papua New Guinean, were adapted for use on fabric.

During the same period, the patterning of fabrics using block printing methods is thought to have existed in China. Certainly, during the third or fourth century AD the use of resist and stencil techniques were introduced into Japan by the Chinese, where they developed into highly sophisticated forms of patterning.

It is harder to ascertain when, or where, resist dyeing was first practised, but the earliest known examples originate from Peru (200–100 BC), and pre-Columbian civilizations of the period AD 700–1500 also developed methods of patterning using resist techniques. Due to environmental and cultural differences this technique evolved in unique ways around the world and its use eventually led to the techniques of 'tie-and-dye' and 'batik' as we know them today.

### Dye in Medieval Europe
With the discovery that coloured stains from plants and berries could be made more permanent if applied with other chemicals (mordants), or via fermentation processes, the techniques employed for dyeing cloth rapidly progressed. Advances in dyeing techniques during the Middle Ages were developed all over Europe,

and in particular in Venice and Italy. In an attempt to maintain standards, dyers' guilds were established and treatises appeared that described various methods of dyeing. One such volume the *Kunstbuch*, or Nuremburg Book, of 1460 contains 100 recipes and is one of the most important sources for the technology of printed textiles during this period.

### The Growth in Demand for Block Patterned Fabric
The biggest development in the decoration of fabric in Europe occurred in the 17th century. An ever-increasing demand for the hand printed cottons from India, was supplied initially by Portuguese trading ships that carried them alongside cargoes of spices, perfumes and embroideries. In 1631 England's East India Company was granted permission to import these cloths, which were extremely fine, soft, delicately coloured and skilfully patterned – very different from the heavy silks, velvets and brocades used for clothing at the time. These fabrics became known as indiennes, calicos, pintadoes or chintz and rapidly grew in popularity. However, pressure from the silk and wool weavers, who were frightened of losing trade, resulted in the passing of laws in France and Great Britain that forbade the sale of painted, dyed, printed or stained calicos. Despite these bans, many indiennes reached London and Paris and were sold illegally in significant quantities. Many of the Indian designs were considered unsuitable for the market and as a result, English patterns were sent out to India for copying. At the hands of Indian craftsmen these designs became more and more stylized, leading to the creation of a hybrid Western-Indian style known as 'exotic-chintz'.

**Above: Dramatic geometrical designs used in block printing were easily transferred to screen printing techniques.**

Entrepreneurs soon set up block printing factories at the main European ports of entry so they could take a share in this market. By employing large composite wooden blocks, instead of the simple smaller blocks used in India, they were able to print elaborate multicoloured designs. The popularity of block printing as a patterning method continued to grow, so that by the 18th century, hand block printing had become the main technique employed in patterning fabric.

### The Introduction of Automated Printing Machines
By the late 18th century the increase in demand for printed fabric led to the invention of automated printing machines. Around 1750, an Irishman by the name of Francis Nixon created a copper plate printing system using an intaglio technique similar to that used in paper printing. However, it was the discovery of a thickener (during the mid-18th century), suitable for use with mordants, that enabled

**Left: This 19th century European miniature illustrates the typical methods of working in a Medieval dyehouse.**

**Opposite: This chintz shows how Indian craftsmen adapted English patterns giving them a more exotic feel.**

**Above: The detail in this 18th century *Toile de Jouy* shows the quality of work achieved in early automated printing.**

printers to produce washable cloths. These prints were nearly always in a single colour – blue, crimson or purple – but very occasionally extra colours were added using small wood blocks. The designs tended to depict exotic flowers and birds as well as pastoral and classical scenes. The very fine drawing and tonal work, combined with the large bold repeat size, contributed to the popularity of these fabrics. The process slowly spread to France, where some of the finest work was produced by the Oberkamphe company at Jouy.

Because of the skill required to print designs using a flat plate, the next logical step was to convert the technique into a roller mechanism. Various patents were taken out for cylinder systems but it was Thomas Bell, in 1785, who designed the first practical rotary printing machine. Considerable expertise was needed to engrave the rollers and operate the machine, but it enabled the rapid mass production of printed fabric and was soon successful. The speed of this new machinery resulted in the inevitable decline of hand block printing, which survived only in the printing of specialist furnishings and silk work.

It was not until the advent of William Morris that hand block printing experienced something of a revival. Working with Thomas Wardle, he produced 16 hand block printed chintzes using many old dyes and processes that had been forgotten with industrialization. Morris explored techniques using indigo and madder discharge work and the influence of his designs was much in evidence right up to the First World War. Morris's designs and style continue to exert a strong influence on decorated fabrics today. Ironically, they are now produced using the very industrial printing techniques and synthetic dyes that Morris had sought to reject.

## Synthetic Dyes

With the discovery of the first synthetic dye, 'Mauveine', in 1853, the whole dyeing and printing industry changed. Aniline dyes, produced from coal tar, and colours such as chrome yellow and Prussian blue soon replaced natural dyes such as madder and indigo. These new colours were easier to prepare and employ than natural dyes, although they had the disadvantages of being garish and having poor light- and wash-fastness.

## The Revolution of Screen and Transfer Printing

By the 1850s, screen printing had started to evolve as a viable method of patterning. Printers in Lyon, who were pushing the limitations of stencil printing, began to support stencils with screens of finely woven silk. By the 1920s and 30s, hand screen printing had become a cheap and versatile patterning technique, and rapidly became the favoured method of decorating short runs of cloth.

As a patterning process it revolutionized the textile printing industry, liberating designers from the limitations of expensive block printing methods or engraved roller machines. Designs created using blocks or rollers were limited by the size of the block or the circumference of the roller (usually about 35 cm). The introduction of screens made it possible to print designs that were larger and freer, with the average size of a screen reaching 60–90 cm (over twice the size of early repeats).

Subsequently, the role of screen printing increased considerably. In the 1940s, the development of hydrophobic fibres like polyester and nylon meant that greater stability and registration of a design could be achieved. Mechanization of the processes, at first with automated screen printing tables and later with the introduction of rotary screen printing machines, has made the screen process one of the most versatile patterning techniques in the history of decorated fabrics. Superseding copper roller printing methods it is now the main method employed to pattern cloth.

Similarly, the discovery that certain dyes would sublime if heated (originally discovered in 1929, but only developed to its full potential in the 1960s) resulted in the evolution of transfer printing. This became the main method of patterning the new acrylic and polyester fabrics. Today, it continues to be an effective method of patterning synthetic fabrics, and new ways are being explored by which to transfer print images directly onto natural fabrics.

**Right: The versatility of screen printing can be seen in the huge range of colours exhibited in these designs.**

## Using the New Technology

Patterning techniques and materials are constantly changing to meet the demands of modern society. Just as mechanical spinning, weaving and printing machines were the catalyst for the industrial revolution, synthetic fibre engineering and dye technology, combined with micro-electronics and computer-aided design (CAD) and manufacture (CAM), have begun to create materials for a new age.

Advances in fibre, dye and finishing technology have resulted in fabrics with a different look or feel from traditional fibres. Fibre technology has enabled the textile industry to develop 'smart' fabrics that retain a 'memory', a property or quality that is absent in natural fibres. For example, some fibres now contain metal alloys that can retain a 'shape memory' returning to their original form when heated to a certain temperature. Similarly, advanced dye technology has created new and unusual colours, with pigments that are capable of emitting a smell or changing colour with stress, heat or light.

These advances are now linked to a demand for a more environmentally friendly product and a cost-effective but rapid response from the textile manufacturer. All these factors influence the materials and the type of imagery and patterns now used by textile designers.

## Computer-aided Design

Until relatively recently the computer and computer-aided design in printed textiles were seen as a means of

reproducing an existing design that had been created by traditional methods. The use of computers allowed designers to render a design for printed fabric in different colour-ways – a set of colours different from the original design. By scanning in a design, manufacturers could produce instant colour-ways and computerize many of the manual operations linked with the production of a printed fabric. The repeat of a design could be worked out, the scale altered and the number of colours reduced or increased. The design then passed to a computerized manufacturing process with the production of films, screen engraving and automated printing machines. Now, however, both designers and textile artists are exploring computer-generated imagery as the basis for their print ideas, and the computer is being used as a method of producing exciting high quality design.

## Further Developments in Computer Technology

One of the main problems with computer-generated design has been the transfer of colour from the computer screen to the finished fabric. The colour vibrancy achieved on screen and in prints on glossy paper can rarely be successfully transferred to fabric. Most computer-generated designs are transferred to a fabric base by conventional printing techniques, which means that the number of colours used has to be considerably reduced. Some designers have turned to using specialist photocopy transfer papers in an attempt to overcome this problem (see chapter 11), but their use is limited as they produce a harsh handle and the size of the patterned cloth is determined by the size of copy paper available.

The textile printing industry is now looking into ways of overcoming this problem, particularly with the use of ink jet technology – a process already important in the printing of pile carpets and paper. Small ink jet machines have been developed that can print large sample pieces of cloth, but these are still a long way from being capable of mass production. The cost of such machinery is still prohibitive and their use is currently restricted to the design studios of large textile manufacturing companies.

Progress has also been made in the development of devices that retain some of the qualities of freehand drawing, such as the pressure-sensitive stylus and various digitizing techniques to replace the much clumsier computer mouse. Advances in scanning have also opened up a new realm of computer imaging, enabling any two- or three-dimensional object to become the basis of a design after it has been reduced to a digital format.

## Environmental Concerns

There is growing concern about the amount of waste produced by the fashion and textile industries. Recycling has always taken place within the industry, and in the last 10 years or so many interesting fabrics have been made from waste cloth. This has been achieved by traditional manufacturing or by applying newer non-woven, felting and laminating techniques to waste fibres and scraps of material. Also, the necessity to dye the final cloth can often be eliminated by careful colour selection of the waste fabric used.

Polyester is seen by some as the most 'green' textile on the market as it can be melted down and recycled again and again, and some fibre manufacturers are successfully producing new polyester fibres from recycled plastic drink bottles. Polyester is an extremely versatile material and is available in a wide range of thicknesses. By employing various finishing processes its use will continue to grow. Many innovative designers are already making use of its thermal properties, which allow fabrics to be heat set, moulded, textured and embossed.

## The Future in Sight

Modern designers are also finding solutions to the interlinking problems of environment, time efficiency and innovation, and are beginning to push conventional boundaries by using equipment designed for non-textile processes.

Widespread concern over the acid sludge, a waste that is a by-product of many of the techniques, has prompted research into the use of lasers and ultrasound as a way of moulding, burning, welding and cutting natural and synthetic fibres, thus eliminating the effluents produced by wet finishing. The advantage of the laser is that it can be used to etch or cut patterns into a broad variety of fabrics and materials, while accurate computer control can produce geometric, lace-like effects. Other technology, such as ultrasound, metal plating and etching techniques, can be used to bond, stiffen and pattern many fabrics to create visual and tactile effects.

Advancing technology will have an ever-increasing influence on the fashion and textile world (as well as our environment) but it is unlikely that it will replace altogether the traditional design elements and techniques that have been built up over centuries. Rather, traditional textile design is being combined with the new technology to create a new generation of patterning techniques.

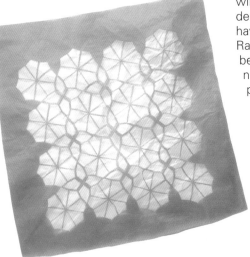

**Left: Janet Stoyel employed a laser cutting technique to create these delicate lace-like effects.**

**Opposite: Sharon Baurley used heat-setting to mould the fabric into a three-dimensional head.**

# CLOTH AND COLOUR

*The success and tactile qualities of decorated textiles rely upon both the selection of the base fabrics and the employment of the appropriate dyes or pigments in their coloration. This section offers essential information on the basic ingredients required before embarking upon the patterning process.*

*The first two chapters deal with the correct choice of materials (fabrics, dyes and colorants) for the patterning techniques described later in the book. The third chapter details methods of preparing and dyeing cloth prior to patterning, while the final chapter introduces the different types of thickeners available and the recipes necessary to make them.*

**Opposite: At Yateley Industries for the Disabled, blankets used to cover block printing pads are hung up to dry. A separate blanket is used for each colour printed.**

# 2

# FABRICS AND FIBRES

## Fabrics

Fabrics come in many forms: thick, thin, coarse, fine, smooth, textured, transparent or opaque. They can be made by one of three processes: woven, knitted or 'non-woven'. To identify a fabric, it is necessary to look at its structure. A woven cloth will consist of two sets of threads – the 'warp' threads run down the cloth and the 'weft' runs across its width. Fabrics produced by this method can be simple or complex in their construction. Simple fabrics are produced by using plain weaves and twills, for example sheeting, hopsack, denim and flannel, while complex weaves – velvet, damask, brocade, corduroy and towelling – use compound structures of many layers. A knitted fabric is formed by interlacing loops of yarn, and it can be produced either by warp or weft knitting. It is often referred to as a jersey, double-jersey, piqué or Jacquard. The term 'non-woven' is used to describe any fabrics that have

**Opposite: This beige and gold cross-dyed fabric by Georgina von Etzdorf brings sophistication to the spot design.**

not been created by weaving or knitting; these are normally produced from a web of fibres that are tangled and bonded together by mechanical, physical or chemical methods to form felt-like structures. Non-woven fabrics may also be found in the form of plastic or rubber sheetings.

Success in the dyeing and patterning of cloth begins with the correct selection of the fabric base – choosing the right weight, fibre type and weave of cloth for the fabric's final use. Some of the dyes, pigments and processes are specifically appropriate to certain fibres and before using them it is necessary to establish what fibres make up the base fabric. You should keep records of any dyed samples, good and bad, as much can be learned from mistakes and what might be a failure on one cloth can often be turned into an interesting technique or design on another.

## Fibres

For identification, fibres can be classified into two groups: natural and man-made. Natural fibres can in turn be subdivided into two main categories: those derived from plants and com-

posed of cellulose; and those derived from animals and composed of proteins. Man-made fibres include regenerated fibres and synthetics. There are many variations in the names and properties of these fibres depending on the manufacturer; for example nylon is also known as Antron or Tactel.

To ease identification, the table on page 20 gives a summary of the main fibre types, but the trade names used for many of the synthetic fibres are too numerous to list adequately here.

**CELLULOSE FIBRES**
**1 Hemp**
**2 Linen twill**
**3 Cotton Jacquard**
**4 Viscose rayon**
**5 Cotton muslin**
**6 Hemp and recycled cotton**

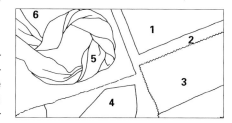

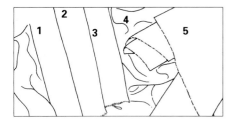

**PROTEIN FIBRES**
1 **Pleated silk organza**
2 **Ribbed wool**
3 **2 x 2 plain weave silk**
4 **Stonewashed silk**
5 **Wool flannel**

### Identification of Fibres

The simplest ways to identify the fibres used in fabrics are by sight, touch and a burn test. The look of a fabric gives a good indication of its fibre content. If the yarn is a continuous filament it must be either silk or a man-made fibre. An irregular fibre length suggests a natural fibre, while a regular length suggests a man-made staple; wool may have a hairy appearance, while rayon is likely to be shiny. The handle of a cloth may also give some indication of the fibre present. Wool will feel warm, linen feels cool, silk is smooth and angora is soft.

A burn test is a good way of identifying fibres. Before starting, separate the warp and weft in woven fabrics and, as far as possible, the yarns of a knitted fabric. The points to note are: whether the fibres burn or melt, the rate of burning, the type of flame, the type of smoke, the smell given off, and finally the type of ash or residue (see the Fibre Identification chart opposite).

### CELLULOSE FIBRES

Cellulose fibres, especially cotton, linen and hemp, have been used to make textiles for many centuries. These fibres originate from plants and their basic chemical structure is cellulose, a carbohydrate similar to starch.

Cellulose fibres are used to produce a vast range of cloths, from heavy fabrics such as denim, canvas, velvet, corduroy and towelling, to fine muslin, organza and jersey. They may be used alone in fabrics but are often found mixed with other fibre types that alter the properties of the cloth. For example in polyester-cotton sheeting the polyester improves the washing and ironing qualities of the cloth resulting in an 'easy-care' fabric, while the wool in Viyella, a cotton-wool blend, imparts warmth and a softer handle to the cloth.

### FIBRE TYPES

NATURAL FIBRES

**Cellulose**
Cotton, hemp, jute, linen, nettle, pineapple, ramie, sisal

**Protein**
Alpaca, angora, camel, cashmere, mohair, silk, wool

**Mineral**
Asbestos

MAN-MADE FIBRES

**Natural Polymer and Regenerated**
Alginate, cellulose acetate, cellulose triacetate, cuprammonium rayon, Modal, rubber, Tencel, viscose rayon

**Synthetics**
Acrylic and modacrylic, chlorofibre, elastane, polyamide, polypropylene, polyester, polyethylene,

**Others**
Carbon, ceramic, glass, metal

## Cotton

Cotton is the downy fibrous substance obtained from the cotton plant, *Gossypium*. It is available in many varieties ranging from the fine Egyptian cotton to thick Indian homespun. Varieties are grown for their natural colours which eliminate the need for dyeing.

Cotton has many characteristics that make it ideal for cloth. It is durable, soft and absorbs large amounts of moisture. It can also be processed at high temperatures, which makes it easy to wash and iron.

## Linen

Linen is produced from the flax plant, *Linum usitatissimum,* and is the oldest fibre known to man. Although composed mainly of cellulose it also contains lignin, which gives it a brownish colour, and its main characteristics are coolness, a silky lustre and durability. It is less pliant than cotton which causes it to crease more, but crease-resistant resins applied to the fibres will reduce this problem.

## Other Fibres

Hemp, jute, ramie, nettle, pineapple and sisal are employed throughout the world on a small scale. Their use is limited but may increase following the results of current research into finding alternatives to cotton that are natural and environmentally friendly.

## PROTEIN FIBRES

These fibres originate from animals and the majority are composed of the protein keratin, which comes from hair fibres. These fibres can be spun into yarn then woven, felted or knitted into a vast range of fabrics. Those used mainly for printing or handpainting are crepes, lightweight plain weaves and twills, jerseys, velvets, flannels and felts.

## Silk

The numerous varieties of silk can be divided into two categories: cultivated and wild. Cultivated silk is produced from the silkworm, the caterpillar of the moth *Bombyx mori*, which feeds

### FIBRE IDENTIFICATION

| Fibres | Burns/Melts | Burning rate | Flame | Smoke | Residue | Smell |
|---|---|---|---|---|---|---|
| **Natural cellulose** | | | | | | |
| COTTON | Burns | Fast (crease resistant finish: less rapid) | Yellow | Grey | Small amount of fine, soft grey feathery ash | Burning paper |
| LINEN | Burns | Fast (crease resistant finish: less rapid) | Yellow | Grey | Small amount of fine, soft grey feathery ash | Burning paper |
| **Natural protein** | | | | | | |
| WOOL | Burns | Slow | Irregular, splutters | Grey | Brittle, spongy black, easily crushable ash | Burning feathers or hair |
| SILK | Burns | Slow | Irregular, splutters | Grey | Brittle, spongy black, easily crushable ash | Burning feathers or hair |
| **Man-made regenerated** | | | | | | |
| CELLULOSE ACETATE | Melts | Fairly slow | Yellow | Grey | Crushable black bead | Acetic acid or vinegar |
| CELLULOSE TRIACETATE | Melts | Fairly slow | Yellow | Grey | Crushable black bead | Acetic acid or vinegar |
| TENCEL | Burns | Fast | Yellow | Grey | Small amount of fine, soft grey feathery ash | Burning paper |
| VISCOSE RAYON | Burns | Fast | Yellow | Grey | Small amount of fine, soft grey feathery ash | Burning paper |
| **Man-made synthetic** | | | | | | |
| ACRYLIC | Melts | Rapid | Very hot, luminous | Black | Irregular black bead | Acrid, sharp, unpleasant |
| MODACRYLIC | Melts | Very slow, extinguishes when removed from flame | Not really noticeable | Black and irregular | Rubbery black bead | Sweet, rubbery |
| POLYAMIDE (NYLON) | Melts | Fairly fast | Yellow | Grey | Hard uncrushable brown bead | Cooked celery |
| POLYESTER | Melts | Fairly fast | Yellow | Grey | Hard uncrushable black bead | Hot oil, aromatic, sweetish |
| POLYETHYLENE | Melts | Fairly fast | Luminous | Waxy vapour | Hard black bead | Molten wax |
| POLYPROPYLENE | Melts | Fairly fast | Luminous | Waxy vapour | Hard black bead | Molten wax |

on the leaves of the mulberry tree. The silk has a fineness, lustre, strength and softness that produces fine shiny cloths. Wild silk, also known as raw silk, tussah, shantung or honan, comes from a wild variety of silkworm that feeds on leaves. This silk is irregular in appearance, with a harsher handle, and is not as lustrous as the cultivated variety.

The silk fibre is spun by the silk-worm into a continuous thread and wound into a cocoon structure. It is a pale yellow, buff or white colour and has an outer coating or envelope of gum called sericin. The fibre can be made into two types of yarn: the first is made by combining the threads of several cocoons into a continuous filament yarn, while the second is made from waste or damaged cocoons that are chopped into short fibre lengths and spun on conventional machines.

## Wool

Most wool is obtained from the domestic sheep. It is found in many colours and qualities, with fibre lengths varying depending upon the breed of sheep. As a fibre it is flexible, elastic and curly, giving the final fabric a natural resilience and elasticity that stops excessive creasing. A wool fibre is capable of absorbing a large amount of water without appearing damp, but it is susceptible to heat and if washed in hot water may felt. This property can either be exploited in felt making, or overcome

by treating the cloth with a shrink-proof finish. Wool fibres will readily accept dyes and bright vibrant colours can be achieved.

## Other Fibres

Alpaca, angora, camel, cashmere and mohair are employed throughout the world on a small scale. They are obtained from the hair of various animals and are normally combined in mixes with wool and silk to add a luxury feel to the cloth.

## MAN-MADE REGENERATED FIBRES

Regenerated fibres were the first man-made fibres to be produced and, in an attempt to copy nature, experiments were made to produce both 'artificial wool' and 'silk' type fibres.

### Cellulose Acetate and Cellulose Triacetate

Cellulose acetate was discovered in 1918 by breaking down the cellulose in wood with acetic and sulphuric acids, but it was not until the 1920s that a fibre could be extruded. This was achieved by chemically altering the acetate to yield the fibre cellulose triacetate (secondary acetate). By the 1950s more efficient ways to extrude cellulose acetate were discovered and the fibre Tricel was developed. Fabrics made from Tricel are shiny or matt, woven or knitted, and when pleated with heat retain their shape.

### Tencel

In recent years the search for a 'green' artificial fibre has culminated in the manufacture of Tencel, the first

new, man-made fibre for 30 years. Tencel is viscose produced using wood pulp (from environmentally sustainable plantations) and mixing it with a solvent that can then be recycled after use. It has been called the 'chameleon of fibres' and is capable of taking on the qualities of other fibres perfectly. Fabric produced using Tencel can be made stronger than cotton, with a handle like velvet and the drape quality of silk.

### Viscose Rayon

Discovered in 1892, viscose rayon is produced by breaking down wood pulp with a strong alkali. It was used for many years as an alternative to cotton and silk, and it has many of the properties of a natural cellulosic fibre as well as the shiny lustre of silk. However, it does have a tendency to crease very badly, but this can often be overcome by combining viscose with other fibres.

## SYNTHETICS

Synthetics are man-made fibres derived from coal or oil. In the 1930s, after the discovery of regenerated fibres, chemists set out to produce polymer chains, the first being the polymer 'nylon'. This was discovered by a specialist team set up in the USA by E. I. du Pont de Nemours. In 1934, the team leader Wallace Hume Carothers discovered the formation of long polymeric chain molecules and used this principle in the formation of nylon. The synthesis of this fibre led to a whole range of man-made fibres. Unlike natural fibres, synthetics can now be produced with characteristics to meet specific purposes, and if combined with each other and natural fibres, the qualities of cloth that can be produced are almost infinite. A recent development are microfibres which are so fine that they exhibit properties, like softness of handle and drape, that natural fibres cannot compete with.

**Left: Using a fabric containing different fibres, Sally Weatherill has burnt away the viscose pile leaving areas of silk behind.**

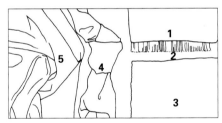

**SYNTHETIC FIBRES**
1 Acetate velour
2 Polyester lurex
3 Polypropylene with polyester
4 Polyester
5 Cellulose acetate satin

## Acrylic and Modacrylic

Acrylic was first discovered in the 1940s by E. I. du Pont de Nemours. It was produced from a liquid derivative of natural gas and air, and it is the most wool-like of all the man-made fibres. As a result it can be made into high-bulk yarns with warmth and softness. Acrylic is often blended with other fibre types to add softness and stability at a low cost. Modacrylic is an adapted acrylic fibre that has the advantage of having flame-retardant properties.

## Polyamide

Originally known as nylon, polyamide was developed in the United States. However, due to the subsequent development of many different types of nylon the fibre's name was changed to polyamide, which gives a more accurate description of the fibre's chemical structure.

These were the first fibres to exhibit the property of 'cold stretch' (fibres that will stretch without the application of heat) and could be extended, once spun, to three to four times their original length. During World War II this fibre was used in parachutes, tents and tyres, but it soon became popular for hosiery and lingerie. There are now hundreds of polyamide fabrics produced throughout the world.

## Polyester

Polyester was discovered in 1941 by the British Company ICI who gave it the trade name Terylene. Polyester is the most-used synthetic fibre; it is strong, washable and shrink-proof, but generally requires high-temperature pressure dyeing. It can be recycled from clear soft-drink bottles (one popular fabric produced this way is polar fleece). Polyester is used in combination with many other fibre types and is commonly found mixed with cotton, linen and wool.

## Other Fibres

Other synthetic fibres include elastane, polypropylene and chlorofibres. Elastane fibres, based on polyurethane, have the ability to stretch and return to their original shape with great versatility. They can be dyed easily and are mainly used, combined with other fibres, in stretch fabrics like swimwear (well-known examples are Spandex and Lycra). Similarly, polypropylene is used mainly in sportswear and high-performance garments (polar fleeces), while chlorofibres, such as PVC (polyvinylchloride), were used mainly in the 1960s for fashion garments.

Other materials and minerals like glass, carbon, ceramic and asbestos can be melted down and drawn out into a fibre. These fabrics tend to have mainly industrial uses and are not suitable for dyeing or colouring. Metals in the form of fine wire can also be incorporated into fabrics in combination with other fibres.

# 3

# COLOUR AND COLORANTS

The human eye is able to recognize three measurable properties of colour. The first property is hue. This is the name given to any one of the main colours of the spectrum, for example, red, green or blue. The second recognizable property is value, which relates to the lightness or darkness of a colour when compared to the grey scale. For example, white can be added to a colour to make a tint, thus making the colour lighter and giving it a higher value on the grey scale; alternatively black can be added to create a tone, resulting in a colour that is darker and of lower value on the scale. The third property of colour is intensity. This refers to the brightness or dullness of a colour, where the closer a colour is to a primary colour the more intense (bright) it will appear.

The theories of light and colour have been well researched and documented and many experiments have been carried out into the mixing of coloured pigments, and light. Today, colour mixing can be divided into two main systems: additive mixing and subtractive mixing. The additive system applies to the direct mixing of the primary colours of light – red, green and blue – which when mixed together in equal amounts will produce white. Subtractive mixing occurs when areas of the spectrum are absorbed or 'subtracted' by a surface, thus scattering and reflecting back the lightwaves that remain. For example, we see a rose as red because all the blue and green lightwaves have been absorbed by the flower and only the red colours of the spectrum are reflected back. A white surface will reflect back all the light, whereas a black surface will absorb all the lightwaves. Rather than red, green and blue, the primary colours

for subtractive mixing are red, yellow and blue, which if mixed in equal proportions will produce black.

The 'subtractive theory' is the most commonly used of the two systems and was first developed by Johannes Itten (1888–1967). In this chapter I will use the subtractive theory as a model to explain basic colour mixing of dyes and pigments. First we must assume that the three primaries are pure colours. This means that they must be of equal brilliance and must not contain any fraction of the other primary colours in their make-up. Secondary hues can then be produced by mixing two primaries in equal amounts, for example:

yellow + red = orange
yellow + blue = green
blue + red = violet

If the secondary colours are mixed with their nearest primary colour a new set of six intermediate hues can be produced.

The simplest way to demonstrate this is with the aid of a colour circle, in which the colour spectrum is curved until its ends touch to form a wheel. All twelve hues can be seen at once and their relationship with each other can be easily understood. Colours opposite each other on the wheel are known as complementary colours. If a complementary pair of colours are mixed a neutral 'grey' will

**Opposite: By handpainting with acid dyes, Sian Tucker was able to achieve the vibrant colours in this geometric design.**

**Right: Elvira van Vredenburgh created this realistic image of foxgloves using reprographic three-colour separation.**

result. This is important to note when mixing dyes, as the addition of black will often 'dull' a colour (make it 'dirty') rather than tone it down (whereby the colour retains its clarity).

The successful application of this theory relies upon the three primaries being pure colours. However, there are always impurities within pigments or dyes which means that many of the secondary colours produced by mixing them are dull. Various colour systems have been devised to overcome this problem and the trichromatic colour system (based on magenta, yellow and cyan) used in paper printing, is one. In this system, an image is separated into the three colours, each made up of very small dots, which when printed, combine to give the impression of a whole range of colours. The colours do not actually mix, hence this system overcomes the problems of mixing. This system is less successful in textile printing as few dyes or colorants are available in a pure enough form, with adequate fastness and reflective qualities, to give bright pure colours in mixing.

## The History of Colorants

Dyes can be divided into two main groups: synthetic and natural dyes. The first substances to be used as colorants were obtained from rocks and plants. Minerals were ground into pigments and mixed with tree resins, waxes, blood, saliva or albumen (egg white) to produce a paste that could be either rubbed or painted onto a fabric. Lime, gypsum and clays were used for whites and creams, and iron ore and other metallic minerals provided yellows, ochres, oranges, reds and browns. Originally, plant dyes were made by boiling and crushing berries, leaves and stems of plants. Essentially, all these colours were simply 'glued' onto the cloth and would have faded with washing and use. The desire to fix colours permanently onto cloth led to experiments with substances such as urine, mud, ashes and river or sea water in combination with dyes. All these substances helped to create and fix a colour permanently onto cloth.

In Medieval Europe the production and dyeing of cloth grew into a large and profitable industry and its practitioners were organized into guilds. The dyers guilds were divided into the 'black' or 'plain' dyers who worked with simple cloth; dyers of high colours who were allowed to dye brightly coloured fine cloths; and, in northern Italy, dyers of silk. Strict laws regarding the dyes and mordants used maintained the quality of coloured fabrics. Under these laws, many foreign dyes were labelled as 'bastard' dyes and their use was forbidden. The dyes used in the industry altered very little until the discovery in the 1790s of mineral lake colours such as iron buff, manganese brown, chrome yellow and Prussian blue. These are insoluble metallic salts or oxides that are produced by the process of precipitation. These colours were very bright and garish when compared to the softer hues produced with natural dyes and they were immediately seen in the fashions of the time.

By the second half of the 19th century, the increasing mechanization of fabric manufacture demanded ever-greater supplies of natural dyes. Plants such as madder and woad were grown in vast quantities throughout Europe and the dyes indigo, logwood, cattu and cochineal were imported in large quantities from the Far East and the Americas. In 1853 William Henry Perkins discovered the first synthetic dye, 'mauve', which was produced by reducing nitrobenzene (a product of coal tar). With the success of 'Perkins violet', as it was commonly called, many more dyes could be made using coal tar as a base. Subsequently, the dyeing industry evolved rapidly and the process of colouring fabric became a new science. The emphasis in coloration moved away from the use of natural dyes to the increasing supply of man-made ones.

There are now thousands of colours and dyes available with many new ones being added each year. Many types and colours popular 30 years ago are now rarely used, as alternatives have been found with better fastness as well as improved dyeing and printing properties.

The demand for 'greener' living has recently led to an increased interest in natural dyes. Their permanence, however, depends upon the use of mordants, many of which can also cause severe pollution. Similarly, the availability of plant and insect sources for natural dyes is limited and the amounts needed to supply the modern textile industry would take up vast areas of agricultural land and forest. As many of these dyes are unsuitable for printing, their role is limited to small-scale specialist areas of textile production.

If all dyes were classified according to their chemical structure there would be at least 30 different types. They are, therefore, categorized into

fewer groups based upon the method of application used and the type of fibres that each dye will colour.

**SYNTHETIC DYES**
This category can be subdivided into the groups briefly described below. There are other synthetic dyes, but these are rarely used and are unsuitable for a small studio set-up.

**Acid Dyes**
The generic term 'acid dyes' includes several different types of dye classified by their wet-fastness properties and the methods required to dye them. As the name 'acid' implies these dyes require hot acidic conditions to fix onto fibres. Most acid dyes will colour wool, silk and other protein and polyamide fabrics. They are extremely predictable and easy to

use and are available in a wide range of bright colours, although careful selection is necessary to achieve a specific shade or required fastness. Specific dye ranges for handpainting are made from mixtures of acid dyes under brand names such as Jacquard, Sennelier and Dupon.

This large group of dyes is then subdivided into four main classes: acid levelling or equalizing dyes; acid milling dyes; perspiration-fast or half milling dyes; and supermilling or fast dyes. Acid levelling or equalizing dyes will give good, bright and level dyeing and are employed mostly for dyeing wools, although some can be used on silks and polyamide. Fast acid, perspiration-fast dyes exhibit superior wet-fastness to that of acid levelling dyes but share some of their equalizing properties. Acid milling dyes require

more control and care during use as they tend to dye unevenly. The range of colours in this group is limited but they are bright and can be used very successfully on silk, wool and polyamide fibres. Finally, supermilling or fast dyes consist of a small selection of bright dyes. It is difficult to dye evenly with them but they are very wash-fast. They are also often referred to as 'brilliant' dyes.

**Azoic Dyes**
These are known as 'ice colours' (see page 186) and were mainly used for the printing of cellulosic fashion fabrics (predominantly cotton). Their main feature is that they are created *in situ* within the fibres of a cloth. They were originally employed in popular African prints which imitated wax batik, but their use has declined in recent times owing to the expense or unavailability of certain key products.

**Basic and Modified Basic Dyes**
These were the first synthethic dyes ('Perkins violet' belongs to this group) produced, but they are now rarely used because they exhibit poor wash- and light-fastness. They can be employed to produce bright colours on silk, wool and acrylic, but their main use today is in the dyeing of modacrylic and acrylic fibres. Astrazone, Maxilon, Sandocryl and Synacril are some of the brand names.

Basic dyes can often be found in silk handpainting dyes because they are simple to use, but their poor fastness can limit their use; however, it is possible to overcome this problem by coating the finished piece of fabric with an ultraviolet-light protector.

**Direct Dyes**
These dyes are so called because they will colour cellulose without the need of pre-treatment or mordant. This makes them some of the easiest dyes to use on cellulosic fabrics. They are also referred to as application

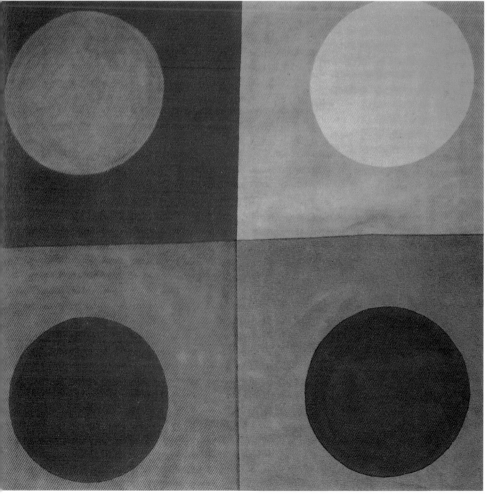

**Left: Using acid dyes, Sian Tucker has created a bright, but subtle colour composition on this woollen blanket.**

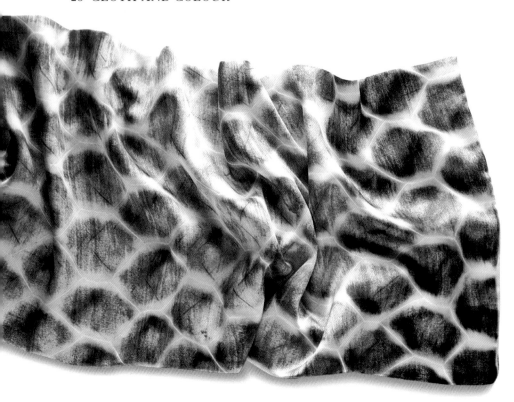

Left: Rebecca Earley used heat transfer (see chapter 11) and disperse dyes to transfer the lines of wire to polyester.

Opposite: James Ward used reactive dyes and discharge processes (see chapter 14) to produce a delicate plaid effect.

dyes because they are simply applied to cellulose, but do not chemically react with it. Direct dyes are inexpensive and available in a wide range of colours that can be intermixed. They are mainly used to dye cotton fabrics, although they can also be used to dye silk and are often used to produce a dischargeable print ground (see page 139). The disadvantage of this type of dye is its poor wash- and light-fastness and recently the available range has been limited to those colours offering the best fastness. They are rarely used for printing, having been superseded by reactive dyes which offer better fastness and processing time.

Direct dyes have to be applied at temperatures of 85–90ºC which makes them unsuitable for batik as the heat would cause the wax that is used in the process to melt. The addition of a salt, such as common salt (sodium chloride) or Glauber's salt (sodium sulphate), is necessary to improve the take-up of the dye. If silk or wool is to be dyed, the salt is replaced by a small amount of acetic acid.

## Disperse Dyes

Disperse dyes were developed in the 1920s to dye the new synthetic fibres that would not colour with traditional dyes. They are used almost solely for the colouring of synthetics and sublime from a solid state to a vapour under the influence of heat, thus allowing cloth to be coloured without the use of water. Disperse dyes have been developed in powder and liquid/paste forms and also used in inks and crayons (e.g. Deka iron-on paints and Crayola transfer crayons) for craft use. This is discussed in chapter 11.

Many interesting fabrics are now made from synthetic fibre mixes – made up from a mixture of synthetic fibres and natural fibres like wool or cotton. These can be coloured with a mixture of disperse dyes and other dyes using exhaust dyeing, provided that a carrier is employed with the dye. The dyes are absorbed into the fibres only at high temperatures (90–100ºC), so particular care needs to be taken when dyeing a wool-polyester mix as the wool will felt if treated roughly at high temperatures. The carrier must be used in a well-ventilated room as fumes are often given off when they are used.

## Pigments

These products are insoluble in water, but they can be applied to all types of fabric through the use of a resin, emulsion or dispersion (see page 115). They are used mainly for printing, handpainting or stencilling fabrics and may be found in either a concentrated form that can be used to colour various binders, or ready-mixed with a base for use as a fabric paint. Special effects can be produced using heat- and light-sensitive pigments or pearlized metallics (a range of metallics that have a pearl finish to them).

## Reactive Dyes

These dyes are, perhaps, of most use to a textile designer/artist as they can be used to colour a vast range of fibre types without the need of any specialist fixing equipment.

Reactive dyes take their name from the fact that they chemically react with the fibre molecules to form a covalent dye-fibre bond. This strong bond between the dye and the fibre imparts excellent wash- and light-fastness properties. First marketed by ICI in 1956, under the name Procion, they were primarily designed to colour cellulose, although some types are suitable for silk, wool and various fibre blends. Nowadays, this type of dye is available from other manufacturers in a variety of forms. Some are less reactive and are suitable for painting and printing onto fabric, others are more suited for dyeing. The more reactive types of dye can be used cold for batik dyeing (see page 131) or when little equipment is available.

Dyeing with reactive dyes has three distinct stages: absorption of the dyes into the fabric; fixation of those dyes onto the cloth; and the washing-off of any unfixed dyes. The dyes require two auxiliaries. The first is salt, which can be either sodium chloride or Glauber's salt (some blue and green dyes will give better results if the latter is used). The salt acts as an electrolyte that reduces the

solubility of the dye. This causes the dye molecules to move around and seek suitable dye-binding sites. If the dissolution of the dye is controlled in this way, over a period of time, a more even dyeing will take place as the dye will be absorbed into the fibres at a steady rate, rather than all at once. The second auxiliary employed with reactive dyes is an alkali – normally sodium carbonate. This increases the pH of the dye bath which enables the dye to react with the fibre molecules and fix onto the cloth. The amount of salt or alkali required depends upon the shade wanted; pale colours will require less than darker shades. There are different methods of dyeing fabric with these dyes and the method chosen will depend upon the reactivity of the dye you are using.

It should be noted that reactive dyes in powder form can sometimes cause respiratory allergic reactions. It is therefore important that a suitable dust-excluding respirator is worn when handling the dyes in a powdered state. Many dyes are now sold in granular or liquid form to overcome this problem.

## Vat Dyes

Vat dyes are mainly used to colour cellulose and are rarely used on wool because the alkaline conditions that they require damage protein fibres. Vat dyes are insoluble in water so they need to be made soluble before they will dye fibres. Using an alkali-solution of caustic soda and sodium hydrosulphite the dye is converted, by a chemical reduction, to a 'leuco' – alkali-soluble – form (this solution may be a different colour from the final dyed colour). In this form, the dye enters the fibres of the cloth and, once absorbed, is then exposed to the air to oxidize back to its insoluble state. At which point the dye is permanently fixed within the cloth.

Indigo is a natural vat dye that has been used for centuries to colour fabric. Indigo was originally derived from plants, but synthetic indigo is now employed in vat dyeing. The dyeing procedures are complex and time-consuming, but the effects that can be achieved through tie-and-dye and resist printing (see chapter 13) are worth the trouble. Indigo was the first vat dye to be synthesized but a large range is now available under various trade names – Caledon, Cibanone, Durindone, Indanthren and Sandothrene.

## MULTI-PURPOSE, DOMESTIC OR UNION DYES

These are readily available in various forms. Some are for dyeing with hot water and may be applied simply in a washing machine, whereas others are designed for cold water application. They are simple to use and will dye most fabrics because they contain a combination of dye types. This is also their disadvantage, because a considerable amount of dye is wasted through being washed away since it has no attraction for the type of fibre being coloured. It is difficult to obtain dark, rich colours using these dyes but they are very useful for dyeing pale-to-medium ground shades or for use in resist patterning techniques (see chapter 13).

## DYES FOR HANDPAINTING

Some companies produce their own dye systems for handpainting. The dye types used may vary but they are normally acid, basic or reactive dyes and they are often made up

Below: A range of natural dyes. Clockwise from bottom left: weld, sumac, turmeric, indigo, madder, alkanet and juniper.

into easy-to-use solutions. Some dyes are dissolved in alcohol, others in water, and a few are sold in powder form. These dyes are readily available from craft shops and although sold mainly for handpainting silks they can also be diluted for dyeing cotton or silk fabrics. There are many systems with slightly different methods of use and fixation so it is advisable to follow the manufacturer's instructions supplied with the dye.

Pigment-based paints are available in many colours, including fluorescents and metallics. They are combined with binders of various viscosities and softness, and can be used as paints or to mimic dye solutions. These are fixed with heat – normally a hair drier or an iron.

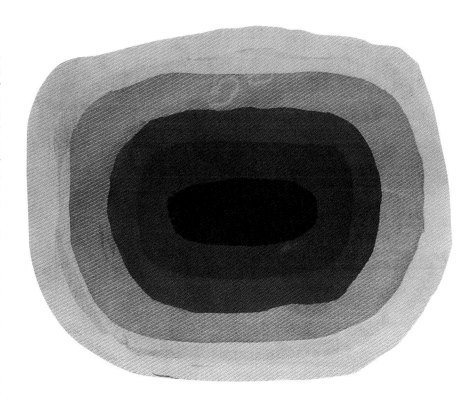

## NATURAL DYES

Natural dyes were the only ones available until synthetic dyes were discovered in the mid-19th century. They are obtained from various plant, animal or mineral sources and are often named after the source from which the dye material originated.

One of the oldest animal dyes was the 'Tyrian Purple' (extracted from shellfish) used by the Phoenicians, 2–1000 BC, and bright red dyes can be extracted from the dried bodies of several insects – cochineal from the cochineal beetle is perhaps the best known. Vegetable dyes are extracted from plants. The dye indigo is found in the form of the chemical indican in a range of plants grown throughout the world. Madder is produced from the crushed roots of the madder plant (*Rubia tinctoria*) and produces fast reds, but requires the mordant alum to fix it. Its red dyeing element is known as alizarin. Many dyes can also be extracted from the wood of various trees. Logwood, produced from the heartwood of the tree *Haematoxylon campecianum*, native to South America, will produce a range of colours from blue, violet, grey and purple through to black, depending upon the mordant used.

Other plants and lichens yield yellows, oranges, pinks, greens, browns and black. Yellows may be obtained from weld (*Reseda luteola*), safflower (*Carthamus tinctorius*), saffron (*Crocus sativus*), turmeric (*Curcuma longa* or *C. tinctoria*) and fustic (*Morus tinctoria* or *Chlorophora tinctoria*). Orange dyes may be obtained from dandelion (*Sambucus ebulus*), onion (*Allium cepa*), annato (*Bixa orellana*) and bloodroot (*Sanguinaria canadensis*). Pinks and greens come from the leaves and berries of the blackberry (*Rubus fruticosa*) and blackcurrant (*Ribes nigrum*); and browns/black can be obtained from walnut (*Juglans nigra*), tea (*Camellia sinensis*) and iris (*Iris pseudacorus*).

The dyes in this section are suitable for base colours and for patterning with resist techniques (see chapter 13); most of the dyes, however, cannot be used for the direct printing style (see chapter 12). Many simple pleasing effects can be obtained using indigo or mineral dyes and these are covered in chapter 13, 'Dyed and Printed Resists'. Natural dyes can be used to dye any organic fibre but the dyes and methods vary for protein and cellulose types. Most natural dyes are unsuitable for synthetic fibres. As with the synthetic dyes, natural dyes can be classified as 'fast' or 'fugitive' types.

**Above: Emma-Louise Fathers used mineral dyes with the mordant 'K' salt for soft rust tones and concentric rings.**

There are few natural substantive dyes (most will be attracted to the fibres only with the help of a mordant) and these will behave differently towards cellulose and protein fibres. They are normally applied by boiling the dyestuff with the fibres in water over a period of time.

### Mordants for Natural Dyes

Most natural dyes are known as 'adjective' dyes which means that they require the presence of a mordant to fix them to the fibres of the cloth. The term 'mordant' is generally applied to metallic salts, but it can be used to describe any substance that fixes onto a fibre to enable colouring. Different mordants will often yield different colours from the same natural dye type.

### Alum

This is the most commonly used mordant and has been in use since ancient times. It is obtained from aluminium sulphate or potassium aluminium sulphate. When used in

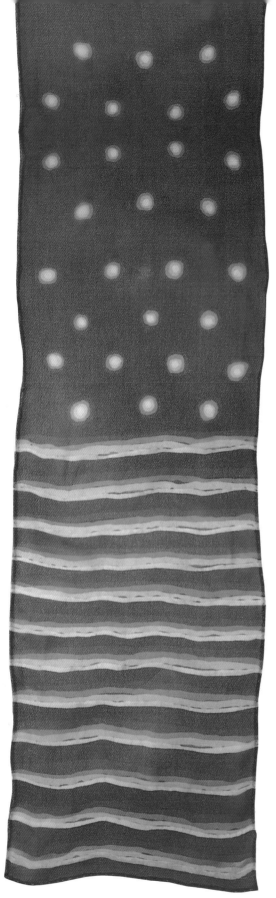

combination with cream of tartar (potassium hydrogen tartrate), alum helps to reduce the amount of mordant needed for fixation and brightens and evens the final colour of the cloth.

## Chrome

This mordant is now mainly employed for the dyeing of cotton. However, its use is limited because of increased environmental concern about its disposal and the fact that many people are sensitive to it – if used in clothing, any chrome not permanently fixed to the dyes or fibres may cause an allergic skin reaction. Using chrome in association with formic acid, however, virtually eliminates these adverse allergic effects, while the fastness properties are increased. The most common chrome mordants are bichromate of potash or potassium and sodium dichromate. These mordants are light sensitive and must be kept in dark containers

## Copper

Copper is little used in home dyeing, but has been used as a mordant by the dyeing industry for centuries. It was originally used in the form of verdigris, a basic copper acetate. Copper sulphate, sometimes known as 'blue vitriol', can also be used. It is a poison and care should be taken when handling it. The addition of acetic acid to the bath will reduce the amount of copper required and increase the fastness of the dye.

## Iron

This was one of the first mordants discovered. It may even have been discovered accidentally, as the iron salts present in water used to dye a fabric would have affected the final colour of the cloth. Iron was commonly used to produce black and greys in combination with the tannic substances found in tree barks and nuts, but now it is often used as an after-mordant in order to 'sadden' (tone down/darken) the colour of a dye. The easiest form to use is ferrous sulphate, a green crystalline powder also known as copperas or green vitriol because of its colour.

## Tannic Acid

Tannic acid acts as a mordant for cellulose fibres or as a fixer in combination with other mordants. It was originally obtained in its natural form from a number of plant sources such as sumac, oak galls and myrobalans, but it can now be obtained in a pure form as a powder. Unlike the natural forms, which require lengthy boiling to extract the acid, this powder will simply dissolve in water. Tannic acid, in combination with ferrous salts, will produce a brown/black colour. The shade of this colour will depend upon how much iron is present and the purity of the tannic substances.

## Tin

This is mainly used as a modifying agent for other mordants towards the end of the dyeing process, and it intensifies and brightens the cloth's colour. It is usually obtained from stannous chloride, tin crystals, other tin salts or murate of tin. It is a poison and an irritant so great care must be taken when using it. If used with the dye cochineal a bright scarlet colour is produced.

## CLASSIFICATION OF DYES

In 1924, to ease the selection and specification of dyes, a standard, international colour index was created. A supplement to the first edition of the Colour Index International was published in 1928. Since then, the Index has been updated by a quarterly publication of additions and amendments to keep all the sections up to date. It is an important reference work for all dyers and colourists.

The Colour Index now consists of nine volumes and is divided into three parts. Part I covers all known commercial names under which dyes are sold, their usage, their fastness properties, the methods of application and other basic data. In Part II, the chemical structure of each dye is given and, where known, the inventor and any literature, including patents, are stated. Not all dyes are featured in this section, as a dyemaker has the right to protect, by exclusion, the formula of a new product. Part III gives lists of the abbreviations used in the index, a list of dye and pigment makers, an index of commercial names, details of fastness tests and a patents index. A copy of the Colour Index International has recently been issued as a CD-ROM.

Most textile designers and colourists do not need most of the information in this index, but it is useful to know that by referring to it, chemically equivalent dyestuffs can be identified, along with information on a dye's dischargeability and fastness.

## Dye Reference

The Colour Index categorizes dyes by their trade names, followed by the colour, which is suffixed by a series of numbers and letters. We can derive considerable information about the dye colour from a dye's name.

Each of the dye types is given a different trade name by different manufacturers. These trade names are then associated with that particular type of dye, for example, the trade names Procion and Remazol both signify reactive dyes, but they are from different manufacturers. (All trade names are listed in the Colour Index, Volume V.) All dyes of the same type and colour are given the same Colour Index number. This ensures that if this number is known an equivalent dye can be found, no matter where in the world you are working. I have used this number whenever possible when specifying any dyes in subsequent chapters.

The colour, given after the trade name, will tell us what hue to expect – yellow, orange, red, violet, blue, green, brown or black – and the numbers and letters that follow the colour tell us more about the dye, for example, its brightness, wash- and light-fastness, solubility and so on. The first set of suffixes relates to the colour; they are derived from the German names for the primary colours: R = Rot (red), B = Blau (blue)

and G = Gelb (yellow). If a dye is labelled with an R it will have a leaning towards red; if B, it will be bluer and a G implies a yellower shade. The number accompanying this letter is an indication of how far towards a primary the hue is positioned. The higher the number (on a scale of 1–10) the more of that primary colour is present in the dye, for example: a dye labelled Yellow R, will be an orangy-yellow; and Blue 8G will be a turquoise, greenish-blue compared with Blue 2R which will be a purplish colour. Blue B will contain more pure blue than the others and will be closer to the true primary colour.

Other suffixes, once they have been decoded, will provide all the specific information you will need about the properties of a dye, but it is often easier to consult the manufacturer's literature and their technical staff are always extremely helpful and informative.

## Fastness

The selection of a specific dye is important when the end use of the fabric is considered. A clothing fabric requires good wash- and rub-fastness, as well as fastness to perspiration. However, its fastness to light will be of less importance. On the other hand, a fabric used as a hanging or as curtains will require good light-fastness properties with wash-fastness being less important.

Industrial pattern books are useful for finding out the fastness of a dye. They include a range of information, including the depth of a dye's colour (which is given as a percentage shade) as well as its wash- and light-fastness. All levels of fastness (wash, perspiration etc.) are measured in ratings of 1–5, where 5 is very fast and 1 is fugitive. The only exception is light-fastness which is measured on a separate scale of 1–8, where 8 represents the highest level of fastness.

**Right: Using iron dyes and tannic acid solutions, Kate Wells has created a geometric pattern on a silk haboti fabric.**

# 4

# DYEING THE BASE COLOUR

This chapter covers the preparation of cloth before patterning, the methods used to dye fibres with commercial dyes and, finally, specialist methods for dyeing with natural dyes.

Some of the recipes involve caustic solutions so care should be taken when making up the solutions. Always add acid/alkali to water, rather than water to acid/alkali, or the resulting reaction will force fumes upwards and possibly into the face. It is also advisable to wear eye protection, rubber gloves and suitable protective clothing (a large plastic apron, or overalls) as caustic solutions can cause serious burns. A respirator might also be needed when handling and weighing dye powders and chemicals.

## SCOURING AND BLEACHING

Before a piece of fabric can be decorated or dyed it is essential that any

**Opposite: Indigo-dyed lengths of cotton oxidize in the air, turning from yellow-green to a permanent deep blue colour.**

impurities such as dirt, wax, size or machine oil are removed. Some suppliers provide fabric that is prepared for printing or dyeing but most fabrics require some kind of washing to enable an even absorption of the dyestuff. The process of cleaning cloth before dyeing is known as scouring and entails washing with a detergent to remove impurities. Sometimes, as in the case of cotton, impurities are not easily removed and the fabric may require further treatment with a hot alkali to dissolve the starches present; however, fibres such as wool or silk will be permanently damaged if scoured in this way.

Bleaching is often carried out to make the fabric whiter. A number of bleaching powders and chemicals such as sodium hypochlorite, ammonia and hydrogen peroxide are used.

## Cotton and Other Cellulose Fibres

Cotton and linen can be bought in many states: the fabric may have been de-sized, scoured, bleached and

mercerized (see page 36) in preparation for use. Cheaper supplies are sometimes sold in 'grey' or 'loom' states. These need thorough scouring to remove impurities and may need to be bleached to improve the colour.

If the cloth has not been prepared for dyeing or printing it will require further cleaning to remove any dressings that may be present. For a lightweight cotton this is done by soaking the cloth for a few hours in cold water (this removes most of the substances), then boiling the fabric for 30 minutes in a solution of softened water (use a softener like Calgon), sodium carbonate (washing soda), and pH neutral detergent – use 5 g of sodium carbonate and 2 g of detergent per litre of water. A suitable commercial detergent is Metapex, but any domestic brand designed for hand-washing, that says 'pH neutral' on the label, can be substituted. The fabric is then rinsed before dyeing. If the fabric is to be printed it must also be dried and pressed smooth before using.

---

## SCOURING COTTON

**1–2 Soak the cotton for a few hours in cold water to loosen and remove most of the dirt particles. Then measure out the sodium carbonate (washing soda).**

**3–4 Add the sodium carbonate to boiling water, making sure you have enough water to cover the fabric, and measure out a suitable neutral detergent.**

**5 Immerse the fabric in the softened water and boil for 30 minutes. The fabric must then be rinsed – and dried if you wish to print on it – before dyeing.**

## BLEACHING

**1–2 To whiten the scoured fabric use a cold solution of domestic bleach (4% sodium hypochlorite) in water, and immerse the fabric for 30–40 minutes.**

**3 Remove the fabric from the bleach solution and rinse it thoroughly. Gloves, glasses and protective clothing should be worn, as bleach is a caustic solution.**

## NEUTRALIZING BLEACH

**1 To neutralize any alkalinity remaining from the bleaching that may effect later dyeing, measure out the acetic acid (or vinegar) and add to the water.**

**2 Immerse the fabric for a short while, agitating the cloth for a thorough soaking. Then remove the fabric and give the cloth a final rinse before drying.**

For a whiter cloth the scoured fabric can be bleached using a cold solution of standard domestic bleach (containing 4% sodium hypochlorite). This should be used in a ratio of 10 ml of bleach per 1 litre of water. The fabric is immersed in this solution for 30–45 minutes, and then rinsed to remove the bleach. Treat with acetic acid (1 ml of acetic acid, at 20% strength, to 1 litre of water) or a little white vinegar to neutralize any alkalinity, before finally rinsing and drying.

### Mercerizing
Mercerization was discovered in 1844 by John Mercer, and most cotton yarns and fabrics are now given this treatment. It involves the application of a strong alkali, which improves the uptake of dye – giving brighter colours – as well as the strength and handle of the cloth. The majority of pre-dyed and finished fabrics will have been mercerized, but some cottons and calicos may not have gone through the process and hence will not dye as well. Mercerization requires specialist industrial machinery but it is possible to 'causticize' a fabric with less complicated equipment. Causticization will not give the same degree of lustre to the dyed fabric, but it will enormously improve dye take-up.

One method of treating the cloth is to boil the cotton in a solution of 5 g of sodium carbonate per litre of water for 30 minutes, then remove the fabric and carefully add 150 g of sodium hydroxide per litre to the solution. Return the cloth and boil for a further 15 minutes. The cloth is then removed and treated with acetic acid or vinegar which neutralizes the alkali.

### Wool and Other Hair Fabrics
Woollen and hair fabrics contain natural oils, and unless scoured they will have poor 'wetting-out' properties and consequently will not absorb dyes easily. Scouring can be done by gently washing the cloth in a solution of 100 parts warm water (40°C), to 1 part of a pH neutral detergent. This will rinse out of the fabric and, being neither acid nor alkali, will not affect

subsequent processes. Avoid rough handling and the use of water that is too hot as this will damage the wool fibres and cause them to felt.

The bleaching agents used for cotton are unsuitable for wool. If the fabric needs to be bleached this can be done using weak solutions of hydrogen peroxide, which are readily available from chemists. Alternatively, the wool may be treated in a bath containing a solution of 2% formic acid (at 85% strength) with 5% C.I. Reducing Agent 2 (sodium formaldehyde sulphoxylate) and 10% Glauber's salt. (Using the equation on page 41 and the percentage weight of the assistants above you can calculate the amount of assistant required.) The temperature of the solution is slowly raised to 90°C and maintained for 30–45 minutes, after which the fabric is rinsed and dried.

## Silk
Silk fabrics are normally de-gummed, but raw silks may contain natural gums and weaving oils which must be removed before dyeing. Most of the natural gum will be sericin, which is removed by de-gumming. The fabric must be treated at 95°C, over a period of one to one-and-a-half hours, in a solution containing 10 ml olive oil soap per litre of water. Follow by rinsing in warm and cold water before the silk is dried and pressed.

Some silks can be bleached in the same way as wool, using a solution of hydrogen peroxide, but wild silks will never bleach to a pure white colour. If the fabric has been de-gummed but is soiled it will only need a light wash in warm water and neutral detergent before it can be dyed.

## Regenerated and Synthetic Fibres
Viscose, cellulose tri-acetate, polyamide and polyester need a simple wash to remove any yarn lubricants or size that may be present on the fibres. The fabrics are treated for 30 minutes at 70°C in a solution containing 15 ml detergent and 20 g sodium carbonate per litre of water. The fabric is then rinsed and dried.

Acrylic and cellulose acetate, on the other hand, are simply washed with a neutral detergent at 50°C and rinsed well in warm water.

## DYEING THE GROUND COLOURS
It is essential to choose the right dye for the fibres in the base cloth to ensure that the dyes meet the fastness levels required. It is common to have problems of poor colour yield when dyeing natural/synthetic mixes, for example, with cheaper cottons that contain some polyester. Use the correct dischargeable dyes (see chapter 14 for discharge techniques) for the dyeing of the base cloth and any other coloured pattern that may need to be discharged out at a later time. The choice of dyes is limited and mixes of different dyes may be necessary to achieve a specific shade. If the dischargeability of a dye is unknown it is important to test dye colours on different bases, as a dye may produce different shades on different fibres. This happens with acid dyes applied to wool and silk: the colours appear bright on silk, but dull on wool.

Various faults can arise from the dyeing process. A fabric with lighter coloured or white patches generally results from one or more of the following: failure to soak the cloth fully before dyeing; the use of too small a container which restricts the cloth causing folds, that resist the penetration of the dye; failure to agitate the cloth during dyeing so areas of fabric do not remain immersed in the dye solution. Dark patches are caused by the dye bath being too hot at the beginning of the process or by hot spots forming at the base of the container. A speckled appearance is nearly always caused by failure to dissolve the dye powders before adding them to the dye bath.

It is very important to rinse the cloth thoroughly before proceeding to any other technique, otherwise any unattached dye will bleed in subsequent wet processes and may stain white areas of the design.

**Right: Various protein fabrics dyed in a solution of madder root show how differently each fibre type took up the colour.**

Various methods are used to dye cloth in the textile industry, but most suitable for colouring small quantities of fabric are the exhaust (hot or cold), azoic, vat and natural dyeing methods.

## Dyeing Auxiliaries and Additives

Each type of dye (see chapter 3) may be used with one or more auxiliary or additive agent to enhance their effectiveness. Acids are used to reduce the pH value of the dye solution, which assists in the creation of the dye-fibre bonds. Different types and strengths of acid are used within the industry, the most common types being acetic, formic and sulphuric acids.

All safety precautions should be followed, but it is also advisable to prepare diluted solutions of these acids and keep the concentrated forms locked away. This process should also be carried out in a well-ventilated room and a respirator should be worn.

An acid solution of 20% is a safe working strength. To make up 1 litre of dilute acid at 20% strength, measure out 800 ml of cold water into a large plastic or glass container and very slowly add 200 ml of the concentrated acid, stirring gently to evenly disperse the acid in the water. The resulting chemical reaction will generate heat, so allow the solution to cool before transferring it to a suitably labelled bottle.

Acetic acid can be replaced by white malt vinegar, which has a standard strength of about 4%. The quantity required will be five times the amount of acetic acid stated in recipes.

Alternatively, alkalis are used to increase the pH value of the dye bath, which enables the fixation of reactive dyes with cellulose. The most common alkali used is sodium carbonate. It is supplied in its purest form as a white powder; in its less pure crystal state it is known as washing soda. Another alkali, lime water, is produced by soaking calcium hydroxide in cold water. The resulting water is alkaline and the sediment is thrown away.

Many processes require sodium hydroxide, more commonly known as caustic soda, which is supplied as grains, flakes or pellets. It is advisable to make up a solution to a standard strength, which can be kept until required. This is prepared by dissolving 441 g of sodium hydroxide crystals in one litre of cold water and when the solution has cooled the viscosity can be checked. This needs to be 38° Bé (72° Tw), and can be measured using specific hydrometers.

Other auxiliaries like levellers and wetting agents usually come in the form of solutions. These solutions coat fibres of the cloth, and attract dye molecules, preventing patchy, uneven dyeing. They are chemically similar to detergents and a small amount of washing-up liquid will often achieve the same results. Most dye manufacturers will produce specific wetting agents and levellers for their dye ranges.

Two types of salt are also used in dyeing processes: common salt (sodium chloride) and Glauber's salt (sodium sulphate). Both are available in a powder or crystalline state. As electrolytes they aid the absorption and levelling of dyes.

## Exhaust Dyeing

This method relies upon the dye reacting with the fibre until all the dye has been absorbed, leaving an 'exhausted' dye bath – at this stage the dye liquor should be clear. Complete exhaustion rarely occurs, but it is a goal to aim for as it means that all the dye has been transferred to the fabric and none is wasted.

The correct calculation of the amount of dye needed is a major factor in successful exhaust dyeing. Too much will leave a lot of dye loosely attached to but not bonded with the fibres and, if not removed completely in the rinse, it will bleed whenever the fabric is rubbed or washed. Too little dye will result in patchy colour or a lack of depth. To aid the selection of a desired colour, shade dye sample (pattern) books are produced by the dye manufacturers. These show actual dyed samples covering the

**Left: By varying the dye strength, fibre type and dyeing time, a wide range of blues can be produced using indigo dye.**

manufacturer's entire range of dyes, with the shade of each dye expressed as a percentage, or a scale from 0.05% (the palest shade) to 4% (the full shade). At one time a large range of shades for each dye was covered, using different base fabrics to show how the colour varied with each cloth type. Now, however, with increased production costs, only one base fabric is used and only one or two shades of a dye are shown. Please note that these pattern books are produced under controlled conditions and the cloth used will have been chosen to give the best colour yield possible, so use the shades only as a general guide.

Using these guides, the amount of dye you require can be calculated relatively simply. The shade percentage figure indicates the amount of dye required to colour 100 units of dry material. For example a 1.5% shade indicates that 1.5 g of dye will be needed to dye 100 g of material that colour. If the weight of your fabric is greater or less than 100 g then the following equation should be used to calculate the amount of dye needed:

(% shade÷100) x dry weight of fabric (in grams) = amount of dye (in grams)

A dye is normally assumed to be a standard strength, expressed as 100%. However, to reduce the costs of transporting bulky powders, producers sometimes make dyes in a concentrated form. These strengths are normally expressed in percentages, such as 125%, 150%, 200% or 300%, that need to be taken into account when calculating the amount of dye required. For example a dye with a strength of 200% will be twice as strong as the standard dye and therefore half as much is required to achieve the same shade.

Unless you have very accurate scales it will be difficult to measure small amounts of dye precisely and repeat dyeing may become a rather hit and miss affair. This is easily overcome by producing stock solutions of a known concentration that can be measured out using a small measur-

ing cylinder or syringe. The solutions are made by dissolving a known amount of dye in a set amount of water. For example, if a stock solution of 1% is required, 5 g of dye can be dissolved in 500 ml of liquid; or 1 g of dye made up with water, to 100 ml of liquid. Once these are made up, a proportion of the solution can be used to produce weaker solutions, for example a 0.1% solution can be formed by taking 100 ml of the 1% stock solution and adding to it 900 ml of water. By using the following equation you will be able to calculate how much of a stock solution you will need to dye the fabric a certain shade.

**Above: Using a variety of silk fibres and a madder dye, a huge range of colours can be achieved, from ochre to pale peach.**

(Weight of material x % depth of shade)÷strength of the solution = volume of dye solution needed or (W x D)÷S = V.

*For example*: to dye 60 g of fabric a pale shade of 0.3% depth using a solution of 1% strength, (W x D)÷S = V becomes (60 x 0.3)÷1 = 18 ml of 1% dye solution.

## HOT WATER DYEING

**1 Weigh the fabric to calculate the amount of dye required (see page 41). Pour the water into a heat-proof container and soak the fabric in it.**

**2 Put the dye into a heat-proof jug and mix to a paste with a small amount of cold water. Add sufficient boiling water to dissolve the dye thoroughly.**

## DYEING THE FABRIC

**3 Heat the water to a hand-hot temperature (40ºC), and add the dissolved dye solution. Stir the dye bath to ensure that the dye is evenly dispersed throughout.**

**4 Immerse the fabric and stir for 10 minutes. Remove the fabric, disperse the auxiliaries, and replace the fabric. Heat to boiling and stir for 30–60 minutes.**

The same principles apply to calculating the amount of dye for a print paste. Manufacturer's shade cards can be used as a rough indication but the percentage of dye is normally calculated on the amount of print paste required instead of the weight of the material to be dyed:

Amount of dye needed (in grams) = (% shade x amount of print paste)÷100.

*For example:* if 250 ml of print paste is needed for a dye at 2% depth of shade, then:
(2 x 250)÷100 = 5 g of dye.

The same applies when a stock solution is used, but the water content of the paste will have to be reduced by 150 ml or the paste will be too runny.

Volume of dye solution needed = (volume of print paste x % depth of shade)÷strength of the solution or (W x D)÷S = V.

*For example:* to mix 500 ml of print paste a pale shade of 0.3% depth using a solution of 1% strength:
(W x D)÷S = V becomes (500 x 0.3)÷1 = 150 ml of 1% dye solution.

To enable the dyes to fix and take evenly, various auxiliaries are needed in the dye bath. Their roles vary; some aid level dyeing, while others assist in fixing and attracting the dyes to the fibres of the cloth. The amount of auxiliary can be calculated in two ways. The first method is based on the dry weight of the fabric to be dyed:

Dry weight of fabric x (percentage of auxiliary÷100) = amount required.

*For example*: to dye 200 g of fabric you will need 20% salt to assist with the up-take of direct dyes:
W x (A%÷100) = amount required becomes 200 x (20÷100) = 40 g of salt.

The second method is based upon the volume of water in the dye bath and the amount of auxiliary required for the depth of the shade:

Volume of water x (percentage of auxiliary÷100) = amount required.

Exhaust dyeing can be divided into hot and cold water methods. The techniques described in this book have been simplified, providing very general methods for the range of dyes available. Refer also to any instructions given by the dye manufacturer.

## Recording and Sampling

It is often difficult to obtain pattern books from the dye manufacturers. If this is the case it is important to keep records of your own dyeing experiments and the colouring pastes you use. This can be done simply by filing a piece of the fabric you have coloured together with any relevant information. This should include the name, the shade of the dye used and the dyeing time, the volume and temperature of the water in which you dyed the fabric, and the recipe of any print paste and patterning method used. This information will be invaluable if you wish to repeat this colour or effect. It is also useful to carry out a small sample dyeing with any new colour you buy. This will enable you to build up your own sample books. These records are ultimately one of the most important points of reference for successful dyeing and patterning.

## Hot Water Dyeing

Before starting consult the safety precautions, and make sure you are suitably dressed. To begin, fill a heat-proof dyeing container with enough soft water to cover the fabric. A liquor ratio of 20:1 (2 litres of water for every 100 g of fabric) is needed for direct dyes and 30:1 for acid, basic and disperse dyes. This will allow for free circulation of the dye liquor around the cloth. The dye bath should be no hotter than 40°C. If the water is too hot at the start of the dyeing process the dye will fix too rapidly to the fabric's fibres, causing a patchy uneven colour. A small amount of wetting agent, for example detergent, or a specific levelling auxiliary can be added to the bath to aid even dyeing.

INDIGO DYED SAMPLES - HYDROSULPHITE VAT.
DYED DAY AFTER MAKING: TEMPERATURE 22° C; P.H. READING 11.7

TUMMERIC DYED SAMPLES
DYED IN 50% SOUTION FROM TUMMERIC AT 100°C FOR 45 MINUTES

**Above: Simple dye charts will help you record the results achieved using a variety of dyes and fibre types.**

Weigh the fabric (in grams) to determine the amount of dye needed, and before dyeing make sure that the fabric is free from any impurities. Then wet the cloth and place it into the prepared dye bath. Select the dye for the fibres you are dyeing (see chapter 3), along with the colour and shade you require. If the fabric is later to be discharge patterned (see chapter 14), verify the dye's dischargeability. (Some suitable colours have been listed on page 139–141.) Then using the following formula, calculate the amount of dye you require:

Amount of dye required =
(% shade÷100) x dry weight of fabric (in grams)

Weigh the dye out into a stainless-steel or heat-proof glass jug, then mix into a paste with a small amount of cold water before adding sufficient boiling water to dissolve the dye (most colours will require 20–40 times as much water as dye in order to dissolve satisfactorily). It is important to ensure that all the dye particles have dissolved (or dispersed); if in any doubt sieve the solution, because undissolved dye will cause dark spots on the fabric. Most dyes only require hot water to dissolve completely, but some may need boiling for a short period. If you are using a dye mixture, the different dye components should each be dissolved separately.

To dye, remove the fabric from the dye container and add the pre-dissolved dye solution, ensuring that it is evenly dispersed in the water before replacing the damp fabric. Stir the fabric for 10 minutes, and it will begin to absorb the dye. Meanwhile calculate the amounts of auxiliaries you require. Each type of dye will need different types and amounts of additives to aid even absorption and fixation. Auxiliaries for each dye type are listed (see right), along with any further steps required.

After 10 minutes remove the fabric from the bath and add any auxiliaries, dispersing them well in the dyeing liquor. Return the fabric to the dye bath and slowly increase the temperature over a period of 30 minutes until it is nearly boiling (80–100°C). Maintain this temperature for 30–60 minutes. (Do not exceed 85°C when dyeing silks and wools as this may damage the fibres.) If using a mixture of dyes, allow sufficient time (approximately 30 minutes, but consult the manufacturer's information for the specific dye time of different dyes) during dyeing to enable the dyes to achieve an equilibrium. For level dyeing the fabric must be kept moving. Agitating the fabric throughout dyeing prevents the dye from taking faster in the hotter spots near the bottom of the bath and avoids pale patches where the fabric has not been completely submerged.

**Right and Opposite: Using different protein fibres, the yellow dye samples exhibit the effect of weld dyes, whilst the pinks represent a range of effects achieved with cochineal dyes.**

**BRANDED AUXILIARIES FOR REACTIVE DYES**

| Range of dyes | Auxiliary product | Ammonium sulphate | Retarding agent |
| --- | --- | --- | --- |
| Drimalan F | Lyogen FN (1–4%) | – | 10–5% sodium sulphate |
| Lanasol | Albegal B (1–2%) | 4% | 10–5% sodium sulphate |
| Hostalan | Eganol GES (5%) | 2% | – |

*NB: All percentages are given in relation to the weight of the fabric being dyed (see previous equations).*

Once the desired shade has been achieved, cool the dye bath to 70°C before removing the fabric. Rinse the cloth thoroughly to remove any excess which may bleed out and spoil a final piece. Rinsing must be done with care as sudden temperature changes will felt most protein fibres and leave permanent creases in some synthetics. For best results, therefore, rinse the fabric first in warm water and then in cold until the water runs clear. Lightly spin-dry and press.

## Auxiliaries for Hot Water Exhaust Dyeing
To calculate how much of an auxiliary is needed for each of the following dyes, apply the percentages given to the formulas on pages 40–41.

*Acid dyes*: Each dye range has its own specific make of leveller but liquid detergents are chemically very similar and can be substituted if the correct type is not available. The amount of leveller added normally equates to 1% of the dry weight of fabric. For levelling and fast dyes (pH 3–4) use 10% of sodium sulphate (Glauber's salt) and 4–8% of acetic or formic acid (at 20% strength). For acid milling dyes (pH 5.2–6.2) use 10% sodium sulphate (Glauber's salt) and 4–12% of acetic acid (at 20% strength), or 3% ammonium sulphate or ammonium acetate and 6% acetic acid (at 20% strength). Metal complex and supermilling dyes (pH 5.5) require 2–4% ammonium sulphate or ammonium acetate or 6% acetic acid (at 20% strength).

*Basic dyes*: Use 10% sodium sulphate (Glauber's salt) and 4% of 20% acetic acid solution.

*Direct dyes*: For cellulose, use sodium chloride (common salt) or sodium sulphate (Glauber's salt) in an amount equivalent to 10–20% of the dry weight of fabric. Some colours perform better with sodium sulphate (check with the manufacturer). For silk and

wool use a 20% acetic acid solution in an amount equivalent to 5–10% of the weight of fabric.

*Disperse dyes* (pH 4–5): Use 6% acetic acid (at 20% strength) and 6–12% dye carrier equated to the weight of fabric. Soap flakes or the dye manufacturer's recommended dispersing agent can be used in the proportions of 1 g per litre of water.

*Reactive dyes for protein fibres:* Hot water reactive dyes for wool require a slightly acidic dye bath. The pH is determined by the depth of shade required: light shades are dyed at pH 5.5–6.0 and dark shades at pH 4.5–5.5. If the pH is too high exhaustion will be poor; too low and there will be unevenness as the dye is taken up too quickly by the fibre.

Acetic acid is the commonest auxiliary used to control pH, but ammonium sulphate is often employed because it slowly releases acid during the dyeing process. To ensure even dyeing, a levelling agent is employed – each dye manufacturer produces its own brand (see the table opposite).

*Reactive dyes for cellulose and silk fibres:* Reactive dyes (Procion H, H-E and HE-XL) in powder form can cause allergic respiratory reactions and so it is important that a suitable dust-excluding respirator or mask is worn when handling the dyes in their powdered state.

Sodium chloride (common salt) is normally used as an auxiliary but some blue and green dyes will give better results if sodium sulphate (Glauber's salt) is used. The second auxiliary is an alkali, sodium carbonate (washing soda). Add 80 g of sodium chloride and 20 g of sodium carbonate per litre of dye liquor for a deep shade, and 60 g of sodium chloride and 10 g of sodium carbonate for a mid-to-pale tone. If using these auxiliaries you will need to follow a different method after dyeing as the salt and the alkali are added in two stages.

After 10 minutes of dyeing add the salt in three stages – 10%, 30% and 60% – over a period of 20 minutes. Stir the fabric thoroughly after each addition. During this time increase the temperature of the dye bath to 80°C. When all the salt has been added dye the fabric for a further 20 minutes, keeping the fabric constantly moving. Over the following 10 minutes gradually add the alkali solution to the dye bath in small amounts, stirring well after each addition. The fabric is then dyed at 80°C for a further 30–60 minutes depending upon the shade you require and must be kept constantly moving for a further 15–20 minutes after that. For the remainder of the dyeing period you need to stir the cloth only every five minutes.

Once the desired shade has been achieved the fabric should be carefully removed from the dye bath and rinsed thoroughly in warm and then cold water until the water runs clear. Then boil the fabric for 10 minutes in a bath containing 3 ml of detergent per litre of water, after which the fabric can be rinsed again and dried.

## COLD WATER DYEING

The dyes used in cold water dyeing are highly reactive (e.g. Procion MX) and have a shelf-life of about one week once mixed with water, so mix only as much dye as you require at any one time. The method described below is very similar to the hot water reactive dyeing method. However, the main differences to note are: only use cold water in the dye bath; the dye is dissolved in warm rather than hot water; and there is no need to heat the dye bath during the dyeing process. All the other steps described still apply.

## Alternative Cold Water Dyeing

A few types of dye are suitable for dyeing with a cold water method. Because there is no heating process

## COLD WATER DYEING WITH REACTIVE DYES

**1** Weigh your fabric and calculate the amount of dye required. Mix up the dye and dissolve it in warm water. Weigh out and dissolve the auxiliaries.

**2–3** Add the dye solution and sodium chloride to the water in your dye bath. Stir the solution to ensure that the dye has dispersed in the bath.

**4** Immerse the fabric in the dye bath and gently agitate. The fabric needs to be agitated to ensure that the dye is taken up evenly and does not appear patchy.

## FIXING THE DYE

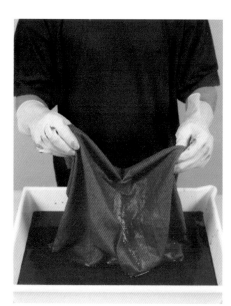

**5** After 20 minutes remove the fabric from the dye bath, allowing any excess dye to drip back into the bath. Do not wring the cloth out.

**6** Put the fabric to one side and add your sodium carbonate to the dye bath. Stir this into the bath thoroughly, before you replace the fabric.

**7** Return the fabric to the dye bath for fixing. You will need to leave the fabric in this solution for 60 minutes to ensure that the dye has fixed properly.

very little equipment is required and any plastic, enamel or stainless-steel container can be used as the dyeing vessel. This type of dyeing is useful for resist patterning techniques and batik work. The methods included in this section cover cold water azoic and vat dyes.

## Azoic or Naphthol Dyes

These can be used for batik and resist work. Although developed for cellulosic fabrics, they will also work on some synthetics but are unsuitable for protein fibres. These dyes are applied in two stages; first by dipping the fabric in a base solution then in a salt solution, the dye is formed within the cloth. The best type of container to use is a large shallow plastic bath and you will need two separate sets of equipment for the two stages. The table on page 46 gives some of the salts and bases available and shows what colours can be produced by combining different naphthol bases and diazo salts. The following recipe describes how to prepare 1 litre of each solution.

For the naphthol base solution prepare a strong solution of sodium hydroxide using the method described in the section on dyeing auxiliaries and additives (see page 38). Transfer 100 ml of this solution to a small bottle or measuring cylinder and keep at hand for the next step of the process.

The naphthol bath is prepared by dissolving the naphthol base in water. For a mid-shade, weigh out 2 g of naphthol base into a plastic or glass jug and mix to a smooth paste with a little methylated spirit or boiling water. To this paste add 250 ml of boiling water, stirring well to dissolve. Then add the sodium hydroxide solution immediately, a drop at a time, until the solution clears and appears yellow in colour. It will normally require about 2 ml of the sodium hydroxide solution for every gram of naphthol base used, but it may take up to 10 times this amount to clarify the solution. If the solution does not clear immediately reheat it to boiling point and stir. (Note: Naphthol AS will not completely clear.) Allow to cool

## NAPHTHOL DYES

**1–2 Weigh out the naphthol base into a suitable container. Mix it into a smooth paste with a little methylated spirits or boiling water.**

**3–4 Add boiling water and stir to dissolve. Immediately add the pre-prepared sodium hydroxide solution, a drop at a time, until the solution appears yellow.**

## THE NAPHTHOL DYE BATH

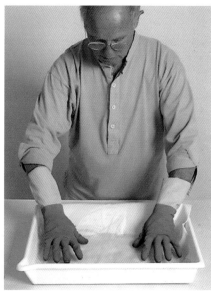

**5 Allow the solution to cool for five minutes before adding it to the water in the first dye bath. The naphthol base and water need to make 1 litre of solution.**

**6 Wet-out the fabric in cold water. Place it in the naphthol dye bath. Agitate for 5 minutes. Remove and allow to drip-dry before transferring to the diazo salt bath.**

**AZOIC DYE COLOUR COMBINATIONS**

|  | Naphthol AS | Naphthol AS. G | Naphthol AS. GR | Naphthol AS. LB | Naphthol AS. BO |
|---|---|---|---|---|---|
| **Fast yellow GC** | Red-orange | Lemon | Magenta | Tan | Bright red |
| **Fast scarlet RC** | Pink | Bright yellow | Red-violet | Cocoa brown | Claret |
| **Fast scarlet GG** | Scarlet | Yellow | Red-violet | Brown | Deep red |
| **Fast red B** | Light crimson | Orange-yellow | Purple | Red brown | Maroon |
| **Fast violet B** | Violet | Brownish-yellow | Dark green | Bordeaux | Violet-black |
| **Fast blue B** | Blue-violet | Ochre | Green | Deep violet | Blue-black |
| **Fast blue BB** | Bright blue | Gold | Blue-green | Purple | Blue |

for five minutes before adding enough cold water to make up a litre of solution. Transfer to the dye bath and keep it out of direct sunlight.

The diazo salt solution is then prepared in a second bath. For a mid-shade, weigh out 4 g of a fast colour salt into a litre jug and mix to a paste with a little cold water. Then make up to a full litre with more cold water and stir the solution until completely dissolved.

Dyeing is in two main stages. Wet-out the fabric with cold water and place it in the first dye bath containing the naphthol base. Agitate for five minutes and remove, allowing the excess base solution to drip off into the bath. Leave the fabric to drip-dry for 15–30 minutes before proceeding to the next stage.

The cloth is then passed through a salt rinse (made up in a separate vessel) containing 50 g sodium chloride per litre of water, followed by a rinse in clean water if desired. The sodium chloride will neutralize any excess naphthol base in the cloth. Next, carefully enter the cloth into the second bath containing the diazo salt and agitate gently. The colour will begin to appear immediately on contact with the base solution. Allow the dye to develop fully over a period of five minutes before removing the cloth from the bath. Allow the cloth to drip-dry for five minutes before rinsing it in cold water until the water runs clear. The process can be repeated to build up deeper shades. When the desired

**Opposite: Noel Dyrenforth's dramatic batik 'Recoil' (137 x 173 cm) shows the vivid effects that can be achieved.**

## THE DIAZO SALT SOLUTION

**1 Make up the diazo colour salt and add this solution to the second dye bath. Stretch the fabric out flat and slowly lower it into the second bath.**

**2 As soon as the treated fabric enters the diazo solution, the colour should appear immediately. Agitate the cloth gently in the bath for five minutes.**

**3 Remove the fabric from the bath and allow to drip-dry for five minutes before rinsing in cold water. This design was created using resist techniques.**

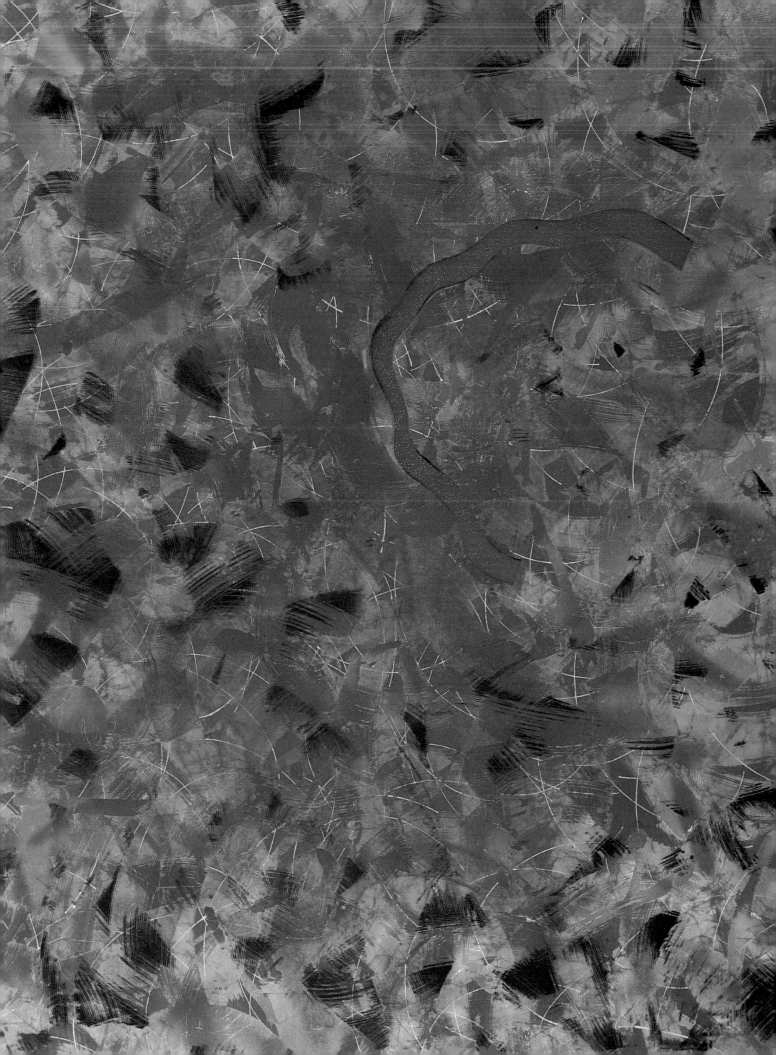

## PREPARING AN INDIGO VAT

**1 Measure out 40 litres of warm water (25ºC) into a large plastic vat. Add the sodium chloride to the water and stir until it has dissolved evenly.**

**2–3 Carefully mix the sodium hydroxide separately (remember to add the sodium hydroxide to the water and not vice-versa). Stir this solution into the vat.**

**4 Sprinkle the sodium hydrosulphite powder slowly onto the surface of the vat. Again, stir the vat to ensure an even dispersion of the powder.**

**5 Finally, add the indigo, a small amount at a time, stirring gently to ensure that air bubbles do not form. Cover and leave for at least two hours before use.**

shade is achieved the fabric is given a final hot wash in soapy water before rinsing and drying.

### Vat Dyeing

A vat dyeing method is where the dye is held in solution in a large container. It is used for dyeing fabric with indigo, mineral, and vat dyes, often in conjunction with batik and resist patterning techniques. With vat dyeing, the shade of a fabric is determined by how often a piece of cloth is dipped into the vessel and for how long. A vat is normally made up with an excess amount of dye and the vat is used repeatedly until the dye has been exhausted. At this point the contents of the vat are discarded and a new vat is prepared. Again, the chemicals employed in making a vat must be handled with special care; protective clothing and a suitable respirator should be worn, especially when sprinkling chemicals or dyes onto the surface of the vat.

The fabric must be clean before you begin the printing process so it should be soaked and wrung out before dyeing. Submerge the fabric gently into the dye vat to avoid trapping pockets of air in the cloth as these may cause patchy and uneven dyeing. Once in the bath it must be kept under the dye surface and gently agitated for an even take up of the dye solution. To ensure that the maximum amount of dye is fully fixed onto the fabric, the cloths are exposed to the air for several hours (overnight if necessary) before giving them a final rinse. Once the dye has been fixed the cloth is washed thoroughly to remove any excess colour that might bleed out, spoiling the final piece.

Indigo is one of the oldest vat dyes. Although originally derived from various plants, it is now available in both natural and synthetic forms. Indigo will dye all natural fabrics but the following method is used mainly for dyeing cellulose and silk. One of the main applications of indigo is in resist patterned fabrics (see page chapter 13).

The dye must be reduced to its leuco form before it can be used. There are many methods of reducing the dye, but the simplest to control is the caustic soda and sodium hydrosulphite method. These measurements make 40 litres of solution. If a smaller amount is required, divide the measurements accordingly.

Place 40 litres of water at a temperature of 25°C in a large plastic vat. Add 850 g of sodium chloride to the vat and stir until dissolved. Remove 1 litre of this solution and add to it 50 g of sodium hydroxide pellets, then carefully return this solution to the main vat, stirring well to disperse evenly. Then sprinkle 150 g of sodium hydrosulphite powder onto the vat surface and slowly stir to dissolve. Add the indigo (200 g of indigo powder or grains; this can always be increased for a stronger blue) to the vat, a small amount at a time, stirring gently to ensure that air bubbles do not form. After about five minutes a brilliant purple sheen will have formed on the surface. This is excess indigo oxidizing on contact with the air at the surface of the vat. Cover the vat and leave for at least two hours before using (it is better to allow it to stand overnight).

Before dyeing with the indigo, you should check that it is in good condition. This type of dyestuff is affected by the cold, and an imbalance in the alkalinity or reducing agent will also prevent it from working correctly. Carefully take a sample of the dye, using a transparent container (try not to get excess air into the vat). If the sample is a clear greenish-yellow colour with a temperature of 20°C and a pH value of 10.5–11.7 it is in good condition and can be used. If the temperature of the dye has dropped below 20°C, it can be warmed up with hot water or an immersion heater. A greener colour indicates a lack of the reducing agent, which can be corrected by adding a small amount of sodium hydrosulphite until it turns greenish-yellow. A cloudy appearance indicates a lack of alkali, so sodium hydroxide solution should be added until the pH value is between 10.5 and 11.7, and the vat is clear. If the vat is pale and watery it has gone off and should be discarded.

## DYEING THE FABRIC

1 First, wet-out fabric in a solution of ammonia and sodium hydrosulphite. Wring out, then lower it slowly into the dye vat. Try to avoid pockets of air.

2 Agitate the fabric under the vat surface before removing. The wet fabric will appear to be greenish-yellow – the colour of the dye in its leuco state.

## OXIDIZATION

3 As soon as the dyed fabric comes into contact with the air it will start to oxidize, turning the indigo dye from greenish-yellow back to its deep blue state.

4 To ensure that the oxidization is even, the fabric needs to be spread out on a line as quickly and flatly as possible. Colour can be intensified by repeat dippings.

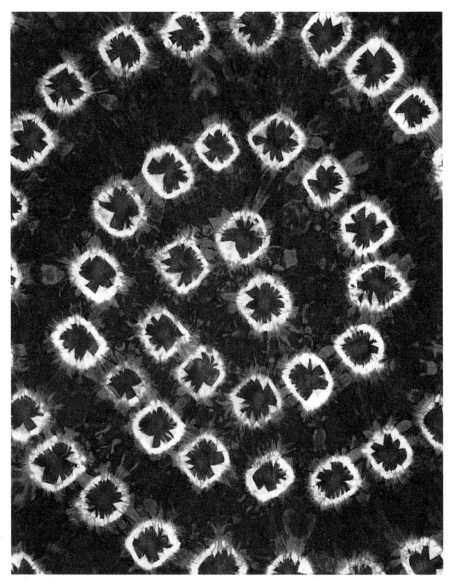

**Above: Kate Wells produced this traditional tie-and-dye by tying soya beans into a cloth and then dyeing with indigo.**

Before dyeing, ensure that the cloth has been wetted in warm water containing a small amount of ammonia and sodium hydrosulphite to acclimatize the cloth to the vat liquid; then wring it out to a damp state. If the cloth has been patterned using a resist paste it is best to dye it from a dry state to prevent the resist from being damaged. To avoid marking the fabric with oxidized indigo the purple scum on the top of the vat should be carefully drawn to one side using a piece of paper and the fabric slowly lowered into the bath. To avoid making air pockets, attach small weights or sinkers (these are supplied for fishing and can be clipped or pinned onto the edge of the fabric) to large pieces of fabric. This helps to keep them below the surface of the dye.

The fabric is then gently agitated for 1–2 minutes before being carefully removed. As soon as the dyed fabric comes into contact with the air the dye will begin to oxidize, converting the indigo back to its blue state. Once removed from the dye vat the fabric needs to be spread out on a line as quickly and flatly as possible to allow it to oxidize evenly (leave overnight if necessary). The colour can be intensified by repeat dippings of 1–5 minutes until the desired shade is achieved. Rinse out any surplus dye in cold water followed by a hot soapy wash. Spin and dry.

The dye vat can continue to be used until exhausted. At this stage it will look a bluey-grey colour when tested. If more fabric needs to be dyed, the bath can be revived by adding sodium hydroxide, sodium hydrosulphite and indigo in the amounts recommended for a new vat. However, it will be necessary to adjust these amounts if the vat is no longer full. Leave for a few hours before re-using.

Insoluble vat dyes are available in two forms: grains and liquid. The liquid will generally consist of about 10–20% dyestuff in water and a small quantity of dispersing agent. The grains have replaced the earlier powder forms and contain a solid diluent and a small amount of dispersing agent. Common brands are the Caledons, Cibanone, Indanthren and Sandothrene. In order to use these dyes, a strong solution is prepared which is then added to the dye vat as required. The following recipe is for 100 g of fabric to be dyed 1% shade in 3 litres of water. The recipe can be multiplied for larger amounts of fabric, in which case a larger container will be needed.

Measure 3 litres of cold water into a plastic container or bucket for the main vat solution. To this add 40 g of sodium chloride or sodium sulphate and stir to dissolve. Then carefully add 2.5 ml of sodium hydroxide solution at 38° Bé (72° Tw) and 2 g of sodium hydrosulphite. Stir to disperse all the chemicals evenly throughout the vat liquor.

For the stock solution weigh out 10 g of dye and place into a heat-proof container. Mix to a paste with some water or methylated spirits, then slowly add 100 ml of warm water (45°C) and stir well. To this solution carefully add 5 ml of sodium hydroxide solution at 38° Bé (72° Tw) and 2.5 g of sodium hydrosulphite. Place the container in hot water and stir gently; maintain the solution at 45–60°C for 5–10 minutes until all the dye has dispersed. The dye should convert to its leuco form and appear an orange colour. Slowly pour the stock solution into the main vat, stirring to disperse the dye evenly. Leave for about one hour before dyeing.

Ensure that the cloth has been wetted in warm water containing a detergent; then wring to a damp state. (If the cloth has been resist patterned it is best to dye it from dry.) Lower the fabric slowly into the bath, taking care to avoid creating air bubbles in the vat. Again, small weights will help to keep larger pieces of fabric below the surface of the liquid. The cloth is then agitated for 1–2 minutes before being removed and allowed to oxidize.

Vat dyes do not react as fast as indigo, consequently the colour change is slower and more even. Allow the cloth to oxidize as long as possible, overnight if necessary. The process can then be repeated to intensify the colour until the desired shade is achieved. Rinse out any surplus dye in cold water, followed by a boil wash with detergent. Rinse and dry.

## DYEING WITH NATURAL DYES

The colours obtained with vegetable and mineral dyes are often rich, but they can also produce softer shades than those of synthetic dyestuffs. They are not as light- or wash-fast as synthetic dyes, but with the careful use of mordants these characteristics can often be improved. The dyeing processes for natural dyes are often complicated and require patience and time before they can be fully mastered. Only a brief overview of the methods involved is given in this book, but further reading on the subject is included in the bibliography. Natural dyes can be divided into two classes: substantive dyes, which have a direct affinity for the fibre; and adjective dyes, which require a mordant to fix the colour upon the cloth.

### Substantive Dyes

These dyes can be used without any additional chemicals, but they may not produce as strong or as fast a colour as they might if a mordant is employed during the process.

The amount of dyestuff required is calculated on the weight of the dry fabric. It is then weighed out into a suitable dye container and boiled in water for 30 minutes to extract the dye. The wetted-out fabric is then submerged in the dye liquor and boiled for a further 45–60 minutes before being removed from the dye, rinsed well and dried.

### Adjective or Mordant Dyes

These dyestuffs require a mordant to fix the colour onto the fibres of the fabric. A mordant can be applied to the fabric before or during dyeing, or afterwards as a modifier. Different mordants will, of course, produce different colours and shades with the same dye, and separate mordanting techniques are required for protein

## PREPARING AN ONION DYE

1 Calculate the amount of dyestuff needed based on the weight of fabric. Then peel the necessary number of onions and place the skins in a heat-proof container.

2 Cover the onion skins adequately with water and bring to the boil. Leave for 45–60 minutes to extract the dyestuff from the skins. Do not allow to boil dry.

3 The resulting dye liquor needs to be strained through muslin to get rid of the skin pulp. Allow the liquor to cool before attempting to use it for dyeing.

**MORDANTS FOR PROTEIN FIBRES**

|  | Mordant | Auxiliary |
|---|---|---|
| **Alum** | 8% Aluminium sulphate | 7% Cream of tartar |
|  | or aluminium potassium sulphate | – |
| **Chrome** | 1% Potassium dichromate | 10% Formic acid at 20% strength |
| **Copper** | 2% Copper sulphate crystals | 10% Acetic acid solution at 20% strength |
| **Tin** | 7% Stannous chloride | 8% Oxalic acid |

*NB: All percentages are given in relation to the weight of the fabric being dyed (see previous equations).*

and cellulose fibres. The dyes and the methods of application will also differ for the two different fibre types. Protein fibres, such as wool and silk, are the easiest to use when exploring this method of dyeing for the first time. All the mordants and dyes needed are calculated on the dry weight of the fabric and are then expressed as a percentage of the weight of the dry cloth. The following formula is used:

Amount of dye÷mordant (in grams) =
(% shade÷100) x Dry weight of fabric (g)

## DYEING WITH ONION DYE

**1 Submerge the pre-mordanted fabric in the onion dye. Place on a hot plate and bring to the boil. Boil for a further 30–45 minutes, stirring occassionally.**

### Mordanting of Protein Fabrics

Wet-out the fabric using warm water containing a detergent, then rinse and wring out or spin-dry to a damp state. Remember mordants are toxic so protective clothing must be worn. Put enough cold water to cover the fabric into a non-metallic container. Dissolve the requisite mordant and auxiliary in a small amount of warm water. Then add them to the bath and stir well to disperse the two solutions. (See the table above for mordants and auxiliaries.)

**2 Allow to cool before removing the fabric from the dye liquor. Rinse the fabric and allow to dry. The dye bath may be re-used for lighter shades.**

Immerse the wetted-out fabric in this solution and slowly bring to the boil over a period of 30 minutes. Simmer for a further 45 minutes and then let the mordant bath cool before removing the fabric. When using stannous chloride or potassium dichromate you must cover the container while mordanting to reduce exposure to the fumes given off. (A respirator may need to be worn during this process.) Rinse thoroughly and dye immediately.

When employing alum as a mordant on woollen cloth, some natural dyes will dye to brighter shades if the cloth is 'aged' before use. This can be achieved by keeping the fabric in a damp state wrapped in plastic for 3–5 days before dyeing.

Modifiers and additives for protein fabrics are: acetic acid, ammonia, iron, sodium chloride and tin. When added to some plants, acetic acid will help to extract more dyestuff and the final colour will quite often be enhanced. Ammonia will alter the pH of the dye bath, making it more alkaline, and often causes the colour of a dye to shift from red or yellow to a green. Iron, in the form of ferrous sulphate, is used as a modifier and is added to the dye bath after the majority of dyeing has taken place. This process is known as 'saddening' and will dull the colour of the dye bath. It also has the effect of hardening protein fibres and will cause damage if too much is applied – an amount equal to 5% of the fabric's weight is normally adequate. Sodium chloride can be added to cochineal dye baths when alum is used as a mordant, and tin (stannous chloride) is used as a modifier. Added to the dye bath after most of the dyeing has taken place, stannous chloride acts as a brightening agent; again, 5% of the fabric's weight is normally adequate. The fabric must then be washed thoroughly after dyeing.

### Mordanting of Cellulose Fabrics

When using these toxic chemicals you must observe all the general safety precautions. The basic method is the same as for protein fibres but

**MORDANTS FOR CELLULOSE FABRICS**

| | Mordant | Auxiliary |
|---|---|---|
| **Alum** | 25% Aluminium sulphate | 6% Washing soda (Sodium carbonate) |
| **Tannic** | 5% Tannic acid or 60% pre-soaked oak galls | – |
| **Alum-tannic-alum** | 1. 25% Aluminium sulphate | 6% Sodium carbonate |
| | 2. 5% Tannic acid or 60% pre-soaked oak galls | |
| | 3. 25% Aluminium sulphate | 6% Sodium carbonate |

*NB: All percentages are given in relation to the weight of the fabric being dyed (see previous equations).*

**PRE-MORDANTS**

| | Mordant | Auxiliary |
|---|---|---|
| **Chrome** | 1% Potassium dichromate | 10% Formic acid at 20% strength. |
| **Copper** | 2% Copper sulphate crystals | 10% Acetic acid solution at 20% strength |

*NB: All percentages are given in relation to the weight of the fabric being dyed (see previous equations).*

the cloth is left in the mordanting solution overnight. When using the alum-tannic-alum mordanting recipe (see the table of cellulose mordants, above) on cellulose, the processes are repeated three times with the appropriate mordants and additives.

### Pre-Mordants and After-Mordants
With pre-mordants the fabric is first mordanted with tannic acid and then treated in a boiling bath with any of the pre-mordants shown in the table above for 30 minutes before being rinsed well and then dyed.

With after-mordants the fabric is mordanted, dyed and then treated in a boiling bath of any of the after-mordants in the table on page 54. The fabric is boiled for 10 minutes before being rinsed well and dried. When using stannous chloride or potassium dichromate, remember to cover the container to reduce the risk of fumes.

### Natural Dyes
Once your cloth has been mordanted you can proceed to the dyeing stage. The following method outlines the general procedure for obtaining dye from plants and insects. The table on page 55 indicates some of the many dyestuffs available and which mordants and auxiliaries to use to obtain particular colours and effects.

Using the equations given earlier (page 39), calculate the amount of dyestuff required based on the weight of the dry fabric. Weigh the material out and place in a suitable

dye container. Cover with water and boil for 45–60 minutes to extract the dyestuff. However, if using madder to obtain reds, the dye bath must be kept below boiling point or you will produce only oranges and browns. Strain off the resulting dye liquor and allow to cool before dyeing the fabric. The wetted-out fabric is then submerged in the dye liquor and boiled for 30–45 minutes. Allow it to cool before removing it from the dye solution, rinsing well and drying. The dye bath may be re-used for paler shades if there is enough dye remaining in the solution.

### Mineral Dyes
The yellow and gold colours of iron rust are produced from iron salts. Iron has an affinity for cellulose and by simply immersing the fabric in a solution of its salts and then exposing it to the air, a golden yellow colour can be obtained. The easiest method to produce this colour is with iron sulphate crystals.

## MORDANTING

**1 Weigh out the mordant and auxiliary into separate containers. Remember that mordants are toxic so you will need to wear protective clothing.**

**2 To dissolve the mordant and the auxiliary, add some warm, not boiling, water to each and stir well to ensure even dispersion.**

|  | Mordant | Auxiliary |
|---|---|---|
| **Chrome** | 1% Potassium dichromate | 10% Formic acid at 20% strength. |
| **Copper** | 2% Copper sulphate crystals | 10% Acetic acid solution at 20% strength |
| **Iron** | 2% Ferrous sulphate | – |

NB: All percentages are given in relation to the weight of the fabric being dyed (see previous equations).

Ensure that the cloth is wetted-out in warm water containing a detergent, then wring to a damp state. In a stainless-steel or enamel pan dissolve 500 g of ferrous sulphate in 5 litres of warm water and heat to 95°C. Then submerge the wetted-out fabric in the solution and stir constantly for 5–10 minutes, maintaining the temperature of the bath just below boiling point.

Carefully remove and allow to oxidize in the air. When dry, pass through a bath containing an alkali, such as sodium carbonate, ammonia or a weak solution of sodium hydroxide. This will convert the green-gold colour of the unoxidized salt to the final rust colour of ferric hydrate. Wash the fabric to rinse out the alkali. A final soak for 10 minutes in a sugar bath (one tablespoon of brown sugar or molasses dissolved in 5 litres of water), will give the fabric a soft, slightly silky feel.

Iron greys and blacks are formed by converting iron salts into iron-tannins, which are grey to black in colour. Any iron salt can be altered with the mordant tannic acid, but most success is achieved with the salts ferrous sulphate and ferrous acetate.

The recipe for iron rust can be used to produce ferrous sulphate on the cloth, but omit the oxidizing and the alkali. Instead, the fabric is soaked in a hot solution containing 10% tannic acid powder for 10 minutes; this will chemically bond with the yellow iron salt in the fabric to form a black iron-tannin. Afterwards, wash and dry the cloth.

A solution of ferrous acetate can also be used. Mix 500 g of ferrous sulphate with 250 g of lead acetate (a poison) in a litre of hot water. The solution is allowed to stand for an hour, after which time a precipitate of lead sulphate in the form of a sediment will have formed in a solution of ferrous acetate. The ferrous acetate can then be poured off for use in the dyeing process. (The waste lead sulphate must be disposed of safely.)

The fabric is soaked in the solution and then treated with a tannic acid bath as described above. A crude version of ferrous acetate can be made by dissolving scraps of iron in vinegar, or fermenting iron scraps in a sugar solution for a few weeks.

It is possible to start with a cloth pre-mordanted with tannic acid and then dip this into the iron salts. Extra care should be taken when handling tannic-mordanted cloth as any trace of iron from your hands will make black marks on the cloth.

The rich brown colour of manganese bronze is developed from the chemical manganese chloride. It is difficult to achieve an even colour on plain cloth but it is useful in tie-and-dyeing and will give interesting effects if patterned with a citric acid discharge (see page 144).

Ensure that the cloth has been wetted-out in warm water containing a detergent and then wring it out to a damp state. Dissolve 30–100 g of manganese chloride in 1 litre of warm water in a plastic container. Multiply this amount accordingly if you require a larger bath. Immerse the wetted-out cloth and leave for about five minutes to absorb the salt, then remove and hang up to dry. Make up the fixing bath containing 2% sodium hydroxide solution at 38° Bé (72° Tw). When the fabric is nearly dry, pass it through this solution, followed by a cold rinse. Then wash it in hot soapy water before a final rinse and drying.

## MORDANTING (continued)

**3 Pour enough water into a container to enable you to cover the fabric. Then add the dissolved mordant and auxiliary and stir well to disperse the two solutions.**

**4 Immerse the wetted-out fabric in this solution and slowly bring to the boil. Simmer for a further 45 minutes and then allow to cool before removing the fabric.**

**NATURAL DYES**

| PLANTS | % | Part Used | Mordant for Cellulose | Colour on Cellulose | Mordant for Protein Fibres | Colour on Protein |
|--------|---|-----------|----------------------|---------------------|---------------------------|-------------------|
| **Blackberry** | 200% | Berries | – | – | Alum | Blue-grey |
| | | Shoots | | | Chrome | Green-grey |
| | | | | | Copper | Mid-green |
| **Black Walnut** | 100% | Leaves | None | Browns and creams | Alum | Yellow ochre |
| | | Hulls | Alum-tannin–alum | Greyish-brown | Chrome | Ochre |
| | | | | | Copper | Light brown |
| | | | | | Iron | Slate grey |
| **Brazilwood** | 100% | Heartwood | Alum + washing soda | Brownish-red | Alum | Deep red |
| | | | Alum-tannin-alum | Deep red | Chrome | Black |
| | | | Tannic | Brownish-red | Copper | Bordeaux |
| | | | Copper + tannic | Greyish rose pink | Iron | Blue grey |
| | | | | | Tin | Dull pink |
| **Bur Marigold** | 100% | Leaves | Alum-tannin-alum | Grey fawn | None | Brilliant orange |
| | | Flowers | | | Alum | Orange-yellow |
| **Cochineal** | 25% | Ground bodies | Alum + washing soda | Grey rose | Alum | Red |
| | | | Alum-tannin-alum | Deep magenta | Chrome | Purple |
| | | | Tannic | Grey-pink-rose | Copper | Maroon |
| | | | Tannic + copper | Dull violet | Iron or tin | Blue-grey |
| **Coffee** | 100% | Beans (ground) | None | Cream | Alum | Browns and buffs |
| | | | | | Iron | Grey |
| **Cutch** | 100% | Leaves and twigs | None | Light pinky-brown | Alum | Warm brown |
| | | | Alum-tannin-alum | Dark copper | Iron | Grey |
| **Fustic** | 100% | Heartwood | Alum + washing soda | Corn yellow | Alum | Bright yellow |
| | | | Alum-tannin-alum | Dark yellow | Chrome | Orange |
| | | | Tannic | Yolk yellow | Copper | Golden brown |
| | | | Tannic + copper | Brownish-yellow | Iron | Brown-black |
| | | | | | Tin | Soft yellow |
| **Heather** | 100% | Flowering tops | – | – | Alum | Warm yellow |
| | | | | | Chrome | Warm brown |
| | | | | | Copper | Fawn |
| **Henna** | 100% | Tops | None | Yellow | Alum | Beige |
| | | | Alum-tannin-alum | Dull greenish-yellow | Chrome | Ochre |
| **Logwood** | · 50% | Heartwood chips | None | Fawn | Alum | Blue black |
| | | | Alum-tannin-alum | Plum purple | Chrome | Black |
| | | Extract | Alum- washing soda | Dark violet | Copper | Navy |
| | | | Tannic | Dull violet | Iron | Blue grey |
| | | | Tannic + copper/chrome | Dark plum grey | Tin | Red violet |
| | | | | Dark purple-black | | |
| **Madder** | 100% | Root | None | Dull pink | Alum | Bright red |
| | | | Alum + washing soda | Brown red | Chrome | Red brown |
| | | | Alum-tannin-alum | Turkey red | Copper | Dull pink |
| | | | Tannic | Brown red | Iron | Grey brown |
| | | | Tannic + copper | Brownish purple-red | Tin | Scarlet |
| **Onion** | 50% | Outer skins (brown) | None | Tan | Alum | Yellow |
| | | | Iron | Yellow greyish-brown | Chrome | Orange |
| | | | | | Copper | Bronze-brown |
| | | | | | Tin | Bright orange |
| **Persian berry** | 20% | Unripe berries | – | – | Alum | Cream |
| | | | | | Alum + tin | Pale yellow |
| | | | | | Chrome | Peach |
| | | | | | Copper | Warm grey |
| | | | | | Iron | grey |
| **Safflower** | 200% | Petals | None | Creamy yellow | Alum | Yellow |
| | | | Alkali | Bright pink | | |
| | 400% | | | Fluorescent pink | | |
| **Sandalwood** | 100% | Heartwood | Alum-tannin-alum | Brownish-orange | Alum | Golden brown |
| | | | | | Chrome | Red brown |
| | | | | | Copper | Grey fawn |
| | | | | | Iron | Slate grey |
| **Tea** | 100% | Dried leaves | None | Buffs | None | |
| | | | Alum-tannin-alum | Pinkish fawn-brown | | |
| | | | Alum-tannin-alum | Camel brown | | |
| | | | Tannin + chrome/copper | Fawn | | |
| | | | Iron | grey | | |
| **Turmeric** | 50% | Powdered plant | None | Bright Orange-yellow | Chrome | Deep orange |
| | | | | | Tin | Bright orange |
| **Weld** | 100% | Roots | Alum-tannic-alum | Mimosa yellow | Alum | Yellow |
| | | | | | Chrome | Old gold |
| | | | | | Copper | Greenish-yellow |
| | | | | | Iron | Green-grey |
| | | | | | Tin | Lemon |

From the above table you will notice that very few natural dyes will produce the colours green or blue. They are obtained from a limited number of plants that contain indigo. Woad (*isatis tinctoria*), indigo (*indigofrea tinctoria*) and the polygonium (*polygonium tinctorium*) will all produce a blue dye. The methods of extraction are more complicated than for other natural dyestuffs and the dyeing recipe can be found in the section on dyeing with vat dyes (see pages 48–50).

# 5

# GUMS, PASTES AND BINDERS

A thickener is used to control the dyes, colorants and auxiliaries in a print paste, and to prevent the colour from bleeding in a design. It must not break down during the fixing process and must wash out of the finished piece of fabric without leaving a residue. Thickeners are grouped into three types: high solid, low solid and emulsion. They can also be categorized as natural, modified and synthetic. Some are starches and gums that have been used for centuries; others are new derivatives, emulsions and synthetic polymers. This book cannot detail all the gums, binders and pastes available, but this chapter will cover the main ones needed for any of the patterning methods in this book.

## NATURAL GUMS
### Alginate Gums
These gums are derived from sodium alginate, which is obtained from seaweeds. They were developed to overcome the problems that arise with reactive dyes and other thickeners. They are available in different grades and different viscosities and are known by the trade names Manutex and Lamitex. The most commonly used are Manutex F and Manutex RS or Lamitex L. These gums store relatively well so can be made up in large quantities and stored in an air-tight container in a cool place until required. The choice of Manutex F or RS depends on what fabric you are patterning and the effects you are trying to achieve.

Manutex F has a high solid content and low viscosity. It is used to overprint (placing one colour on top of another to create a third colour) or to achieve high definition of line on fine fabrics such as silk and cotton. Manutex RS, on the other hand, has a low solid content and is employed when a print or pattern contains no overprints. It is most commonly used with thicker fabrics.

---

RECIPE
1 litre cold water
10 g sodium hexametaphosphate
100 g Manutex F powder
or
44 g Manutex RS powder

---

For 1110 g (gums are usually expressed in weight) of Manutex F add the sodium hexametaphosphate (Calgon) to the water and stir until dissolved. Slowly add the Manutex F in a constant stream, stirring continually for five minutes, then leave to thicken for 1–2 hours before using.

For 1054 g of Manutex RS the same recipe applies, except you add Manutex RS powder (instead of Manutex F) when the sodium hexametaphosphate dissolves. Stir continually for five minutes and then leave to thicken as above.

### Crystal Gum
Crystal gum is often known as Nafka crystal gum and is made from vegetable gums like gum karaya. It is used mainly for acid and discharge printing and is a high solid gum that is very soluble and easy to mix.

---

RECIPE
1 litre cold water
200 g powdered crystal gum

---

For a quantity of 1200 g, sprinkle the powdered gum onto the surface of your water base, stirring constantly while doing so. Leave to stand overnight and strain through a sieve before using. If required for use sooner, the suspension can be boiled for five minutes, allowed to cool and then strained.

### Guar Gum
This gum is extracted from the guar plant (*Cyanaposis tetragonolobos*), a leguminous plant which has been grown for centuries in India and Pakistan for food. The gum is very similar to locust bean gum and can also be used as a thickener (Gum 301 Extra is one brand that is easy to mix).

---

**ALGINATE GUM (MANUTEX)**

Opposite: Karen Johnstone uses a silk screen that has been masked out with molten wax and gums for printing.

**1 Carefully weigh out the correct amount of Manutex gum powder and sodium hexametaphosphate, keeping them in separate containers.**

**2 Measure out the cold water into a jug and add the sodium hexametaphosphate to it (this will soften the water). Stir to ensure that it dissolves properly.**

RECIPE
1 litre cold water
130 g Gum 301 Extra

For acid dyes, discharge, and a few resist printing techniques, use Gum 301 Extra, which is stable in acidic conditions. Measure out the water and sprinkle Gum 301 Extra onto the surface, to create 1130 g of thickening paste. Remember to stir constantly when adding the gum and then leave to thicken for 1–2 hours.

## Gum Tragacanth

This gum is obtained from slits in the bark of *Astragalus gummifer*. In its raw state it was often called Devil's toenails or Dragon gum because it was sold in the form of curved, horny white or yellow scales. These scales were soaked for 2–3 days and then boiled to obtain a paste. However, the gum is now available in the form of a powder that can be mixed with warm water to produce a paste. It is widely used as a thickener – both on its own and in mixtures with starch – for discharge prints, but can be used with most dyes.

RECIPE
930 ml warm water
70 g gum tragacanth powder

Measure out the warm water and slowly sprinkle gum tragacanth powder onto the surface, mixing well (with a high speed mixer if available). Leave to stand for 24 hours before using. If you wish to use this gum as a marbling medium, dilute with more water in the approximate proportions of four parts water to one part gum paste until the consistency of thick cream is achieved.

## Locust Bean Gums

Sometimes known as gums gatto or carob gum, these gums are extracted from the kernels of the nuts of the carob tree, *Ceratonia siliqua*. The gum is treated with chemicals to make it readily soluble in water and is used for most types of printing as it is very stable in all ranges of pH. The various trade names include Printel, Meyprogum and Guaranate. Good results can be obtained if the correct grade is employed, but due to their availability in different grades – which require different proportions of gum – it is necessary to consult the manufacturer's instructions on how to make them up. Only one recipe follows, for Indalca PA/3-R.

RECIPE
1 litre cold water
100 g Indalca PA/3-R

Indalca PA/3-R is stable in acidic conditions and is used with acid and in pigment discharge printing techniques. Measure out the cold water into a container and slowly sprinkle the gum onto the water's surface, stirring constantly. Then leave to stand for 1–2 hours before using.

## Starch and Cellulose Ethers

Most starches and cellulose are not very soluble in water, but by modifying their chemical properties they can become useful thickeners. Cellulose is treated by etherification, a process that enables it to dissolve in water or other solvents. Solvitose is a modified starch and the thickener Celacol is a cellulose ether; to make it up, consult the manufacturer's instructions. Recipes for Solvitose C5 and Celacol are included below. These gums are used for many processes in this book and will keep for several weeks once made up, provided that they are stored in a sealed container and kept in a cool place. Larger quantities may be made up to save time.

RECIPE 1
1 litre cold water
250 g Celacol powder

RECIPE 2
1 litre cold water
120 g Solvitose C5 flakes

Celacol is very stable in acidic conditions. It tends to be used as a component in pigment print resist pastes

## ALGINATE GUM (continued)

**3 Pour the water into a suitable container. Then using a wooden spoon stir the water to create a vortex and slowly add the Manutex in a steady stream.**

**4 Stir the gum mixture well for about five minutes to dissolve the Manutex. Then leave the paste to thicken-up over a period of 1–2 hours before using.**

and as a thickener with acid resists. For 1200 g of gum, sprinkle the Celacol powdered gum into cold water and stir constantly. Then leave to stand for a few hours or overnight before using.

For strong alkali conditions use Solvitose C5 and mix up a paste as above. Solvitose is a starch ether capable of withstanding strong alkalis without breaking down, and is used mainly with vat dyes, where it will give a high colour yield. It is also used in crêpeing and wool devoré. It is easy to mix and has a texture similar to wallpaper paste.

## Gum Arabic
Gum arabic was traditionally used for printing silk (because it produced very sharp prints) and as a table gum adhesive (see below). If used as an adhesive the powder needs to be mixed with water; for a normal table gum a 40% solution (four parts gum to six parts water) is adequate. Ready-mixed solutions are easier to use and, being very pure, avoid problems that may arise with the gum going off. In some resist processes a solution can be used either by itself or mixed with another thickener.

## TABLE GUMS
Table gums are applied in a thin layer to a print table surface, allowing the fabric to be temporarily fixed in place for printing or painting. They do not effect the fabric and can be easily removed from the table with water or a solvent. Gum arabic was a commonly used table gum, but this has now been replaced in many cases with diluted alginate gum (Manutex). Synthetic glues are used in the printing industry. Once applied these glues remain permanently sticky and can be cleaned with water until they need to be removed with a solvent.

## EMULSION THICKENERS
Emulsion thickeners are found in a variety of forms for use with pigments, reactive dyes and disperse dyes. Pigment binders once required large amounts of white spirit to produce soft prints but solvent-free alternatives are now available that give similar results and can be safely used in small workshops or at home.

In industry these half-emulsions, consisting of a combination of white spirit and a water-based alginate gum, were used to print reactive dyes. They produced sharper prints and the emulsion could be washed off easily once the print was fixed. In recent years, their use has declined with the introduction of water and synthetic polymer solutions.

## RESIST PASTES
Various starches, gums, waxes and resins can be used as resists in the dyeing and printing processes. Experimentation is recommended as different effects can be produced by varying the thickness and the drying times of each paste. Starch pastes have been used for many centuries and mixtures can be applied by brush or feathers, or can be stencilled onto the cloth before drying and dyeing. Various flours (e.g. rice flour, corn flour, wheat flour, cassava flour and soya flour) may be mixed to different consistencies, with hot or cold water, to create different effects. Most of these flours will have a tendency to crack when dry, which will result in a crackled effect on the dyed fabric. If a smoother image is required, the flours can be cooked and mixed with gums to produce a more fluid and flexible paste.

## British Gum
British gum (also known as Dextrin) is often employed as a resist under other prints; it will produce some interesting cracked print effects when used as a resist paste under some dyes.

RECIPE
500 g Dextrin powder
500 ml boiling water

For 1000 g of gum, weigh out the Dextrin powder into a heat-proof container. Carefully add the boiling water,

**BRITISH GUM (DEXTRIN)**

1 Weigh out the required amount of British gum (Dextrin) and place it into a heat-proof container, ready for heating in a double boiler or a *bain-marie*.

2 Slowly and carefully add the boiling water to the British gum powder, stirring constantly to prevent any lumps from forming in the paste.

stirring all the time, and then heat in a double boiler or *bain-marie* for 20 minutes. Allow to cool to 60°C before using as a resist.

## Cassava Paste

This paste resists indigo. The copper sulphate is optional but acts as a preservative and gives the paste a pale blue colour that enables it to be seen when used on white cloth. It may also act as a chemical resist when dyed with indigo.

---
RECIPE
250 g cassava flour
5 g copper sulphate crystals
500 ml hot water

---

To make up the paste, weigh out the cassava flour and the copper sulphate crystals (if desired) into a saucepan and mix to a smooth paste with a little cold water. Slowly add the hot water, bring to the boil, stirring all the time. Simmer for 30 minutes, stirring occasionally to stop the paste sticking

to the pan. Allow the paste to cool and strain through a piece of muslin. The consistency of the paste can be altered with a little water, depending upon which method of application you wish to use.

## Flour and Gum Arabic

This paste is suitable for handpainting and block and screen printing. For 300 g of resist paste, mix 100 g of plain flour with 100 ml of cold water and heat until thick. Allow to cool slightly and slowly mix in 100 g of gum arabic solution (100% strength). If too thick dilute with a little water.

## Japanese Rice Resist Paste

The following recipe is a simplified version of a rice paste that can be drawn or stencilled directly onto the surface of the cloth. The paste will keep for one month in a refrigerator.

---
RECIPE
300 ml cold water
250 g rice flour

---

150 g sodium chloride (salt)
5 litres boiling water
Calcium hydroxide solution: 30–45 g calcium hydroxide dispersed in 100 ml water (do not add the sediment).

---

Slowly add the cold water to the rice flour until it forms a soft ball. Knead well, and form into 3–4 doughnut shapes. Add the sodium chloride (salt) to 5 litres of boiling water and drop the paste shapes into the water and heat for 15–20 minutes; remove when they begin to float. Beat to a paste adding the remaining hot salt water until a sticky glutinous consistency is achieved. Continue to beat until smooth. Gradually add the calcium hydroxide solution until the paste changes colour from light tan to a pale yellow. Beat until smooth adding more warm water if needed.

## Gutta, Cold and Hot Waxes

Various ready-made substances will serve as a resist paste. Gutta (a glue-like substance) is available from craft shops and can be used in a similar way to rice paste. It is available in many colours, including metallics, and is normally drawn onto silk using a plastic bottle; when dry it will stop the spread of liquid acid dyes. Some guttas are water soluble, others are alcohol based. The white and clear types will wash away after use but the black and metallic types remain glued to the cloth and cannot be removed once drawn in place.

Cold liquid wax is an emulsion that is normally used as a resist in ceramics. It can also be used on fabrics and may be applied by either painting or printing. Once the cloth has been coloured the wax can be removed by washing in hot soapy water or dry-cleaning.

Two main types of hot wax can be used, depending upon the effects required: paraffin, which is brittle; and beeswax, which is much softer. Many people combine the two in order to get the results they require. The waxes must be applied in a hot molten state, and can be removed once the fabric has been coloured (see pages 131–33).

---

## BRITISH GUM (continued)

**3 Transfer the mixed gum to a double boiler or a *bain-marie* and then heat for 20 minutes. Stir occasionally to ensure that the paste remains smooth.**

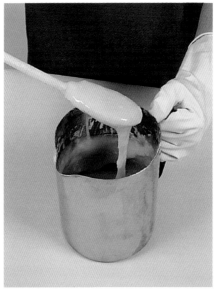

**4 Carefully remove the mixture from the heat and allow the gum to cool to a temperature of about 60°C before using it as a resist paste.**

## BASE THICKENERS FOR MARBLING

Various thickening agents are used to alter the viscosity of marbling mediums in order to control the patterning dyes. Carragheen is the most common but other substances like gum tragacanth, gelatine and wallpaper paste can also be used.

### Carragheen

The seaweed carragheen, which is commonly used as an emulsifier in food, can also be used to thicken the floating bath for marbling techniques. This seaweed is available in granules, chips or powder form. It is always best to choose a variety that requires no heating as such types are by far the easiest to use.

---

RECIPE
75 g carragheen powder
575 ml warm water
3.5 litres distilled water

---

Weigh out the carragheen powder into a blender. Add the warm water, and mix thoroughly until all the seaweed dissolves. Mix this whole solution with the 3.5 litres of distilled water and pour into the marbling bath to a depth of 4 cm, repeating the process if necessary. Then place the bath on a very flat surface and leave to thicken for at least 12 hours before using.

### Liquid Starch, Wallpaper Paste and Gelatine

These can be obtained pre-packaged and should be mixed as directed on the packet. They can then be diluted to make up the marbling medium. The final solution should have the consistency of thick cream.

**Above: Elsa O'Hara used a selection of pigments, binders and foil effects in her layered screen print.**

# PATTERNING

*The aesthetics of many embellished fabrics are governed by the type of image, motif or pattern that has been applied to their surface. These design elements are transferred to fabric using various patterning techniques. The chapters in this section cover some of the different patterning procedures and methods that can be used to apply dyes and colorants, and also many of the processes and recipes included in the subsequent two sections. Some of the techniques discussed will require specialist equipment but most employ simple materials and equipment that are as easily available to the amateur as to the professional designer.*

**Opposite: Block printing a multicoloured parrot design requires a separate block for each colour. The design is slowly built up using reactive dyes.**

# 6

# DEVELOPING A DESIGN

A design is rarely made from scratch. Good textile designers develop an eye for the patterns and colour in the world around them. Inspiration can be gathered from natural and man-made objects and effective patterns can be built up from simple design elements using many of the techniques illustrated in this book.

Good drawing skills are not essential, but a sense of colour and form, and a recognition of potential designs requires time and practice. By accumulating reference material a library of visual information can be built up to aid the development of design ideas. Collect interesting textural or coloured objects such as shells, pebbles, stones, driftwood, grasses and bark. Illustrations and photographs from magazines, plant and seed catalogues, travel literature, product labels and fabric samples can be cut out and filed. Regular visits to exhibitions, art galleries and museums will also provide inspiration.

A successful textile design can take many forms. Not all designs need to be made up from elaborate intertwining motifs. Effective spot, border or all-over designs can be created using simple elements such as stripes, geometric shapes, spots, motifs and, of course, texture.

## DESIGN ELEMENTS
### Stripes
A striped effect, although not necessarily a pattern in itself, can be developed in interesting ways, and will give stability to a design. Stripes need not be a solid colour and can contain different textures. They can be straight or they can bend and vary in width. Bold designs can be made using black and white stripes of equal or varying thickness. Optical illusions are created by altering width or by using complementary colour combinations. The design possibilities are endless and inspiration can be found everywhere: wave patterns left in

the sand, the grain of wood, rock formations, shells, telephone wires, roads and rail tracks.

### Geometric Shapes
Numerous geometric patterns can be found both in nature – crystal formations or the uniformity of a honeycomb – and in man-made objects or landscapes such as aerial views of streets, brick walls, cultivated farmland, tiling, and stained-glass windows.

You can combine different thickness of line with regular or irregular geometric shapes, or alter the size of shapes within a design; for example, checks and plaids can be built up using a variety of lines creating a range of rectangular shapes. Interesting colour effects can be created using one or many colours, or by altering the hue or employing contrasting highlights.

### Spots
A wide range of designs can be built up from spots. Circular forms being one of the most common motifs, and one of the easiest to use. Spots or circles appear everywhere and their symmetrical form is an excellent design element. Patterns range from simple, single-colour dot effects to elaborate 'pointillist' multicoloured designs. Many modern printing techniques rely upon the overprinting of tiny dots to produce half-tone and three-colour separation print effects.

### Textures
Textural effects give depth and interest to a design and can appear rough or smooth, shiny or matt, heavy or light. Different textures can be used to break up flat areas of colour or soften rigid shapes. Inspiration for different textures can be found in objects such as tree bark, stones, gravel, sand, sponges, woven baskets, and polished metals. To create textures within a design rubbings can be made using soft pencils and wax crayons.

The sections 'Patterning' and 'The Rough with the Smooth' include techniques with which specific textural marks and effects can be created using dyes, pigments or chemicals.

### Motifs
Any motif or image can be used in a textile design. However, the choice very much depends upon the end use of the fabric, as the scale and complexity of an image is often different for clothing and furnishing. Motifs for clothing tend to be relatively small and are generally arranged as an all-over repeating pattern, whereas larger, bolder effects are often employed for soft furnishings.

## WORKING UP AN IDEA
The final look and success of a design is affected by the type of pattern, colour, scale and decorative technique used. Before starting to design it is important to know what the fabric's final function will be. The end use of the fabric will dictate the choice of base material and the scale of the design. Lengths of decorated fabric may be used for soft furnishings and curtains or cut up and made into clothes; smaller pieces may be used for wall hangings or scarves.

---

## BLOCK PRINTING

**A repeat design must be carefully aligned when block printing a regular pattern over fabric. The above fabric was printed at Yateley Industries for the Disabled.**

**Opposite: A printed fabric with a bold design was created using just two blocks. Camberwell College of Art and Crafts.**

Fabrics for upholstery and curtaining generally require a pattern that repeats top to bottom and side to side. Motifs are rarely placed in the centre of a width of fabric for furnishings because the cloth will often be cut down the middle when used for cushions or curtains. The images employed tend to be larger and bolder because smaller design elements may become lost in folds and pleats.

Conversely, dress fabrics generally require smaller all-over designs that can be cut and pieced together. If a large motif is used the overall result will be uneasy and give a chopped, broken look. This problem can be avoided if the image is carefully planned and placed onto individual pieces before the garment is made up. The type of base cloth chosen will also influence the final success of a design; a design intended for a fine silk is unlikely to work well on a woollen blanket and vice versa. The decorative technique employed also needs careful consideration. A handpainted set of curtains would take a long time to produce and may not be uniform, whereas a screen printing method would produce a similar effect more efficiently.

To create a design that can be successfully applied to fabric, the elements will need to be arranged into a pattern. In order to achieve this it is often necessary to simplify motifs and reduce the number of colours used. The techniques chosen and the degree of simplification undertaken are influenced by the patterning technique and the materials used.

Ideas for textile designs can be sketched, drawn or painted onto paper using designer's gouache, inks, dyes, watercolours, oil and wax crayons, felt-tip pens, coloured pencils or a collage of various materials – fabric, coloured paper, tissue, flowers and leaves. The degree to which a design is finalized at this stage is determined by the technique employed and the designer's skill in transferring the design onto the fabric. An image intended for a repeating pattern will need to be fully resolved and put into an accurate repeating

**A simple motif placed in the middle of a square network creates a standard spot repeat. The final result, although not complex, can be effective.**

**This simple motif goes to make up a uni-directional, all-over design. As each motif touches the next, a new shape is created by the space between them.**

form before it can be transferred to screen or block. A handpainted design can remain roughly sketched (*croquis*), the design being transferred to the fabric's surface at the painting stage.

To reproduce images as realistically and as naturally as possible they can be copied onto the fabric by one of three techniques. Handpainting every detail directly onto the cloth's surface will create a one-off design (see chapter 7). The use of colour photocopying (see chapter 11) allows a design to be repeated on a limited scale, but works best for spot images. And three-colour separation techniques (see page 26) are expensive and employed only if multiple lengths of cloth are to be decorated. The choice of method depends largely upon the number of times the image is to be repeated.

It is common to simplify a design to enable its transference to fabric. The design motif for a stencil print will require more simplification than a photographic screen print. Patterns for difficult, coarse materials need to be simpler than images applied to fine, smooth fabrics. Stylization of images, such as flowers and animals, is an alternative method of simplification: while limiting the number of colours and creating contrasts between them and textural areas will also

simplify a design. Ultimately, the degree to which an image is simplified is the decision of the designer, regardless of the images and the methods employed.

It is important to be aware of the shapes formed around a motif or image, as they can dominate the intended image in the final work if not considered at an early stage. Some designers exploit this effect to create balance and counterbalance of positive and negative images. A common fault in many designs is the appearance of vertical 'tram-lines' running up the length of the cloth after a repeating image has been printed.

### REPEATS
Repeating designs can be very simple – spot and border patterns – or take the form of complicated inter-cut designs in which it is often difficult to see where a repeat starts or finishes.

### Spot Repeats
Any isolated image, for example a leaf, a bird, a boat, can be used to create a spot repeat on fabric. These can be ordered or random, as you wish.

The ordered placement of motifs relies upon patterning networks which, for most designs, remain hidden but sometimes all or part of them may be included in the final design as

a stripe, check or lattice between the spot elements. There are eight networks commonly used: a square or full-drop, brick, half-drop, diamond, triangle, hexagon, ogee and scale. The most popular are the square and half-drop networks. The size of a network determines the spacing and distribution of a motif. A fine grid will place the motifs close together; while the further apart the grid lines are, the more open the spot effect. With a random spotted effect, spots can be placed anywhere on the fabric – some in groups and others as isolated items – but an awareness of the overall effect needs to be borne in mind.

### Border or Frieze Repeats

The use of borders as a means of repeating a pattern is probably one of the oldest methods of decoration. Simple borders can be made from lines, chevrons, zigzags, spirals, crosses, dots, circles, and more complex ones from twisting, intertwining designs and motifs.

Border designs are simply constructed by repeating one or more design elements in a line. The elements can be placed to form a continuous linked pattern or be separated by a gap or another motif. These repeating elements are often edged with a continuous line of smaller repeating elements such as dots, triangles or squares. Border repeats can be used successfully as an edging on clothing or curtains and larger design elements will often benefit from being surrounded by a simple border.

### All-over Repeats

The characteristic of an all-over print is that the design repeats endlessly in all directions. An all-over repeat can have patterns running in various directions. Uni-directional designs run in one direction only, and normally feature figurative or naturalistic images. They have to be seen from one direction only and if turned around the images will be upside-down. Alternatively, non-directional designs are often textural and can be viewed from all directions. Splattered, marbled, sponged or check effects fall into this category. Finally, multi-directional designs can be viewed from two or more directions.

The spot repeats, motifs or design elements used in networks can be arranged in different ways to produce an all-over print. The choice very much depends upon the type of image used – full- or half-drop networks are the two most frequently employed. To aid a designer with this decision, 'repeat glasses' can be used. These consist of a wooden frame into which a group of glass lenses have been set in either a full- or half-drop configuration. The design can then be viewed in either formation through the different sets. The half-drop repeat glass used on its side will show a brick repeat. If you do not possess repeat glasses, photocopies or tracings of the design can be made and arranged in different ways to help decide the final repeat pattern.

## REPEAT NETWORKS

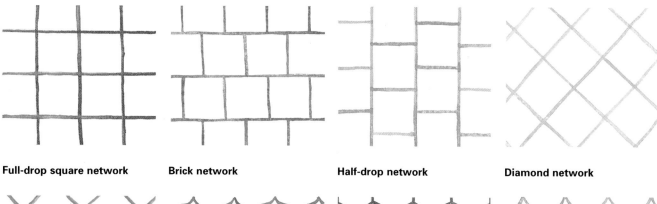

**Full-drop square network**     **Brick network**     **Half-drop network**     **Diamond network**

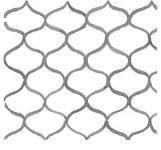
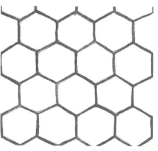

**Triangle network**     **Ogee network**     **Hexagon network**     **Scale network**

The design elements must join accurately from top to bottom and side to side when they are repeated. To achieve this the design is squared-off by drawing horizontal and vertical lines through the main elements of the design to isolate the repeating shape. This shape does not need to be a square, but when repeated it must totally fill the cloth, the size being a multiple of the fabric width.

A cross is then drawn through the centre of this shape – this should be square, however, when you cut through the design you must avoid any major elements – dividing the design into four equal pieces. The design is then cut in half lengthways (see picture 2). The two pieces are then rearranged by lining up the horizontal and vertical lines so that the outer edges meet in the middle of

the design (see picture 3). To hold the pieces in place the design is taped firmly on its back. The cutting process can then be repeated in a horizontal direction if needs be, but this depends upon your design. When all the pieces have been re-aligned any modifications needed to ensure alignment can be made. Once the design is correct, it can be copied and used for a block or screen print.

## CREATING AN ALL-OVER REPEAT

1 First decide on your image – in this case it is entwining leaves. Then draw the design and mark a square cross through the centre for re-alignment.

2 To ensure the design elements match up, cut the design in half lengthways (avoiding any of its major elements) following the lines of your marked-up square.

3 The two pieces are then realigned using the marked-up horizontal and vertical lines. The outer edges should now meet in the middle of the design. Tape to hold.

4 Add any extra design modifications – in our case extra leaves – to make up a design without any obvious gaps. This is commonly known as smudging.

5 Tidy up the design. Now that the repeating element is complete, it can be copied and joined together to create a larger repeating design.

6 Photocopy all the design elements and place them together to create a multi-directional design that can be made into a photographic positive (see page 69).

For large photographic screen prints (see chapter 10) the repeat needs to be multiplied to cover the width of the screen. This is achieved by using photocopies or tracings of the repeating element and joining all the repeats together. It is important that everything is kept 'square' and aligned or the design will not repeat correctly at a later stage. It helps to use a square grid or graph paper under the traced or photocopied repeats. Positives required for photographic screen printing are then reproduced from this layout. Separate positives are required for each colour in the design; these can be copied by handpainting the image in opaque paint onto a polyester or acetate film, photographing an image onto photosensitive film or photocopying the repeating design onto standard photocopy acetate. With colours that butt up to each other, a small overlap is normally allowed. This ensures that no gaps appear between the colours when the design is finally printed. When using film or acetate copies, they must be inter-cut and taped together to avoid any build up of layers in the final positive. Accurate registration crosses, should be added just outside the design at each corner of the finished positive. These are placed square to the design and are exactly the repeating distance of the image apart. Every positive used for a design should have these crosses accurately transferred to them, ensuring that they are all in register when the positives are placed one on top of the other. These positives are then used to transfer the design, using photographic methods, to the screen as discussed in chapter 10.

Specialist machines can produce a photo silk-screen from a single repeat image. These are known as 'step and repeat' machines and will expose a repeat with absolute precision across a photographically sensitized screen, thus eliminating the time-consuming process of handpainting and inter-cutting a full-sized positive. However, these machines are expensive and more generally used in industry.

## REGISTRATION OF DESIGNS

Once a repeating image has been transferred to either block or screen, some form of registration is required to ensure the design can be repeated accurately down the length of fabric.

### Block Printing

The registration of a wooden printing block traditionally relied upon the skill of the printer. The small blocks, still used today (mainly in India), were often registered by eye. Larger blocks used for multicoloured designs relied upon the use of small metal pins, known as 'pitch pins', which were inserted into the corners of the block. When the block was printed each pin would print a small dot of colour onto the surface of the cloth. As the printing continued, the next repeat could be accurately registered by lining up

## A MULTI-DIRECTIONAL REPEAT

**Above: Jonathan Fuller's screen printed, multi-directional design shows perfectly the concept of the all-over repeat.**

the pitch pins with the dots made from the previous impression. Multi-coloured designs would be built up using these dots as guides to accurately print another block over the first image. With the introduction of faster and cheaper methods of printing (roller or screen printing) these marks were copied to deceive the buyer into thinking that the fabric had been produced by the more expensive block printing technique.

It is not always necessary to use pitch pins for simple block printing patterns. Small blocks can be easily registered using a grid system. This can be drawn onto the cloth using a soft pencil or temporary fabric marker, the rectangles of the grid being the same size as the block that is to be printed. An alternative is to use a grid constructed of fine dark thread taped tautly in place at the edges of the fabric. This is easily removed once the printing is completed.

## Screen Printing

A grid can also be used to register small silk-screens. Again, the grid needs to be the same size as the repeating image on the screen. Larger screens, with images that stretch across the whole width of the fabric, will require an alternative method of registration. If the screen is only printed two or three times, the design can be registered by eye. The screen is placed squarely on the fabric and the image printed. Allowing time for this print to be absorbed, the next print can be aligned with the help of the registration crosses at the edge of the design. This is easier with the help of an assistant at the other side of the screen. To keep the selvages of the cloth clear of marks, the edge of the fabric can be protected with masking tape which is removed after printing. Other colours can be registered in the same way and printed over the first image after it has dried. This system is slow and time-consuming if large amounts of cloth are to be printed.

To pattern long lengths of cloth, the screen must be printed many times and so a bar registration system is commonly employed (see diagrams

on page 98). A long straight bar, no higher than the edge of the screen, is fixed to one side of the print table. This can be constructed from wood but a straight piece of steel or metal angle is normally used. Attached to this are registration stops firmly clamped in place and set at the repeating distance of the image. The screens employed for this registration technique are slightly modified with adjusting bolts and a T- or L-shaped bracket attached to one end. The bolts allow accurate alignment of the screen against the registration bar and ensure that the design prints squarely on the table. The shaped bracket is used to register the screen against the repeat stops, thus enabling rapid registration of the design on the cloth during the printing process. Wooden screens can be simply modified, using large wood screws as bolts and a right-angle bracket – available in many hardware shops – for the L-shaped bracket. Most metal screens will come with the correct bolt and bracket holes already in place, but check with your

**Above and Opposite: The above design has been executed on paper, using paint and resist techniques. The design has then been transferred to cloth using first a devoré process (above right) and then a discharge process (below right). This shows the importance of technique and colour to the overall 'feel' of a design.**

supplier before purchasing, as they cannot be added once a metal frame has been stretched with mesh.

To ensure precise registration of a design, the images on all the screens used must be aligned accurately with each other and the registration bar of the print table. This can be aided by drawing a pencil line onto the backing cloth. This should be perpendicular to the bar, across the width of the table. If a backing cloth is not being used, a piece of masking tape can be stuck across the table and removed after all the screens have been aligned.

To register a set of screens, choose one screen that contains the largest part of the design as a master. Using this screen, align the perpendicular

lines of the registration crosses in the image with the line on the table. The horizontal lines of the registration crosses are then transferred to the perpendicular line on the table by rubbing a soft pencil or piece of chalk over the cross marked on the screen. Reinforce the transferred image of the cross with a black pen, making sure that the lines you use are not too thick or the other screens in the design will not register as accurately. The first screen can then be fixed in position by adjusting the bolts on the end of the screen. These should rest firmly against the registration bar and be secured in place with a locking nut tightened against the edge of the screen. The T- or L-shaped bracket can then be attached to the screen with a registration stop clamped to the registration bar touching the bracket. The bracket can touch either the left or the right side of the stop, but it is essential to be consistent or the design will misregister. Other screens in the design can then be aligned in the same way with the crosses drawn on the table and the registration stop.

To set the correct repeating distance for the screens, the width of the image is accurately measured and the registration stops set to this distance along the table; a 'stop-bar' is useful for this purpose. This is a metal bar with adjustable clamps that can be fixed at a set distance and used as a standard measure. The accuracy of a repeat can be checked by rubbing French chalk or talcum powder through the mesh of the screen with a soft cloth. This will leave an impression of the design in white dust on the surface of the table. The process is repeated for the next repeat in the design. Any mistakes in the registration can then be noted and rectified before the actual print is undertaken. Surplus chalk left in the screen will normally fall out of the screen mesh or can be washed away before using. It is advisable to print a strike-off onto cheap fabric or paper to ensure there are no mistakes and that all the designs register correctly before embarking on long lengths of cloth.

# 7

# HANDPAINTING

A limitless variety of exciting designs can be produced by painting dyes and textile paints directly onto the fabric. The diversity of techniques gives the designer freedom to experiment with colour, shade, texture and form.

Handpainting requires very little equipment; a variety of brushes, nibs, sponges, rollers, pens, bottles and sprays can be used to apply the dyes. The cloth must be taut before it is patterned. This is achieved by pinning it out onto a backing cloth on the print table or stretching it across a frame such as a painter's canvas stretcher.

The type of fabric and the choice of paint, pigments or dyes depends upon the final use of the cloth, and as with all fabric decorating, the type of dye has to be suitable for the fabric base. All the printing paste recipes given in chapters 12 and 13 can be used with handpainting techniques.

Many craft shops sell handpainting dyes in the form of inks, paints, crayons and pens. All these products

**Opposite: Working in her studio, Kim Meyer handpaints a naturalistic design onto a stretched piece of fabric.**

**Below: Caroline Whelan used a white discharge paste in bold brush strokes to give a painterly quality to her fabric.**

can be used very successfully for fabric painting, but it is important to follow the manufacturer's instructions to determine what fabric bases can be used with different mediums and the fixing methods required.

## METHODS OF APPLICATION

A good selection of brushes will help achieve a variety of effects. Large decorating brushes are useful for washes and covering large areas of fabric or thicker cloths. Chinese calligraphy and silk painting brushes will hold a lot of dye at their base but have a fine point for more detailed work, while fine round- or flat-ended sable brushes are useful for more delicate, precise work.

Any print paste, dye or resist can be applied using plastic 'squeezy' bottles which trail dye across the fabric's surface. Small plastic bottles and large syringes are readily available in craft shops and can be filled with dye paste which is then drawn directly onto the fabric. Metal nibs, for gutta work, can be attached to the necks of small bottles and used for drawing fine lines with most print pastes. However, the consistency of the print paste may have to be altered to enable the paste to flow easily through the nib.

### Pens and Crayons

A large range of fabric crayons and pens are now available. These can be used to decorate all types of fabrics, either by themselves or combined with other patterning techniques to create texture and highlights.

Fabric crayons and pastels can be simply applied to the fabric like a crayon to paper. Texture is created by gently rubbing the crayon onto a fabric that has been placed over an interesting surface or object, such as bark or leaves. There are two types of crayon, steam- or heat-fix. The steam-fix crayons produce resist effects when combined with fabric dyes.

Special felt-tip pens, filled with fabric dye instead of ink, are also available; these draw directly onto the fabric. Once the dye has been fixed it is fade-resistant and wash-fast.

### Colours and Additives

Colouring substances react in different ways, and the viscosity of a dye or paint will affect the final patterning. For a wash or watercolour effect, dyes and paints are thinned so that they can spread into each other. Dye pastes can be used without a thickener and handpainting silk dyes are often diluted with solutions produced by the manufacturer. Alternatively, an

## PREPARING THE FRAME

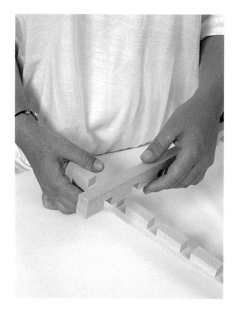

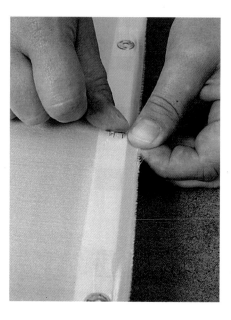

1 By moving the wooden frame of the silk stretcher backwards and forwards make the correct adjustments for the size of the fabric that is to be painted.

2 Line the frame with masking tape to cover the brackets. Then carefully stretch the silk over the frame and secure it with silk pins positioned at regular intervals.

3 It is important to stretch the fabric taut over the frame. This will prevent any creases or ridges from forming, and will ensure a flat surface for painting.

## METHODS OF APPLICATION

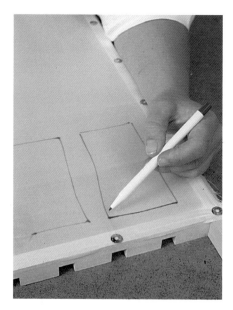

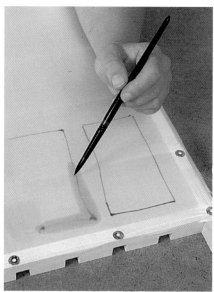

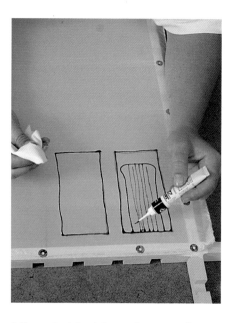

1 When the fabric is secured in place take a soft pencil or one of the specialist fabric pens and draw the design directly onto the surface of the silk.

2 Alternatively, acid silk dyes can be applied directly to the silk using a soft brush. This should produce a more delicate watercolour effect.

3 To control the inks, and prevent the colours from mixing, gutta is used to outline the design. Coloured gutta is then left on the fabric after patterning.

alcohol (methanol or isopropyl) and water solution, in a ratio of 50:50, can be used. Fabric paints and pigments can also be thinned with water.

For more controlled work, dyes, pigments and paints can be used undiluted or thickened. Most craft fabric dyes and paints can be thickened using glue-like substances such as Epaississant or Superclear. After application and fixing, the thickener can be washed out of the fabric.

When handpainting with solutions of dye and paint, specialized effects and textures can be produced by adding various substances to the dye. Alcohol, for example, can give greater depth to a design. A small amount applied at the centre of a painted colour, causes the dye to migrate away from the middle, leaving a paler shade surrounded by darker rings. This technique will work with steam-fixed dyes but not with fabric paints. Similarly, weak bleach solutions will remove colour from a design. These can simply be painted onto the fabric and left until the colour fades.

In the gutta (also known as serti) technique fine lines of a glue-like substance are painted onto the fabric. These act as a resist, stopping colours that are painted next to each other from mixing and producing a stained-glass-window effect. Gutta is used mainly on silk but can also be used on lightweight cottons and wools. It is available in two forms: water-based and solvent-based. The water-based type can be removed by washing; whereas the solvent-based gutta is removed by dry-cleaning. They are applied using various nibs with a pipette or plastic bottle; some are available in tube form to ease application. The gutta is applied to the stretched silk in a continuous, unbroken line and allowed to dry. Once the gutta is dry the silk dyes and paints are carefully applied within the gutta outlines. Gutta is also available in colours and metallics. However,

**Left: Kim Meyer used lines of gold gutta and a variety of acid silk dyes to produce a painting of shells and seaweed.**

these are meant to be left on the fabric after patterning and if the cloth is dry-cleaned they may disappear.

Marbled patterns can be achieved if salt or sugar is sprinkled onto the fabric after painting. These substances attract moisture and pull the dye in various directions creating interesting textures. Different types of salt create distinct patterns: sea-salt crystals or granulated sugar will produce the most dramatic effects; table salt a fine feathery effect; and pearl-salt grains a more rounded pattern. If the fabric is soaked in a strong salt or sugar solution, containing 250 g of sodium chloride or granulated sugar to every litre of water, and then left to dry, the fabric will be impregnated with tiny crystals that produce a fine spotted effect when painted.

If a sugar solution is applied to the fabric before the dye, the sugar will act as a resist and prevent the dyes from spreading. A syrup solution made from equal amounts of icing sugar and water, thickened by boiling to the consistency of double cream, can be painted onto the cloth. The dye will slowly 'creep' around the sugar creating a marbled effect.

## Pads and Rollers

Rubber and decorators' rollers come in a range of sizes and materials. Using these, dye pastes can be rolled directly onto the cloth. Foam rollers can be cut with a craft knife to produce various patterns, and lamb's-wool rollers will create a fine texture.

Both natural and synthetic sponges are readily available and an even layer of colour can be spread across a fabric using a sponge with diluted dye (different effects will be produced if a thickened dye is used). Synthetic and natural sponges produce different patterning effects. Natural sponges are expensive but are softer, and their irregular shape and holes will produce softer textures on the fabric. An alternative is a foam applicator or decorators' paint pad. Available in many sizes these will hold a lot of dye and

## HANDPAINTING WITH GUTTA

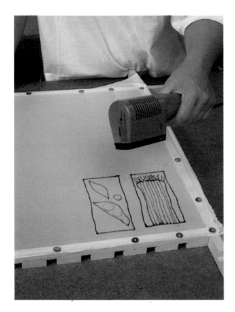

**1** Once the gutta has been applied it must be allowed to dry before painting with dyes. To speed up this process it may be easier to use a hair dryer.

**2** When the gutta is dry, use silk dyes or paint to fill in the outlines you have drawn. The gutta prevents the different areas of dye mixing with each other.

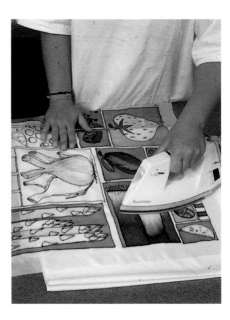

**3** When the design is complete, and the dyes have dried, the pattern needs to be fixed onto the fabric. With a hot iron, iron the underside of the design to heat-fix.

tion (available in specialist shops) on the fabric before spraying. It is important not to saturate the fabric and each layer of colour must dry before applying the next. Choosing the correct dyestuffs for your fabric, make up the dyes into solutions containing the appropriate auxiliaries necessary to fix them onto the cloth. Many specialist craft dyes are available for spraying techniques.

A large, protected working area is needed, as the sprayed dye particles can travel a long way. If possible, spray outdoors on a still day or construct a spray booth out of cardboard or polythene sheeting. A suitable face mask should also be worn. The effect achieved will depend upon what technique and equipment you use, but practise on some waste fabric before embarking on the final piece.

Air guns and brushes are used for a uniform spray of tiny dots. A small bottle or metal container holds the dye and a trigger releases the compressed air, propelling the dye in a

**Above: Karen Johnstone used a discharge technique to create white areas which she later painted with acid dyes.**

## PADS AND ROLLERS

are very useful when applying dye to large areas of cloth, or to thicker fabrics such as wool or velvet.

### Sprays, Atomizers and Air Brushes

Ink sprays are often used in graphic design artwork, but the technique can easily be applied to textiles using dye instead of paint and inks. The equipment required ranges from simple toothbrushes and bottle sprays to expensive air guns and brushes (air guns will hold a larger volume of liquid than brushes). The technique can be used by itself to produce all-over spotted and speckled effects, but is often used in combination with stencils. Spraying works best on thicker fabrics, as thin ones tend to absorb the dye too easily and the particles will blend together. This can be remedied by using an anti-spread solu-

**Print pastes can be applied to the surface of fabrics using a variety of paint rollers. For different decorative effects patterns can be cut out using a craft knife.**

**Specialist handpainting foam pads are used to apply dyes directly to fabric. The foam holds a lot of dye enabling large areas to be painted in one go.**

fine spray. The spray can be directed anywhere you want it on the fabric, and due to the uniformity of dye particles, patterning can be controlled.

A random splattered effect can be achieved with any stiff brush (i.e. a worn-out paintbrush or old toothbrush) by dipping the brush into the dye and flicking it across the fabric's surface. It is difficult to direct the path of the spray and patterning can be patchy and irregular. Finally, plastic plant sprayers and atomizers can be used to produce random jets of colour. They can be filled with the dye and, with a hand-pump action, used to spray the dye onto the cloth.

## Masks and Stencils

The general technique of stencilled patterns may be divided into two categories: masks and stencils. A mask

## PRINTING WITH MASKS

## SPRAY GUNS

1 Create a mask from any object – in this case a leaf – or you can use masking tape, iron-on paper or sticky-back film. Then paint over the mask.

2 When the paint has dried remove the tape or object (whichever you have used). What will appear is a negative image in the form of your mask.

As an alternative to brushes, spray guns can be used. These release a fine, uniform spray of dye particles which makes it easy to control patterning.

is any material that is placed on top of a fabric to protect it from the colour. Objects such as leaves, grasses, flowers, nets and lace can be used. Masking tape, heat-fix, iron-on paper or sticky-backed plastic film can also be cut into shapes and stuck in place. Alternatively, a painted image can be applied using masking fluid, gums or waxes. The dye or paint is then applied around the mask using a stencil brush, sponge or spray technique. Once the colour is dry the mask can be removed to produce a light image on a darker background.

A stencil, however, is made when shapes are cut out of a sheet of paper, card or film and what remains of the sheet protects the fabric from coloration. Oiled manila card was used, but has now been replaced with acetate film or thin plastic sheet. These are transparent, easy-to-cut, waterproof and washable – which aid registration – and last longer.

The pattern is traced onto the back of a sheet of stencil material and the design is carefully cut out using a craft knife and a cutting mat. (Keep your fingers well out of the way.) Simple designs are easier to start with as it is difficult to cut out intricate patterns. Ensure that all the pieces of the design remain joined by leaving small 'bridges' to anchor any floating images. The finished stencil is then placed on the fabric and fixed in place using masking tape or spray mount. Colour can then be applied inside the cut-out shapes using a painting, sponging or spraying technique. A variety of specialist stencil brushes are available. These have flat, blunt ends which help to apply colour evenly and without smudging. Various dyes and pigments can be used, but specialist textile stencil paints are available in a wide range of colours.

**Right: These bright hangings, by Sally Greaves-Lord, are produced by free hand-painting of stripes, spots and spirals.**

**Overleaf: Caroline Whelan's dramatic fabric has been produced using washes of acid dye and discharge processes.**

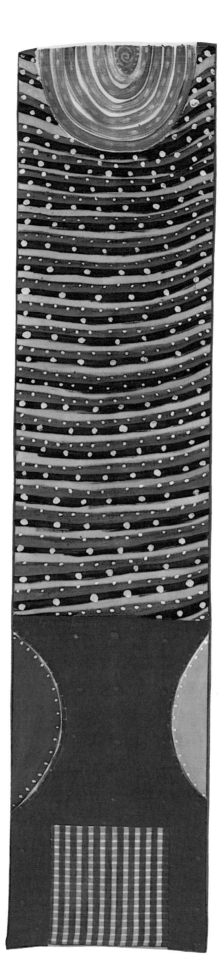

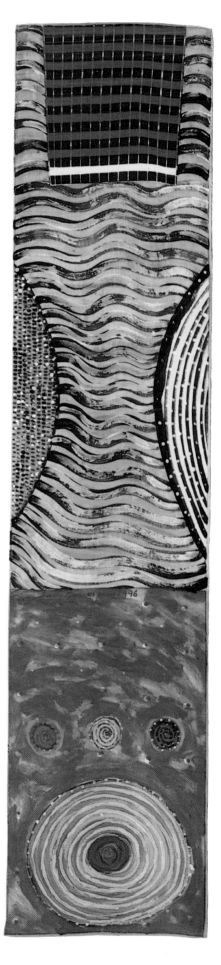

## HANDPAINTING WITH A STENCIL

1 Trace or draw your pattern or image onto the transparent acetate film using a permanent fine marker pen. This film can be washed and used again and again.

2 Using a sharp craft knife and a cutting mat, carefully cut out the design ensuring that all sections of the image remain joined by small 'bridges'.

3 Place the stencil onto your fabric and fix it securely with masking tape or spray mount. Then paint, spray or sponge the colour inside the cut-out shapes.

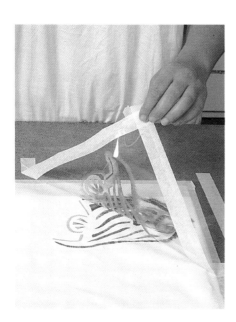

4 Colour needs to be applied evenly and without smudging. Once the design has been completed you can remove the acetate stencil from the fabric.

5 The paint now needs to dry before any other patterning takes place or smudges may occur. A hair dryer can be used to speed up the drying process.

6 In our design we have chosen to repeat the image of the fish. Before doing this the acetate must be washed and then refixed onto the fabric in a new position.

# 8

# MONO-PRINTING

Mono-printing, as the name implies, is the production of a single print – a one-off image or pattern that is unique and cannot be repeated. I use the term for the transference of a non-repeatable image onto a cloth's surface through an indirect patterning method. The dye colours are temporarily applied to another substrate and are then transferred to the final piece of fabric. The final image will print in reverse on the finished piece, and this must be considered at the design stage.

## DIRECT SILK-SCREEN METHOD

Interesting mono-print effects can be achieved when a silk-screen (see chapter 10) is used as the transfer medium for dyes. The technique will work on most fabrics and employs reactive or acid dyes, depending upon

**Opposite: Karen Johnstone applies acid dyes to the surface of an open screen for a direct silk-screen print.**

the fibre content of the cloth (see chapters 2 and 3). To create an image on a piece of fabric, solutions of dye are painted onto the printing surface of a clean silk-screen. The pattern is then transferred to the fabric by pushing a clear printing paste through the screen.

The easiest dyes to use are reactive dyes. They give bright, pure colours that are intermixable and change very little during the fixing process. Both the highly reactive Procion MX and less reactive Procion H or P can be used, but the latter class will require steam-fixing rather than baking (see chapter 17). Reactive dyes can be used on cellulose and some protein fabrics. Acid dyes are used for wool and silks; these work just as well but the colours will not fully develop until the fabric has been fixed by steaming.

The texture of the fabric obviously affects the definition of the transferred image. The smoother the fabric surface, the sharper the design will be. Fabrics that are either fine plain

weave, satins or sateens will give sharp clean prints, and more textural crêpes, twills, hopsacks and velvets will soften the image.

### Preparation

Choose a blank screen slightly larger than the design. Then select the dyes – 2 g of dye in 100 ml of hot water (use a heat-proof jug) will produce a medium strength colour. Stir well to ensure that they have dissolved and allow to cool. Mix the printing paste, following the recipes on page 119 or 122. If you are using acid dyes you will need to use the print paste recipe on page 119, but if you are using reactive dyes you will need the recipe on page 122. For both recipes you will need to omit the dye from the paste.

### Patterning

An outline sketch of the design, placed under the mesh, can be copied from above. The screen is then placed face-upwards on a flat working surface and the dye solutions are

## DIRECT SILK-SCREEN METHOD

1 Paint the acid or reactive dyes onto the printing surface of the silk-screen. If colours are to butt up to each other allow them to dry between each application.

2 Secure the fabric to be printed firmly to the table and place the screen on top. Before printing, create a trough of clear print paste at one end of the screen.

3 Then pull the print paste through the screen using a squeegee. One to two pulls is normally adequate or the dyes may begin to mix.

painted onto the top of the mesh following your design. The way the dye is applied will influence the final design. Dyes can be diluted with water and applied like inks or water-colours, layering the colours on top of each other. As with silk painting, salt crystals can be sprinkled onto areas to give a marbled effect. The salt must be left in place until the dye has dried. Excess dye can be removed from areas using a clean sponge or tissue; cotton-wool buds are also very useful. This method is used if a soft painterly effect is wanted.

For a sharper image the dyes are applied by paintbrush, leaving a small space between each colour to avoid them bleeding into each other. It often helps if the dye is dried before applying the next colour. Once dry, colours will appear faded, the dyes having crystallized around the filaments of the screen mesh. However, they will return to a liquid state during printing. A white outline or other white areas are created by painting the surface of the screen with a gum solution such as gum arabic and British gum (Dextrin). Once dry, they act as resists and prevent neighbouring colours from mixing. Texture can be added to the screen before applying the dyes; wax crayon rubbings carefully taken from surfaces such as wood, bark, sandpaper and stones, will resist the dyes and give an added dimension to the print. The design should be left to dry in a horizontal position to avoid dyes running and spoiling the final piece.

### Printing

When you are ready to print make sure that your fabric is firmly gummed, pinned or taped to the printing table and place the dry patterned screen face-down on top of the fabric, before pulling the paste through the mesh screen using a squeegee (see chapter 10). Two pulls are normally adequate to transfer the dye to the fabric. It is sometimes possible to print a second image but more pulls of the squeegee will be required and the image may not be as clear. The printed fabric is then allowed to dry, after which the dyes are fixed according to the type used. See chapter 17 for the best method to employ.

## MARBLING

One of the easiest types of mono-printing to attempt is marbling, but it is also one of the hardest to master. Over the centuries, it has been used extensively for endpapers in books and for covering and lining boxes. In recent years, it has also been used to pattern textiles and can now be found embellishing everything from cushions to scarves.

The principle of marbling is that some substances repel each other. Traditionally, oil-based inks and a thickened water base were used. As the two media do not mix the inks float on the water surface, forming into swirls and droplets. The design is transferred by carefully laying paper

---

**DIRECT SILK-SCREEN METHOD**

4 Carefully lift the screen to reveal the printed design, making sure you do not jolt the screen and smudge the image. Allow the printed image to dry.

5 Unsatisfactory areas of the design can be touched up after printing to give a better over-all result. This is done using a fine paintbrush and dye solution.

6 The whole design is then allowed to dry (this can be speeded up with the use of a hair dryer), before finally fixing the image by steaming (see chapter 17).

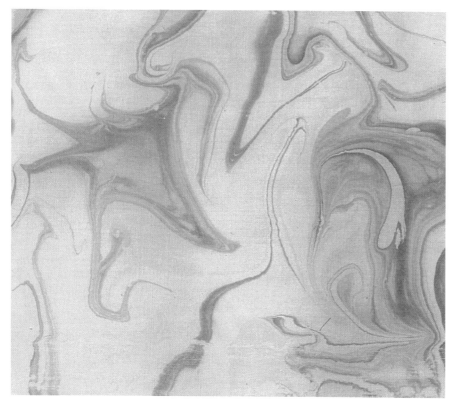

onto the patterned surface of the water. The inks, having little affinity for the water, will then transfer themselves to the paper. This paper is then lifted off and dried.

Marbling equipment is very basic, the most important item being a large shallow bath. Pet litter trays or photographic developing trays are ideal and are available in different sizes. Choose one that is clear or white in colour and slightly larger than the piece of fabric; too large a bath will waste the colouring materials. Dye applicators and patterning tools are also needed. Any small pipette, syringe or plastic squeezy bottle will be suitable for applying dyes. Tools such as sharp sticks, knitting needles and paintbrushes, move the colour around on the surface of the medium; while combs are used to feather and rake

**Left: This swirling design (created in the steps below) has been produced using a marbling medium and coloured inks.**

## MARBLING

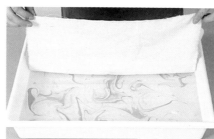

**1** First prepare the marbling medium, making sure it is the right consistency. Pour this into the marbling bath and allow the mixture to settle.

**2–3** Apply droplets of coloured dyes or paints to the bath and move them around to create a pattern. Lay the fabric carefully onto the surface of the bath.

**4** Once the dyes have transferred to the cloth remove the fabric gently from the bath. Rinse carefully under running water to remove the marbling medium.

the colorant. Combs can be made from a length of wood, the same width as the bath, with nails or golf tees spaced evenly along its length to form the teeth.

## Preparation

The most suitable fabrics to use are smooth and absorbent with a fine weave, such as silk pongee, twill, crepe or fine cottons. Better patterning results may be obtained if the fabric is then coated with a solution of alum (25 g of aluminium potassium sulphate per litre of warm water) before marbling. The alum makes the fabric more receptive to the paints. Soak the fabric in the solution, then let it drip-dry. Make sure that there are no creases as these will effect the success of the patterning.

The depth of marbling medium in the bath should be at least 3–5 cm. Refer to the recipes for carragheen and gum tragacanth in chapter 5; or if you are using wallpaper paste, gelatine or liquid starches, the consistency should be similar to double cream. Consult the manufacturer's instructions if you are using a craft marbling medium. The prepared medium can then be poured slowly into the bath and left to settle.

To marble successfully, the ink or paint must be of the correct consistency. If they are too thick they will sink to the bottom of the bath, if too thin they will disperse thinly over the surface of the medium until they are almost invisible. The viscosity can be altered with a little oxgall, available from art suppliers.

## Patterning

Before beginning, make sure the surface of the marbling medium is clean. To do this, skim the surface of the medium using strips of newspaper. Then, using a little pipette or dropper, apply small drops of colour onto the surface. Each drop will spread into a circle of 5–8 cm diameter. If it does not spread evenly or has ragged edges, the marbling medium may be too thick, too hot or too cold and should be thinned with a little water. Always work with the marbling medium at room temperature.

Using a fine paintbrush, a sharp wooden stick or a nail, move the colours around on the surface of the marbling medium; this creates swirling, marbled patterns. If a more controlled, feathered effect is desired, a comb can be drawn through the design in one or both directions. Colour combinations are endless, but care should be taken not to over-mix colours or the resulting design will tend to look muddy.

When patterning is completed lay the fabric onto the surface of the bath, taking care to let the centre of the fabric come into contact with the colours first; then let the edges fall gently into place. Avoid trapping air under the cloth as this will result in plain patches. To ensure that all the colour is transferred to the fabric gently touch the back of the cloth. Most fabrics will become translucent when wet, so if any areas look dry and opaque they may not have picked up all the colour. These areas should be pressed onto the surface of the marbling medium. The fabric is then lifted from the bath, keeping it as horizontal as possible so as not to disturb the design. Rinse it carefully under running cold water to remove any marbling medium that has attached itself to the surface. Do not touch the pattern when rinsing the cloth as the inks will smear easily when wet. Only when the fabric no longer feels slimy can it be hung up to dry.

The colorant must then be fixed onto the fabric. The method used depends upon the type of dyes, pigments or inks that have been

**Left: Pat Parker mono-printed black outlines by direct transfer. Colours were then handpainted within them.**

used. Consult the manufacturer's instructions or see chapter 17 for the best methods to employ.

## INDIRECT TRANSFER

This technique is used mainly for mono-printing onto paper but also works when applied to fabric. The print paste (you can use any recipe in chapter 12) is applied to a smooth, waterproof surface and is transferred to the fabric while still wet. A sheet of glass or polythene, acetate film, varnished hardboard and melamine or laminate-topped tables are all suitable surfaces. The print paste can either be applied directly in a pattern, or in a thin, even layer of colour by using a roller, sponge or large paintbrush. In the latter, the pattern is drawn into the ink using thin pieces of wood and/or combs. The combs designed for applying adhesives can be used, or they can be made from thick plastic or card. Other impressions can be made by pressing pieces of string, fabric or leaves into the ink and then removing them. Work quickly, or the paste will dry on the printing surface before being transferred to the fabric. Once the design is finished the fabric is carefully placed on top and gently rubbed by hand or rolled with a soft roller. Then peel the fabric off and fix the dye. Pigment print pastes can also be used and are available in art and craft shops ready-mixed; they are often called fabric paints or inks.

## DIRECT TRANSFER

This method works like carbon paper. The print paste is applied with a brush to a thick absorbent material such as a backing cloth. The fabric is then placed on top and, using a pencil, rounded stick or the blunt end of a paintbrush, a design is traced onto the back of the fabric. Take care not to lean on the fabric with your hands as this will leave an impression on the final piece. When the design is finished the cloth is removed. The paste will have transferred across where you traced and other areas, where the fabric touched the dye, will have a soft textural effect. The fabric is then fixed and washed.

## DIRECT TRANSFER METHOD

1 To mono-print via direct transfer, coloured dye paint is applied to a padded surface or board. Apply the paste to the board evenly using a large paintbrush.

2 Place the fabric over this padded surface. Care must be taken not to press down too hard on the fabric or it will pick up colour in unwanted areas.

3 The image is then impressed onto the fabric by drawing freehand. You can use a pen, a pencil, a rounded stick or the blunt end of a paintbrush.

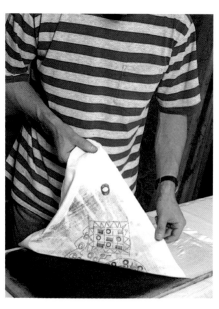

4 When the image is complete, remove the fabric with care. You will see that where you traced your design the colour has transferred to the face of the cloth.

# 9

# BLOCK PRINTING

Block printing, although largely super-seded by screen printing, is one of the easiest methods of producing a repeating image. It is an effective patterning technique that does not employ expensive equipment. Print-ing blocks can be made from a variety of materials including card, string, rubber, metal, lino and wood. The pat-terns achieved range from simple stripes, blocks, circles, triangles and chevrons, to finely detailed figurative scenes that use a number of blocks.

A solid padded table is a good print-ing surface, provided it is covered with a calico backing cloth or a waterproof neoprene or plastic top. The fabric can then be pinned, taped or glued down to create a taut, flat printing surface. To begin, create a grid system of pen-cil lines or coloured threads which will help register the blocks accurately, but these may become unnecessary with practice. Any of the dyes or pig-ments in chapters 12, 13 and 14 can be used for block printing, but they need to be the consistency of single cream (slightly thinner than the pastes required for screen printing) and occasionally their viscosity may need to be adjusted for this process.

Various methods can be used to apply printing paste to a block. Colour can be painted onto the block's surface using a brush, but care must be taken not to fill in any of the cut-out areas or build up ridges of paste along the edges of the block. Rollers can also be used to ink-up the sur-face of the block. The printing paste is rolled out onto a glass or perspex sheet. An even layer of paste is then rolled across the block. The amount of paste applied depends on the type of roller used. A hard rubber roller will leave a thin layer, and a foam or sheepskin roller will apply the most (the softer the roller the more 'ink' is transferred).

**Opposite: These swatches illustrate the wide range of designs block printed at Yateley Industries for the Disabled.**

**Right: Sally Weatherill block printed images of roses in a resist paste. After dyeing, the resist roses are clearly visible.**

Alternatively, you can transfer the printing paste to the block using a printing pad with a slightly convex surface. Printing pads can be made simply by covering a flat piece of wood or blockboard with a piece of high-density foam – 3-4 cm thick and exactly the same size as the board. The foam is then covered with a larg-er waterproof cloth that is tacked securely in place at the back of the pad. Plastic sheeting or neoprene can be used, but I have found that PVC-coated upholstery fabric works very well as its knitted backing allows the fabric to be stretched very taut. All the sides of this covering need to be pulled down firmly to compress the foam's edges, thereby creating a convex surface. The pad is then cov-ered with a removable printing blan-ket. The type of material chosen for the printing blanket depends upon the quality of print desired. Calico, felt and various woollen blankets can all be used. The printing paste is then applied to the pad's surface using a brush, and the block's printing side is firmly pressed against it to be coated with the printing paste. At the end of a printing session the top printing blanket can be removed from the pad,

washed and re-used. It is important to clean off any pastes that may have seeped through to the waterproof cover as these may spoil future prints.

To print your image, the block is carefully placed face down onto your fabric and held firmly in place. To pro-duce a clean, sharp print, precise pressure needs to be applied to the back of the block by, for example, a sharp tap from a clenched fist on the back of the block. A better method is to use a small but heavy maul or mallet such as a sculptor's mallet or a 1-kilo lump hammer with a shortened handle, where the end of the handle is capped with a rubber stop. The back of the block is then tapped sharply with the rubber-capped han-dle. This produces a precise even pressure which will aid even and thorough penetration of the printing paste. The whole process is then repeated until the cloth is covered with your repeating images. Vari-ations in the design can be achieved by rotating blocks to create mirror images or off-setting them in a half-drop repeating formation (see page 67). When a printing session is com-plete the block and pad are cleaned and the fabric fixed (when dry).

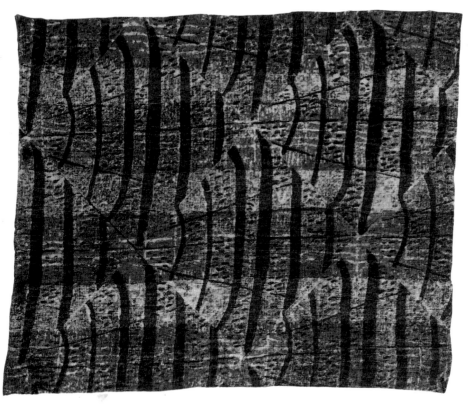

Block printing falls into three different categories: simple relief printing, printing with metal stamps and printing with wooden or lino blocks.

## Wood and Lino Blocks

To make and cut your own wooden printing blocks requires specialist skills and cutting tools. Small blocks with simple designs can be purchased from art and craft shops. Alternatively, you can use one of the old Indian wood blocks that are available in some ethnic shops. These are sold for decorative purposes but if an undamaged block is selected it can still be used to print fabric.

Most block printing is now carried out using lino blocks. Linoleum was invented as a waterproof floor covering and is made from compressed

**Left: In Jacqueline Wauchope's print the diagonal lines of the blocks are as integral to the design as the pattern itself.**

## BLOCK PRINTING WITH LINO

**1 Use lino-cutting tools to carve out areas of design that are not to print. Then mount the lino on the wooden block with a suitable adhesive.**

**2 Ink-up the printing pad using a large paintbrush. This pad can be used again and again if the top printing blanket is washed after use.**

**3 Press your block firmly, printing-side-down, onto the ink pad's surface. The printing paste should now have transferred to the block.**

ground cork particles, resins and other fillers, and oxidized linseed oil. The best sort to use is 'battleship' linoleum. It is thick, with a dull brown colour and has a firm texture that will not break up when cut or etched. This type of lino can easily be purchased in the form of 30 x 30 cm tiles or in a larger sheet from art and craft shops.

To create a block, the carved lino is mounted onto a piece of well-seasoned wood, blockboard or marine plywood. Do not attempt to make the blocks too large as they will not print evenly and will be difficult to handle. Blocks that easily fit in the hand, make an ideal size. Patterns are made by gouging out non-printing areas from the surface of the lino. Sharp craft knives and specialist lino-cutting tools with a variety of blades are readily

**Right: The simple designs of many block prints can be enhanced by the careful choice of vibrant colours.**

**4 Carefully position the inked-up block face-down on the fabric. Apply precise pressure to the back of the block to make a clean, sharp print.**

5–6 More complex designs will use more than one block in the printing process. After printing your first block, allow the ink to dry before printing any further

blocks. These could be in different colours if you wish. Care needs to be taken in fitting together the design elements and you may need to practise first.

available. Always cut away from yourself as the tools are very sharp. To aid cutting, warm the lino's surface but do not overheat as this will make it brittle and crumbly. Design possibilities are endless but it is advisable to start with simple geometric patterns until you have mastered the cutting tools and the printing process.

Lino can also be etched by using a solution of 33 g of sodium hydroxide (caustic soda) dissolved in 100 ml of water. This is painted onto the lino, using a synthetic paintbrush, and burns away the top layer of the block producing soft textural areas. Rubber gloves must be worn as caustic solutions will burn. Other substances such as oven cleaner and paint stripper can be used in a similar way. After etching, wash the block in water to remove any caustic substances.

Lino has a waterproof surface that if left in place will create textural effects when printed. This can be removed by sanding the block evenly before using. Some designers apply a flocked layer to the surface of the block. Flocking fibres are synthetic fibres that help the block hold more print paste, which means more paste can be transferred to the fabric. This is unnecessary in most cases. Lino is a very hard-wearing material and a block will last for years if cleaned and stored properly.

## Relief Printing

This method of printing is one of the easiest and requires very little equipment. In its simplest form objects such as corks, nuts, bolts, nails, leaves, feathers or dried flowers are painted with printing paste or pressed onto an inked-up printing pad and then pressed onto the fabric's surface to create a pattern.

Very simple stamp prints can be made with wire, pipe cleaners and pencil erasers. A length of wire or a

**Above: For a block printed scarf – Jackie Hayes used simple square blocks with different strengths of discharge paste for this chequerboard effect.**

pipe cleaner can easily be bent into a variety of flat patterns and a vertical handle formed out of the two ends of wire; these stamps produce very successful designs when used with hot wax to create a wax resist pattern (see page 131). Small printing stamps can also be made from soft rubber erasers. The surface of the rubber is carefully cut away in a simple pattern with a sharp scalpel or craft knife (as with the lino). Care must be taken not to cut away too much rubber or the eraser will break up when used. These stamps can then be dipped into the printing colour or a resist paste and pressed firmly onto the surface of the cloth.

Larger printing blocks can be made from flat pieces of card, hardboard or plywood. These are used as bases onto which a textured pattern is then created using a variety of materials. String, embossed papers, card, canvas, sponge, felt, dried beans and pulses, or pasta can all be stuck to the base and used for relief printing. It is important to ensure that the objects are securely glued in place with a waterproof adhesive and allowed to dry before using. Any waterproof glue or wood adhesive can be used, on its own, to create a range of spotted and linear

## FLOCKING

**1 To flock the surface of a lino block, first apply a thin layer of glue to the block. Then gently sieve the flocking fibres over the surface of the glue.**

**2 Dry the block overnight before knocking off any excess fibres. The block is then ready for use. A flocked block will absorb more print paste.**

## RELIEF PRINTING

images. The glue is squeezed or dripped in a pattern directly onto a base. It is then left to harden before any printing can begin.

Many vegetables and fruit can also be used for relief printing. Some are used whole or cut in half to produce an impression. Others, for example potatoes, turnips and swedes, are best cut in half and then patterned by cutting out sections with a sharp knife. Again, it is important to dry the fruit or vegetables well before inking up their surfaces and printing.

A wide variety of dyes, paints, print pastes and inks can be used with these simple techniques. The type used depends upon the fabric and the effect desired. The paint or print paste is first applied to the printing stamp or block by brush, roller or a padded printing pad. The different inking methods produce very different imprints. A thick layer of print paste can be applied with a brush, whereas a rubber roller will transfer very little ink. However, applying the paste from a printing pad will produce a much more even layer of ink, ensuring a uniform print.

### Metal Stamps

Metal printing blocks can be made quite easily. The vast variety of nails, tacks and metal pinning systems available in hardware stores can be used to create a large variety of spotted, dotted and line effects on a variety of fabric bases.

Using a 25 mm thick piece of softwood cut to the size of the block you require, carefully hammer in a variety of nails, tacks, pins and metal joining strips into any pattern you wish, taking care not to split the wood. It is important to ensure that all the heads are at the same level or the block will print unevenly. Simple blocks constructed in this way can be used with normal print pastes to create a positive image but a molten wax or resist paste (see page 131) will produce a negative image design.

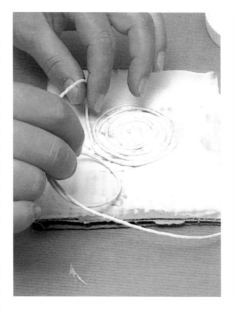

1 Paint a waterproof adhesive onto the surface of some thick card. Carefully place some string in a spiral design on the surface of the card.

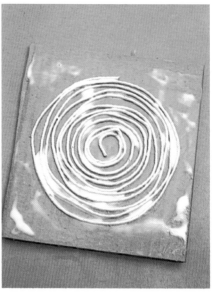

2 When the design is complete wipe off any excess glue that might spoil the print and allow the whole stamp to dry thoroughly before printing.

## PRINTING THE IMAGE

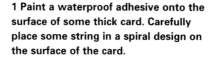

3–4 Roll the printing paste onto a smooth surface, like glass. Then place your block face-down onto the glass to transfer the ink onto your string block.

5 The block can then be printed in a pattern onto the surface of a fine fabric. The print is then fixed and finished according to the dye you have used.

# GALLERY
# BLOCK
# PRINTING

Above
**MELISSA PIETERSON**
For a simple, but dramatic design a bold,
bright block of colour is used as a resist under
an indigo-dyed ground.

Far Right
**CAMBERWELL COLLEGE OF ART AND CRAFTS**
A more complex tile-effect block print is
produced using a simple quarter circle of
a design and an indigo resist technique.

Below
**YATELEY INDUSTRIES
FOR THE DISABLED**
This very traditional border-print
design has been built up using
a series of lino blocks with
reactive dyes.

# 10

# SCREEN PRINTING

Screen printing (or table printing as it is known in America) can be considered a development of the stencilling process that has been practised in Japan since the eighth century. It is one of the most versatile patterning techniques and can be used to produce anything from simple stencilled, wax or gum resist patterns to complex photographic images. It is not difficult to master and can be used for most types of dye, pigment, discharge, resist and texturing effects.

All screen printing techniques use similar equipment, the main requirement being a silk-screen. A silk-screen consists of a rigid square or rectangular frame (wood or metal) with a fabric mesh stretched over it. The size of screen and its mesh depends upon the type of design, fabric and printing technique to be used. Frames can be obtained in a wide range of sizes, materials and mesh types. It is possible to construct your own (see chapter 18), but for a first attempt a small commercially constructed screen is recommended.

Print paste is pushed through the mesh using a squeegee (sponges and pieces of rubber can be used with less success). This is a rubber or plastic strip clamped in wood or metal. For small screens, a simple window cleaning squeegee can be used. Larger screens require a full width squeegee to ensure even images. Squeegees can be bought in standard sizes or as a long strip that can be cut to a specific size.

The basic technique is the same no matter what system of screen printing is used. To print an image, the prepared screen is placed onto the surface of the fabric that has first been stretched and pinned, taped or glued to hold it firmly in place. For a repeating image, ensure the screen is

correctly positioned with the registration nuts and the bracket in the correct position against the registration bar (see page 98).

To prevent the print from smudging, the screen must be held firmly to prevent any movement. The assistance of another person is advisable if you are inexperienced or need to print a large screen. Rest the squeegee at the top of the screen about 5 cm from the screen's inner edge. Using the squeegee as a barrier, the printing paste is carefully poured into the trough between the blade and the edge of the screen. Hold the screen firmly and transfer the squeegee behind a portion of the printing paste. Keeping the squeegee at an angle of 45°, slowly drag the paste across the screen in a smooth steady action. A second pull of the squeegee is normally necessary to achieve a uniform print. This can be done by transferring the squeegee back to the top of the screen and repeating the process with more print paste or by reversing the action. For a reverse pull the squeegee must be held at an angle of 45° facing away from you and smoothly pushed back to the top of the screen. Practice is required to achieve a smooth motion, as any uneven pressure may cause streamers of print paste to trail behind the squeegee. If you are working alone it is sometimes easier to employ a

cross-wise stroke, holding the screen firmly with one hand and pulling the squeegee with the other. The number of pulls of the squeegee will vary with the type of design, screen and cloth. Two pulls is normally adequate when using a standard screen to print on a medium-weight silk or cotton, but thicker fabrics, finely detailed images or specialist techniques may require more. It is advisable to do a test or 'strike off' before commencing on the final piece. This allows one to determine the number of pulls that will be required and spot any faults in the screen or image.

Once the image has been printed, the screen is lifted off the fabric. It is then washed and dried, or placed in another area ready for the next print. If printing a repeat, it is standard practice to print every other image first; this allows time for the printing paste to soak into the cloth and dry before the adjoining image is printed. It also prevents the back of the screen picking up wet paste from the newly printed image, and depositing it as a shadow or mark-off on the next print.

Very large screens will need two people to print the design. They must work as a closely coordinated team as it is necessary to pass the squeegee from one to the other, mid-way through a pull. The same angle and pressure on the squeegee must be maintained or the resulting print will be uneven.

**Opposite: Jonathan Fuller's inspirational design used reactive dyes and a discharge technique to achieve a layering effect.**

**Right: Joseph Burrin used a computer to generate this design, before screen printing it onto Lycra using acid dyes.**

## REGISTRATION OF A SCREEN

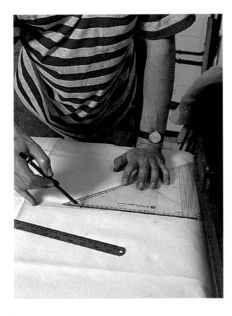

1–2 To align the screens with the registration bar, draw a pencil line onto the backing cloth, perpendicular to the bar and across the width of table. Using this

as a guide, align the registration crosses in the image on the main screen with the line on the table. Then transfer the lines on the screen to the cloth (see chapter 6).

3 Secure the screen by adjusting the bolts at the end of the frame. These should butt up to the registration bar and be secured in place with a locking nut.

## PRINTING A REPEAT IMAGE

4–5 Attach the T- or L-shaped bracket to the screen with a registration stop clamped to the bar. For repeating images measure the width of the screen and set

the registration stops to this distance along the table. Large prints will require assistance. The screen is held securely whilst the image is printed.

6 The squeegee then swaps hands half-way across the screen. When printing a repeat, it is standard practice to print every other image first. This avoids mark-off.

Several methods are available for transferring designs to screens. All of them rely upon the mesh being filled in specific areas to, create a 'stencil' of the design. The blocked 'stencil' areas prevent any print paste reaching the fabric beneath them when the screen is printed. For every colour in a design a separate screen is needed.

## Wax and Gums

Areas of the screen mesh are blocked with wax or gum to create a semi-permanent stencil. This will eventually break down but the stencil can be refilled. If a design calls for different colours to print one on top of another, the palest shade is always printed first. Between each print the screen is washed and dried before being filled a second time (this protects the area of the first colour) whereupon the next colour can be printed. The process is repeated until all the colours have been printed.

First, the design or pattern is transferred to the printing surface of the mesh by placing the screen face-down on top of the design and, using a soft pencil, carefully tracing the main elements onto the screen. The screen is then placed face-up, on a flat table (protect the table's surface with layers of newspaper) and the areas of the design not to be printed are painted out with a suitable filler and allowed to dry. Liquid stencil, shellac, PVA glue, wax or a gum are all suitable mesh fillers.

The choice of filler depends upon how many times a screen is to be printed. For a semi-permanent stencil, use a commercially produced filler or shellac; these can only be removed with a solvent or methylated spirits but will allow repeated use of the screen. Other fillers such as batik or paraffin wax will give a softer effect. Melt the wax in a double boiler or wax pot and apply to the mesh using a brush or tjanting tool (see page 132). When the wax has set, any drips that have formed on the inner surface of the screen can be scraped off using a palette knife. A stencil made this way will last some time provided that the printing paste is not washed

## USING A WAX RESIST

1 To make a simple screen you can block out a design with molten wax. To do this lay the screen face-up and paint the wax resist onto the mesh with a paintbrush.

2 When the wax has set remove, with a palette knife, any lumps that have formed on either side of the mesh. Then seal the edges of the screen to prevent bleeding.

3 Select the dye (some are given in chapters 12, 13 and 14) and print the design onto the fabric. Make sure the screen is held firmly in place during printing.

4 When you have finished the print carefully lift the screen. Where the wax blocked the screen's mesh no dye should have penetrated to the fabric below.

off with hot water. For a textural effect, a wax crayon or candle can be rubbed onto the mesh to create a stencil. The crayon or candle is applied to the screen's inner surface with considerable pressure. The aim is to deposit enough wax on the screen to block the small holes of the mesh. Textural effects can be produced by placing thin objects such as leaves, bark, string or sandpaper beneath the mesh. To remove a wax stencil, place the screen between two sheets of absorbent paper and press the inner surface with a hot iron. Replace the paper as soon as it becomes impregnated with melted wax. Any residue left on the screen is dissolved with methylated spirits or petrol. If a natural gum such as gum arabic or British gum (Dextrin) is used, the image will only last for a single printing session. As soon as the screen is cleaned with water the gum will wash away.

Before printing, the gap between the frame and the mesh is blocked to prevent any seepage onto the fabric. A special filler or masking tape can be used (see pages 99 and 184).

## Paper and Film

Stencils can be cut from a firm paper, such as good quality cartridge paper. The stencil is then placed under the mesh of a prepared screen in the printing position. For repeated prints allow the paste or ink to temporarily glue the paper to the face of the screen enabling the screen to be moved with the stencil attached (for single prints the paper can be fixed to the fabric). For patterns on a large scale, stencils can be cut out of a special heat-fix paper. This is temporarily ironed onto the cloth's surface and a blank screen is placed over the whole area to print. Once the print is dry, the stencil can be peeled off. Paper stencils will only last for one printing session. If the design is to be repeated it is advisable to cut a few copies or use a special pro-film.

**Opposite: Piccadilly Circus, London, inspired David Edmond's photo silk-screen on wool delaine fabric.**

## PAPER STENCILS

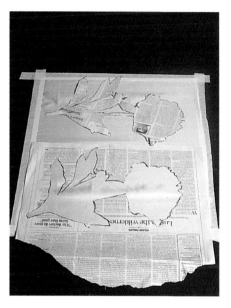

1 Cut your image out of either newspaper or cartridge paper. Tape the stencil onto the fabric. Remember, paper stencils can only be used for one print session.

2 When the stencil is in position, place an open screen over it. Then apply the print paste down one side of the screen, making sure there is enough for a good print.

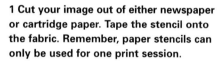

## PRINTING THE STENCIL

3 To print the image pull the dye across the screen using your squeegee. Two to three pulls should be enough to push the dye through the screen.

4 When the image has been printed remove the screen and allow the print to dry. Once the print is dry, peel off the paper stencil.

**Above: Karen Johnstone used a screen that was blocked out with wax to produce this discharged floral design.**

Pro-film is a lacquer-backed film that is readily available in lengths from art and graphic shops. It is cut easily with a sharp craft knife or scalpel. It requires practice to cut only the lacquer layer leaving the film backing intact. The cut stencil is transferred to the face of the screen using a special adhering solution or a hot iron, depending upon the type of film used. Once the stencil has hardened, the film backing can be carefully peeled away leaving behind the lacquer, bonded to the mesh of the screen. This type of stencil is durable and can be used repeatedly. It is flexible enough to allow both bold and intricate stencils to be printed.

## Photographic Stencil

This is the stencil technique used in the textile industry. It is very versatile and can be used for all types of imagery. Specialist equipment is needed to produce photographic stencils, but it is possible to coat and expose your own screen. However, this is only sensible if a large number of screens are required, as you will also need a darkroom and some expensive photographic equipment. There are many screen-making firms that will photographically transfer your image to screen.

To produce a photographic stencil a 'positive' of the image or design is required. A positive is a transparent film onto which the image has been handpainted, photocopied, printed or photographically reproduced. This positive image must be black, and opaque enough to stop light passing through it. For a hand-drawn image, specialist polyester film, like Kodatrace and Permatrace, is readily available from any art or graphics shop. This film is expensive but, if a water-based opaque is used to produce the image, the film can be recycled after washing. Using a hand-drawn positive enables a designer to reproduce many of the painterly qualities of the drawing. The special drawing paint can be applied with pens, brushes and/or sponges. It may help to produce a small test screen employing the different patterning techniques, with varied exposure times, to see the variety of marks that can be printed.

Many photocopiers and computer printers are capable of producing an image on acetate or special film that is opaque enough to be used as a positive. Specialist copy shops will enlarge small images onto a polyester film. This can be very useful for some designs as the same enlargement by reprographic methods is expensive.

Photographically reproduced positives will give the most accurate reproduction of a design but tend to be expensive if used for large images. These can be obtained from specialist reprographic shops. This is the only method capable of producing a 'half-tone' image and accurate colour separation for trichromatic work.

## Avoiding Faults

Tiny specks of colour on the printed fabric are caused by small holes in the photographic coating of a screen. These are known as pin holes, and they are caused by air bubbles in the screen coating or dust on the screen positive or exposure unit. A breakdown of the coating can produce the same effect. Before printing with a photographic screen always check it against the light for holes, which can then be blocked in with a small amount of photosensitive coating, varnish or a small piece of tape.

Uneven printing is often caused by too few pulls of the squeegee or, alternatively, a lack of printing paste – be sure to maintain even pressure with every pull of the squeegee. Too many pulls may cause the printed image to bleed. A similar problem can be encountered in block printing, so it is important to ensure that the block is evenly inked and to maintain this throughout, or lighter and darker areas will spoil the overall design.

**Opposite: Timney Fowler used reprographic techniques and three-colour separation for this classic period velvet.**

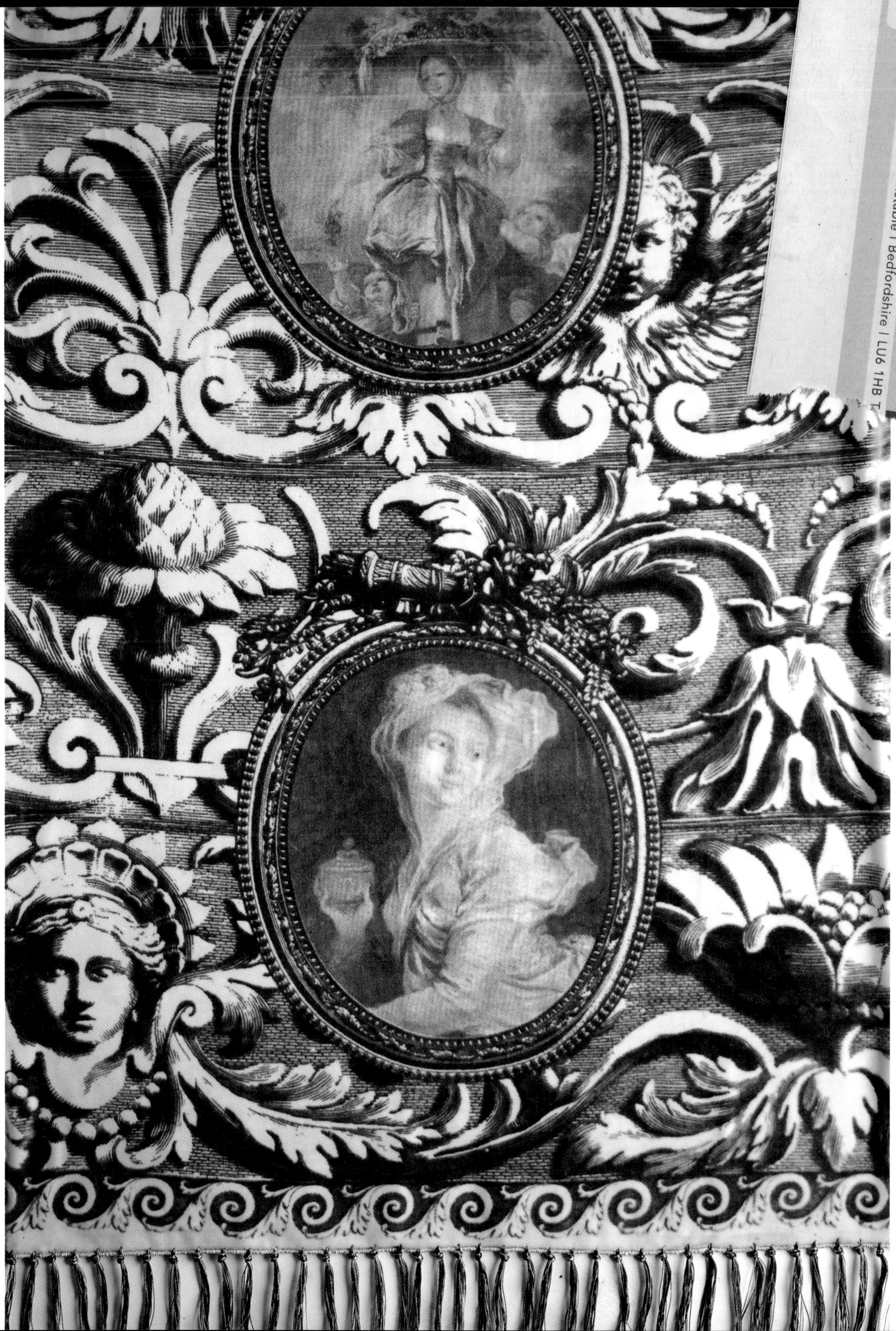

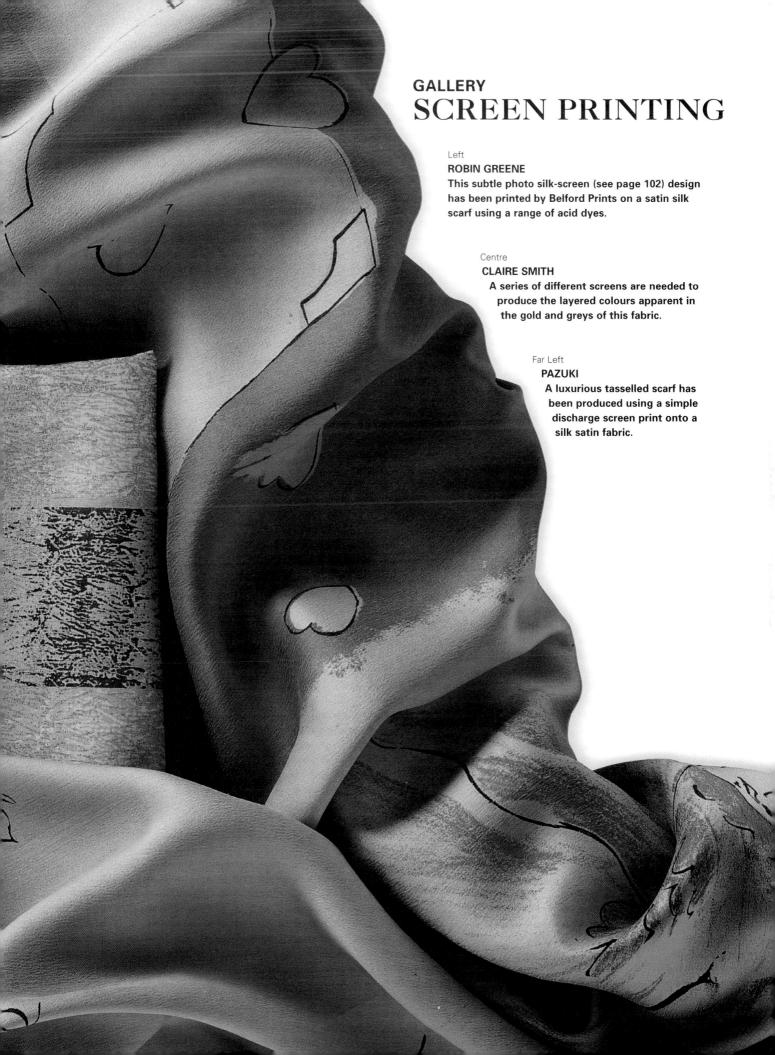

# GALLERY
# SCREEN PRINTING

Left
**ROBIN GREENE**
This subtle photo silk-screen (see page 102) design has been printed by Belford Prints on a satin silk scarf using a range of acid dyes.

Centre
**CLAIRE SMITH**
A series of different screens are needed to produce the layered colours apparent in the gold and greys of this fabric.

Far Left
**PAZUKI**
A luxurious tasselled scarf has been produced using a simple discharge screen print onto a silk satin fabric.

# 11

# TRANSFER PRINTING

Transfer printing is the transference of an image to fabric via a substrate. Dyes, or a resin base containing the coloured pigments, are transferred to fabric via heat and pressure.

## Sublimation Dry Transfer

This technique relies on the fact that disperse dyes sublime when heated. The process is simple and enables the designer to create multicoloured designs without specialist equipment. Only synthetic fabrics can be used, although some fabrics with a high proportion of synthetic fibres will pattern, but the colour yield may be lower.

Transfer dyes can be bought in the form of inks, dyes, pencils and crayons and can be painted, printed or crayoned onto paper and then transferred to the fabric using a hot iron or heat press. Deka iron-on paints and

**Opposite: For a heat photogram, Sarah Batho placed feathers between a coloured transfer paper and this polyester satin.**

Crayola fabric transfer crayons are available in craft shops, and other disperse dyes can be mixed up to a printing paste using certain disperse dyes that will sublime (consult manufacturer's information). All the dyes are transparent, intermixable and can be diluted with water to produce a range of shades. Different papers used as an intermediate substrate give different yields of colour. Specialist transfer papers are available but a fine cartridge paper or newsprint will work equally well. Avoid using thick papers as the heat needed to transfer the dyes cannot pass through them. The colours may seem dull when applied to the paper, but will become bright when transferred to the fabric base. Colour tests with different papers, inks and crayons on small pieces of fabric will provide a guide for colour.

Using any of the above materials, create your design on the paper, bearing in mind that the design will reverse when transferred to the fabric. When the design is completed,

ensure that there are no loose specks of crayon outside the design and allow the dyes to dry completely. Then lay out the fabric on an ironing table or the bed of a heat press, having protected the surface of the table with newspaper to stop any dye passing through the cloth onto the base below. Then place the finished design face-down onto the fabric and cover with another sheet of thin white paper (special silicone-coated sheeting can also be used) to protect the fabric from scorching. Holding the transfer firmly in place, iron the back of the design very carefully at a high temperature until the dyes transfer across to the fabric beneath. If using a heat press set the temperature at around 200°C and press for about 30–45 seconds. The dyes will now be permanently fixed. If a printing paste was used the fabric should be washed in warm water to remove the gums and chemicals present. It can then be dried at a coolish temperature (do not tumble dry).

---

## SIMPLE TRANSFER PRINTING

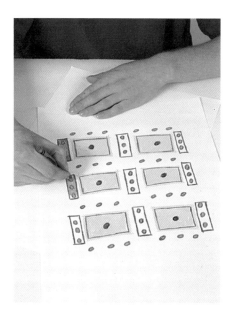

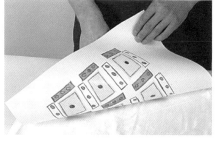

**1 Using Crayola fabric crayons, draw and colour a simple pattern onto a thin piece of paper. You will find photocopy paper is ideal for transfer printing.**

**2–3 Place the paper design face-down onto a synthetic fabric. To transfer the image across to the fabric, press the back of the paper with a hot iron.**

**4 After ironing for about a minute remove the paper backing to reveal the design. The dyes should now be permanently fixed on the fabric.**

**Right: Using specialist photocopy transfer paper Caroline Wright has collaged a large decorative panel on cotton upholstery.**

Not all the dye will have transferred to the fabric and the paper image can often be used again. However, the colour yield for the second print may not be as strong. 'Heat photograms' can be created if objects such as lace, feathers, wire or string are placed be-tween the fabric and a coloured piece of transfer paper; the object acts as a mask stopping the dye reaching the fabric. The final result is a white shadow print on the fabric. This technique works best if a heat press is used.

## Photocopy Transfer

A wet and a dry heat method can be used to transfer either a black and white or coloured photocopy image to fabric. The image is 'glued' with resins to any fabric, but because it gives the fabric a stiffer handle it is best to use

## DIRECT TRANSFER PRINTING

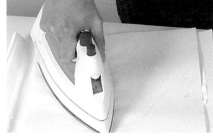

**1 Interesting effects can be created by applying transfer inks to objects with a textured surface (like leaves) and then transferring the dye to a fabric base.**

**2–3 When the ink has dried on the leaves, place them face-down onto the fabric. Cover them with a thin sheet of paper and press with a hot iron.**

**4 After pressing, lift off the paper and carefully remove the leaves from the fabric. The transfer inks will have sublimed directly onto the fabric base.**

this process for small isolated images rather than whole pieces of fabric. Handpainting and screen printing can be used along side this technique.

### Wet Method

The first technique employs a product called Image Maker produced by Dylon. This solution can be used to transfer any standard photocopy but gives a rubbery feel to the fabric. The photocopy will be reversed so avoid writing or numbers in the design.

To transfer your image place the photocopy printed-side up onto a piece of foil or plastic then paint the surface of the photocopy with an even layer of Image Maker solution. Lift the photocopy and transfer it face-down onto the fabric. Cover the back with a piece of absorbent paper and then press the copy down firmly. A rubber roller or rolling pin can be used to ensure that the image has taken.

Leave the copy to dry for at least four hours, and then soak the paper backing thoroughly with water. Once softened it can be carefully removed using a sponge and water – a few attempts may be necessary. When the image is completely free of any paper 'fuzz', leave it to dry. The image can then be sealed with a thin layer of Image Maker painted over its surface. Leave to cure overnight and do not wash for at least 72 hours.

### Dry Heat Method

This requires a photocopy printed on special paper, such as Paracopy and Magic touch. The image is photo-copied onto the paper and placed image-side down onto the fabric. Cover with a clean piece of thin white paper or a silicone-coated sheet and slowly iron with a hot iron, or heat press for 20 seconds at 200°C, to transfer the image to the cloth. Leave the photocopy to cool for a few seconds before peeling the backing paper away and leaving the image behind. Care must be taken at this point as the fabric and image can be distorted if the paper is removed too quickly. Once cool, the image is per-manently fixed and the fabric can be washed with warm water.

## INDIRECT TRANSFER PRINTING

1 Using a paintbrush, apply the transfer inks to a thin piece of paper and allow to dry. Specialist paper that already contains transfer dyes is also available.

2 Choose a variety of interesting objects and place them in a pattern on a piece of synthetic fabric. These will act as a mask when the ink is transferred.

3–4 Using a hot iron, press hard to flatten the objects on the cloth. The transfer inks should now sublime across to the fabric. Finally remove the transfer paper.

5 Remove the objects to reveal a shadow image on the fabric below. For a good result, enough pressure must be applied at the heat transfer stage.

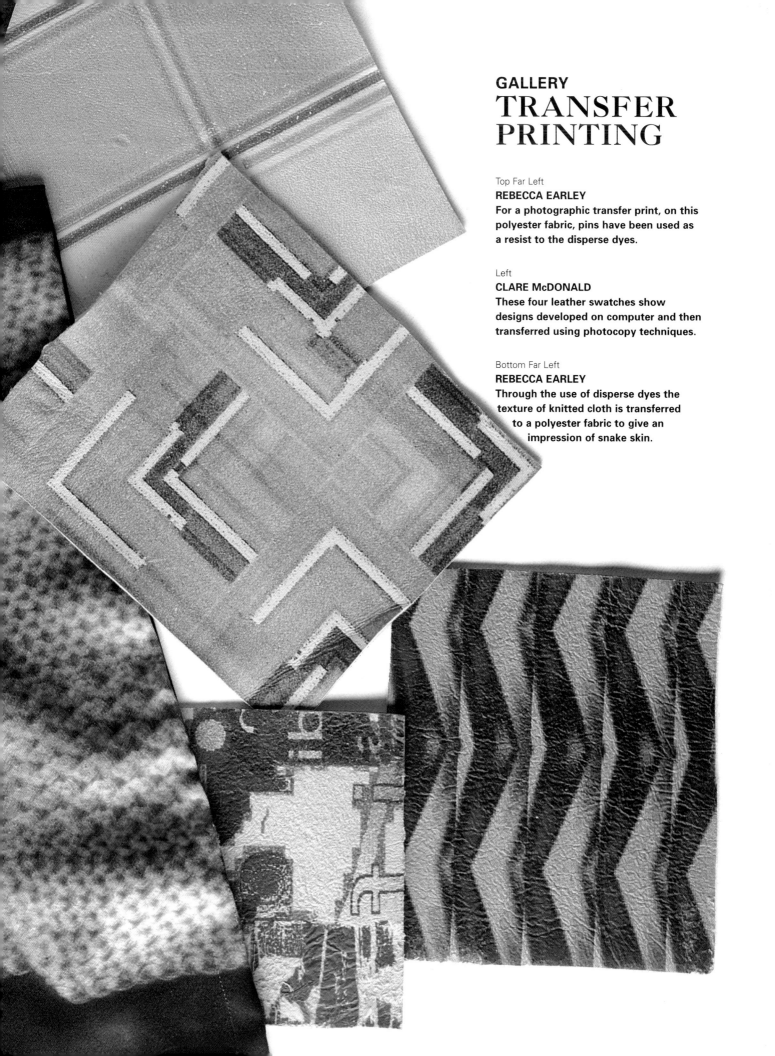

# GALLERY
# TRANSFER PRINTING

Top Far Left
**REBECCA EARLEY**
**For a photographic transfer print, on this polyester fabric, pins have been used as a resist to the disperse dyes.**

Left
**CLARE McDONALD**
**These four leather swatches show designs developed on computer and then transferred using photocopy techniques.**

Bottom Far Left
**REBECCA EARLEY**
**Through the use of disperse dyes the texture of knitted cloth is transferred to a polyester fabric to give an impression of snake skin.**

# POSITIVE AND NEGATIVE IMAGES

*Liberal use of colour can bring depth to a design, making the pattern an integral part of the fabric. This section is a guide to the dye recipes and colouring processes, both traditional and modern, that are employed in the patterning techniques discussed in the previous section. First, it looks into the direct application of dyes and pigments onto a fabric to create a positive image that is darker than the background on which it is printed. The second chapter explores ways in which physical, mechanical and chemical methods are used to control the application of dye solutions. The final chapter explores ways of producing negative patterns on dark or coloured grounds using discharge techniques.*

**Opposite: By tying soya beans into a cotton fabric with strips of raffia, and dyeing with an indigo vat dye, Kate Wells follows traditional methods of resist dyeing.**

# 12

# DIRECT STYLE

The production of positive images is a simple technique and is commonly known as direct style. It involves the use of one or more colours in the creation of a positive pattern upon a white or pale coloured cloth and can be considered a form of localized dyeing with the colourants fixed by steaming or, occasionally, baking (see chapter 17).

## Pigments
Over 50% of all fabrics printed employ a pigment system. Their success relies upon ease of application and a simple fixation/finishing process without the need for a final wash-off. Pigments can be applied to all fabrics but may give the cloth a stiffer handle. This should be taken into account at the initial stages of design. Designs with a small amount of print coverage work best because they minimize this effect; designs with fuller coverage will stiffen the base cloth considerably. A successful pigment print has clean, bright colours, minimum stiffening of the base cloth and acceptable colour-fastness properties. Many suppliers sell a large range of ready-made combinations and systems that will fulfil most requirements.

Pigment printing is the simplest form of direct style. The colour mix is created simply by combining a pigment concentrate with a pre-mixed binder emulsion. Various pigment and binder systems, are designed for the various end uses of a fabric: some are designed for printing furnishing fabrics, others for fashion and knitwear, and specialist binders such as puff or gloss can be used to create a range of textured or shiny effects. Recent developments have introduced light- and heat-sensitive systems as well as pigments with iridescent and reflective properties. Some specialist solvent-based systems are designed for printing on vinyl and plastics and produce high gloss effects. There are also ready-

**Opposite: Norma Starszakowna has screen printed pigments onto a fabric base to create a torn paper effect.**

mixed colours that can be used directly from the pot. Choose a system that suits the end use of the fabric.

## Patterning
As a general guide, the amount of coloured pigment paste you require equals the amount of binder (see page 116). If white or black is required, increase the amounts used by 100 g per litre of binder; both colours can be purchased ready-mixed to give

**Above: Using a stencil, with gold pigment and a devoré technique, Zoë Roberts has created this maroon and gold fabric.**

better coverage. For a matt, opaque or pastel colour, add an opaque white pigment or opaque binder into the paste. It is important not to use more than 50% of an opaque binder or the handle of the fabric will be severely affected.

STANDARD RECIPE
950–999 g pigment binder
1–50 g pigment colour

RECIPE FOR METALLIC PRINTS
850 g metallic pigment binder
100–150 g metallic powder
1–50 g pigment colour (optional)

Special binders are available for metallic prints which will give better fastness and handling properties. Metallic powders come in a range of colours and particle size, the most common being: gold, silver, bronze, pearl and interference pigments. For 1000 g of print paste, mix the metallic pigment binder, the metallic powder and the pigment colour together.

With both of the above recipes, measure out the binder into a non-metallic container and add the pigment colour, mixing thoroughly until the desired shade is achieved. Most pigment colours are compatible and can be intermixed to create desired shades and tones, but excessive use of a pigment colour will affect the rub- and wash-fastness of the print. When mixing metallic pigments, cover the working area with paper and wear a suitable mask and gloves as these powders are extremely fine and will blow around if not combined slowly and with extreme care. The pigment paste can then be applied to the fabric using a handpainting, mono-, block or screen printing technique. The cloth is then allowed to dry before fixing and finishing, especially if a solvent-based system has been employed.

Pigments are fixed via the application of dry heat. A standard pigment or metallic colour will require baking at 150°C for five minutes. Puff prints require a higher temperature of 170–180°C for the same period. (See chapter 17 for methods and equipment.) Pigment prints do not require washing-off, but a warm wash and rinse will improve the cloth's handle. If the fabric has been stuck directly to the printing surface of the table, residue gum will need to be removed.

**Above: In Elsa O'Hara's stunning silverly fabric, metal foils have been used to give the cloth a reflective quality.**

## Foils

This technique enables the application of metallic and patterned foils to the surface of a fabric to produce a reflective mirror-like appearance. The process uses a special, colourless ready-mixed polymer binder like Metran, which is applied to the surface of the fabric by screen printing or handpainting. All equipment must be cleaned afterwards with a solvent-based universal screen wash in a well ventilated area. The adhesive on the fabric is then baked at 170°C for five minutes before applying the foil to its surface. Lay the sections of plastic-backed foil, foil-side down, onto the surface of the dried polymer. Then pass the fabric through a transfer press to bond the two together. The fabric is allowed to cool and the foil's backing film removed. Where the

## PRINTING WITH FOILS

1 Working in a well ventilated area, take the ready-mixed polymer binder (Metran) and run it in a line down one side of the screen printing frame.

2 Screen print (or handpaint) the polymer onto the fabric. Wash the screen immediately with a solvent-based screen wash. Then bake the polymer for five minutes.

3 Cut out a section, or sections, of metallic or patterned foil big enough to cover your fabric completely. This foil should be plastic-backed.

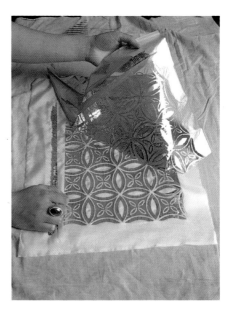

4 Lay the section, or sections, of foil over the printed area of the fabric. This should be foil-side down on the surface of the dried polymer binder.

5–6 Smooth the foil over the fabric, cover it with a plain sheet of fabric and press firmly with a hot iron. Alternatively, you can pass the cloth through a transfer press.

7 Allow the fabric to cool before removing the backing film. Where the polymer binder was printed the foil will have bonded with the fabric.

printed polymer is present the foil will bond with the fabric. This effect can also be achieved by pressing firmly on the fabric with an iron for five minutes, but the final results may not be as fast or as even.

## DYESTUFFS

If a pale-coloured base cloth is required, one of the dye recipes mentioned in chapter 4 can be used, but remember that any base colour will affect other layers of colour. For dark-coloured backgrounds use either an opaque pigment or one of the discharge or resist techniques described in chapters 13 and 14.

Most dyestuffs can be used for direct style but some ranges have been specifically developed for this technique. Nearly all direct patterning processes require fixing with steam. When selecting colours it is important to take into account the end use of the fabric and check the light- and wash-fastness of the dyes, as problems can occur if one dye is not the

Below: Although acid dyes are usually known for their bright colours, this Georgina von Etzdorf scarf shows a range of pastel shades.

same standard as the others. If the colours are to be discharged the dye's dischargeability rating must also be considered (consult the manufacturer's instructions or refer to the dyes listed in chapter 14). When using more than one colour it is advisable to use the same class of dye throughout, as different types may react differently during the patterning process.

To enable successful printing, certain additives are needed. Gums or thickeners control the dye solution on the surface of the cloth and also prevent bleeding of the dye into other areas of the design. Wetting-out and hygroscopic agents aid the absorption of the dye into the cloth's fibres. Wetting-out agents are often added to aid penetration of the print solution, and hygroscopic agents are included to protect some fibres and attract enough moisture into the dry printed film to dissolve the dyes. Some chemicals aid fixation by altering the pH value of the print paste.

## MIXING AN ACID DYE PASTE

1 The acid dye powder is carefully weighed out into a heat-proof container. The amount of dye needed will depend upon the shade of colour required.

2 Mix the dye into a paste using a little cold water. Then add the ethoxylated alcohol (if using) before finally dissolving the dye in hot water.

3 Heat the dye solution to ensure that all the dye has dispersed evenly. If there are any lumps left, sieve the solution and then allow it to cool before use.

## Acid Dyes

These dyes can be applied successfully to all protein and polyamide fabrics (see pages 21–23). Wool that has been prepared for printing is often treated with a chlorination process to assist even up-take of these dyes.

A thickener or gum is used to control the dyes. Gum arabic can be used alone, or in mixes with gum tragacanth or British gum, but it is expensive so alternatives like locust bean gums (Indalca) or guar types (Gum 301 Extra) can be used.

Hygroscopic agents such as urea or thiourea are added alongside auxiliary solvents – ethoxylated alchohol and glycerine – to assist in the dissolution of less soluble dyes. Glycerine reduces the adverse effect of heat (in the steam) on wool, but if added to pastes intended for silk fabrics it may cause bleeding of the dyes. Patterning pastes also need to contain an acid donor for the fixation of the dye. Ammonium sulphate is used but can cause yellowing; ammonium oxalate or tartrate are recommended for polyamide and silk and occasionally acetic acid is added.

---

### RECIPE

5–50 g acid or metal-complex dye
50 g ethoxylated alchohol (optional)
(Glyezin BC)
50–70 g urea or glycerine
250–300 ml hot water
500–600 g thickener
(locust bean, guar or British gum)
30–60 g acid generator
20 g wetting-out agent (optional)
(Matexil WA-KBN)

---

Weigh out the acid or metal-complex dye and the ethoxylated alchohol into a heat-proof container, and dissolve in the hot water. Then measure out the thickener and urea or glycerine into a container and add the acid generator in a solution of 1:2 parts water and mix well. Locust bean or guar-based gums can all be used for the thickener. Slowly add the dissolved dye solution and mix until the paste and solution are thoroughly combined. A wetting-out agent, such as Matexil WA-KBN, is an option if the fabric is difficult to wet-out. The patterning paste can then be applied to the fabric and allowed to dry before the dyes are fixed. Avoid over-drying as a small amount of moisture in the fibres aids the fixation process.

The dried cloth is fixed by steaming in saturated steam for 30–60 minutes at atmospheric pressure (see chapter 17). The fabric is then washed to remove any dyes, thickeners and chemicals. This should be carried out in open width and with extreme care.

For wool and silk rinse the fabric in cold water until most of the dye and thickener has been removed, then rinse in warm water. Wash in a solution containing 1 g per litre of a weak ammonia solution and 2 g of a mild detergent such as Metapex. Finally finish with a cold rinse before drying.

Polyamides must be washed off under mildly alkaline conditions. First, rinse the fabric in cold water con-

---

## MIXING AN ACID DYE PASTE (continued)

4 Measure out the pre-mixed thickener into a plastic basin. The amount of thickener required will depend upon the type of gum used and its viscosity.

5 Then add the acid generator, urea/glycerine and wetting-out agent (if using) to the thickener. Mix thoroughly to ensure that they have all dissolved.

6 When the dye solution is cool, slowly add it to the thickened mixture in the plastic basin. Stir constantly to ensure that the dye and paste are combined.

taining 1 g per litre of sodium carbonate until most of the dye and thickener has been removed. Then follow this with a soapy wash containing 1 g per litre of sodium carbonate and 2 g of a mild detergent such as Metapex. Finish with a cold rinse before finally drying and pressing.

## Direct Dyes

Direct dyes are characterized by their affinity for cellulose fibres, but they can also be used on protein fibres (see page 21). They are readily soluble in water and, in addition, they can be easily applied to fabrics through a thickened gum. Their main disadvantage, however, is that the unfixed dye will readily dissolve in the washing liquor during the final wash-off and may then stain any undyed areas. Special fixing agents are therefore employed in the finishing process.

RECIPE
5–50 g direct dye
50 g urea or glycerine
300–350 ml boiling soft water
500–600 g thickener (guar gums, gum tragacanth, locust bean gum)

10–20 g disodium hydrogen phosphate

ADDITIONS FOR PROTEIN FIBRES
20 g wetting-out agent (optional) (Matexil WA-KBN)

For 1000 g of print paste, weigh out the direct dye into a heat-proof jug and dissolve in the boiling soft water. This solution may then be boiled to ensure that the dye is completely dissolved. Measure out the thickener and urea or glycerine into a container and add the disodium hydrogen phosphate and wetting-out agent, stirring well. Slowly add the dissolved dye solution and mix until the paste and solution are thoroughly combined. The patterning paste can then be applied to the fabric which is then dried before the dyes are fixed.

The dried cloth is then steamed in saturated steam at atmospheric pressure for 30–60 minutes (see chapter 17). After steaming, wash the fabric in open width and with extreme care. Rinse in a large quantity of cold water containing 1 ml of a direct fixing agent (Fixogene) per litre of water,

which helps to protect unprinted areas from mark-off. The fabric can then be given a warm wash before rinsing, drying and pressing.

## Disperse Dyes

Disperse dyes are the only dyes that will colour polyester fibres (see pages 21 and 23). They can also be applied to most synthetic fabrics: polyamides, acrylics, cellulose acetates and tri-acetates but their fastness properties may be reduced. They are applied either by printing or painting onto the surface of the cloth, and are then fixed with steam or hot air at high temperatures (see chapter 17), or by a transfer process (see chapter 11).

RECIPE
5–50 g disperse dye
250–300 ml hot water
500–600 g thickener
(British gum, crystal gum, guar gum, locust bean or alginate gums)
2–5 g oxidizing agent
(sodium chlorate or Matexil P-AL)
1–20 g wetting-out agent
(Matexil WA-KBN)

ADDITIONS FOR POLYESTERS
30–60 g acid donor
3–6 g carrier (optional)

ADDITIONS FOR CELLULOSE ACETATE
30–50 g urea or glycerine

For a steaming recipe of 1000 g of print paste, measure out the dye into a heat-proof jug and disperse it in the hot water. Then measure out the thickener into a non-metallic container. High solid thickeners (gums with a high proportion of gum per litre of liquid) such as crystal gum or British gum give sharp lines, but they do form brittle films that tend to crack off and scatter the

**Left: Motoko Uchimaru used a puff pigment binder to produce this striking textural, as well as graphic, piece.**

**Opposite: Jonathan Fuller's contemporary design illustrates the bright effects achievable with reactive dyes.**

dye particles; the lower solid locust bean gums (Indalca) and alginate gums form elastic films that easily wash out. Then add the oxidizing agent and the wetting-out agent to the mixture.

Slowly add the dissolved dye to the paste and mix until combined, then make any additions specific to your fabric. Polyester fibres will need an acid donor dissolved in a solution of 1:1 with water. Citric or tartaric acid can be used, but disodium hydrogen phosphate is more common due to its compatibility with alginate gums, and if steaming at atmospheric pressure, a suitable carrier will be needed. An additional 30–50 g of urea or glycerine is needed for cellulose acetate. The patterning paste is then applied to the fabric. The fabric is then dried before the dyes are fixed. Avoid over-drying as a small amount of moisture present in the fibres aids fixation.

The dried cloth is fixed by steaming in saturated steam (see chapter 17). To obtain the best results with polyester, pressure steam at 21 p.s.i for 30 minutes. Atmospheric steamers can be used, but a suitable carrier must be added to aid dye migration and steaming times increased to 60 minutes – pale colours may fix without a carrier. A heat-fixing process can also be employed at temperatures of 180–200°C for 45–60 seconds, but the polyester fabric will start to shrink at these temperatures and must be held to width. A simple frame can be fitted to a standard baking cabinet to hold the fabric to its original dimensions, but the size of frame does restrict the size of cloth that can be fixed. Colour yields are 30–50% lower than with pressure fixation methods. Steam cellulose acetate for 30 minutes at atmospheric pressure, and cellulose tri-acetate for 20–30 minutes at 15–20 p.s.i.

The fabric is rinsed in cold and then warm water. This is then followed by alkaline reduction clearing at 40–50°C, which quickly solubilizes any unfixed dyes. Use 1 ml of dispersing agent (Matexil DN-VL 200), 2 ml of sodium hydroxide solution 48° Bé (100° Tw) and 2 g of sodium hydrosulphite (per litre of water). Then rinse in cold water, and a wash at 70°C with 1 ml of detergent per litre. Follow with a final rinse before drying and pressing.

## Reactive Dyes

These dyes give bright colours with very good wash- and light-fastness. Using an alkali, and the influence of heat, fixation takes place by a direct chemical linkage with the fibre. Some reactive dyes are unstable once mixed with water and an alkali, but they are very fast to react and can be fixed without specialist equipment. Others are more stable and can be fixed by steaming or by heat. The best results are achieved on mercerized cottons. The easiest way of applying these dyes is the all-in method described below.

RECIPE
5–60 g reactive dye
100–200 g urea
10 g sodium hexametaphosphate
300 ml hot water
500 g alginate thickener
(Manutex F or Manutex RS)
10 g oxidizing agent (Matexil P-AL)
0–10 g wetting-out agent (optional)
(Matexil WA-KBN)
15–30 g alkali (sodium carbonate or sodium bicarbonate)

ADDITIONS FOR WOOL
10 g citric acid
50 g glycerine

Weigh out the reactive dye (common reactive dyes for this process are Procion MX and P dyes which are specially designed for print, and Remazol), the urea and the sodium hexametaphosphate (Calgon) into a suitable heat-proof container. Slowly add the hot water, stirring the solution until all the dye and urea dissolve, and then allow the mixture to cool. Make up the alginate thickener (see steps on pages 57–8) and combine it with the alkali, oxidizing agent and the wetting-out agent, and then mix well before using. For overprints and designs that require high definition on fine fabrics a high solid thickener, like Manutex F, is advisable; Manutex RS has a lower solid content which is suitable for thicker fabrics. Some recipes call for half-emulsion mixtures, but these are difficult to produce without a high speed mixer. For the alkali, sodium carbonate is normally used with cellulose fibres. Sodium bicarbonate gives a better colour yield with some blue and turquoise dyes

**Left: The safety clip pattern on Charlie Mayes-Baker's silk-satin crepe has been printed with a pigment paste.**

**Right: This contemporary tartan-style fabric by Jonathan Fuller has been produced using reactive dyes.**

and is also used when heat fixing. It is used with protein fibres, too, but can be omitted from the recipe when patterning a chlorinated wool. Other additions for wool are citric acid and glycerine. The paste can then be printed or handpainted onto the base cloth and allowed to dry before fixing.

Most reactive dyes are fixed by atmospheric steaming for 5–20 minutes but some dyes such as Procion P dyes can be baked at 150°C for five minutes. Highly reactive dyes such as Procion MX can be fixed by air hanging for 12 hours or by steaming for 2–5 minutes. Other reactive dyes, especially the vinyl sulphone types (Remazol or Sumifix), can be treated with wet fixation, but it is important to omit the alkali from the patterning paste (see chapter 17).

After fixing, rinse the fabric in cold water. This is followed by a hot wash, and boiling, in a bath containing 1–2 g per litre of non-ionic detergent to remove any excess dye. Give the cloth a final rinse before drying and pressing.

## Vat Dyes

Vat dyes give a wide range of colours with good all-round fastness on cellulose fibres and for this reason they are used in the direct printing of high-quality furnishing fabrics. They can be applied in a single- or two-stage process. The former is described here.

This method uses a patterning paste containing selected vat dyes, an alkali, reducing agent and a hygroscopic agent. During the steaming process the vat dye is reduced to its soluble leuco form and diffuses into the fabric. After steaming, the cloth is rinsed and oxidized returning the dye to its reduced state and fixing it within the cloth. The process is relatively simple, but problems can occur if the quality and quantity of the steam is not adequate to fully reduce the dyes. A typical paste consists of a stock thickener to which a dye paste is added.

STOCK THICKENER
30–75 g glycerine
500–700 g thickener (gum tragacanth, British gum or starch ether)
125–200 g C.I. reducing agent 2 (Formosul)
75–100 g sodium carbonate
or potassium carbonate

PRINT PASTE
5–150 g vat dye
(*C.I. Vat Yellow 2, 4; C.I. Vat Orange 1, 7; C.I. Vat Red 1, 14; C.I. Vat Violet 1, 3; C.I. Vat Blue 4, 5; C.I. Vat Green 1, 3; C.I. Vat Brown 57*; Solanthrene Printing Black 2RB [Mix])
50–150 ml water or thin thickener
800 g stock thickener

Mix up 1000 g of stock thickener. In a separate container, weigh out the vat dye and mix to a paste with the cold water or a dilute solution of the gum used in the stock thickener. Add this paste to 800 g of the stock thickener and mix well. The paste can then be printed or painted onto the fabric. Dry carefully under a moderate heat and steam immediately, or wrap the fabric in polythene and keep in a cool dark place until you are ready to steam.

The fabric should be steamed for 15 minutes, at atmospheric pressure, in an air-free steamer with a constant flow of saturated steam. The time required will vary depending on the fabric and the steaming equipment (see chapter 17). After steaming, the cloth is carefully washed to remove any excess dyes, chemicals and gum. Then rinse in cold water, followed by an oxidizing bath containing 2 ml of 6% hydrogen peroxide solution per litre of water. The fabric is then given a hot soaping at 90°C with detergent and sodium carbonate, if necessary, followed by a final cold rinse before drying and pressing.

# 13

# DYED AND PRINTED RESISTS

There are three main types of resist patterning methods: mechanical, physical and chemical. Most of the ancient techniques fall into the first two categories. These rely upon a physical barrier such as a tight fold, stitch or tie to prevent colour reaching part of the cloth, or the mechanical action of wax, fats or starch. Fabrics are then coloured using solutions of natural, mineral or synthetic dyes.

## PHYSICAL RESISTS

Physical resists can be tied, stitched, clamped or compressed, where the folds in the fabric resist the penetration of the dye. These processes are usually classified under the universal title 'tie-and-dye' but the Japanese name *shibori*, derived from the verb *shiboru*, 'to wring, squeeze, press', is a more accurate description.

The soft, blurred effect produced when dye slowly penetrates into the cloth is one of the special patterning characteristics that gives these techniques their appeal. A design can be made by simply compressing cloth into folds or wrinkles, but folding, knotting and twisting cloth, with the addition of threads, plastic strips, raffia, pegs and clips, can all be used.

Once a fabric has been tied, stitched or clamped, the cloth is dyed. Any of the dye recipes in chapter 4 will work, but make sure you choose the right dye for the fabric you are using. Traditionally, indigo was used for this technique and it still produces a quality of colour not found with any other dye.

## Binding

In bound and tied resists, parts of the fabric are tied up, bound or knotted, thus constricting the cloth and preventing penetration during dyeing. At its simplest, the cloth is scrunched up into a ball or tightly twisted, and wrapped with thread to keep it in place while it is dyed to produce a marbled pattern. A regular striped effect can be produced if fabric is knotted with a simple overhand knot along its length and then dyed. More regular stripes can be created in hori-

zontal, vertical or diagonal directions by pleating or rolling the fabric tightly and then binding sections to stop the penetration of the dye. Bindings of the same thickness at regular intervals will produce an even striped effect, and irregular bindings will produce a varied stripe. A chequered effect is achieved if the fabric is untied after the first dyeing and the process repeated, pleating or rolling in a different direction.

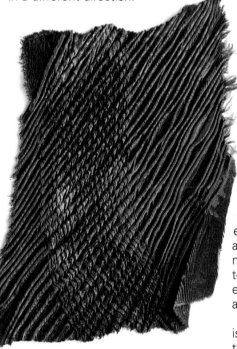

**Above: Nina Domansky's finely pleated silk was made by pole-wrapping and dyeing with indigo and 'K' salt.**

**Opposite: Norma Starszakowna coated a fine silk fabric in wax and then over-dyed with iron rust to produce a crackled effect.**

The most common tie-and-dye pattern is the circle. It is one of the easiest patterns to create and is largely associated with T-shirts of the 1960s and 70s. The fabric is pulled into a point from a central position and bound in sections down its length. By adding additional bindings and over-dyeing the fabric further patterns can be produced. The diameter of the circle can range from 1 millimetre to 1 metre, depending upon the width of

the fabric (larger circles are harder to handle). The shape of the circle can be controlled by careful folding. A square-shaped dot is made by pulling the cloth up into a point and folding it in half (from the tip downwards), this is repeated before binding with a series of half-hitch knots. Spider-web effects are created by pleating the raised section of cloth and binding it with a spiral of thread. Random binding of the raised section will give more irregular shapes.

Small objects can also be tied into the cloth before dyeing. Seeds, beans, rice, twigs, stones, glass marbles and beads, nails or coins can all be used. The material is formed around the object and then tied firmly in place using a strong thread, string, raffia or elastic bands. Various patterns can be built up by objects of different sizes into the same piece of fabric. With all bound or tied resists the selection of cloth, technique and pattern is very much a personal preference. The choice of binding material depends upon the quality and thickness of mark required. It is important to ensure that the ties are tight, otherwise dye will penetrate underneath and ruin the pattern.

Once tied, the fabric can be dyed. It is important to rinse and dry the fabric thoroughly before it is untied or the patterning effect may be spoiled by excess dye bleeding into the design. Different effects can be produced by using different dyes and fabrics.

## Stitching

A strong thread or raffia is required for stitched resists. Using a running or whipstitch, motifs of all shapes and sizes can be built up. When trying this technique for the first time, choose a simple design (circles, squares or diamonds) and trace the pattern with a soft pencil onto the fabric as a guide for stitching. Using a strong thread, knot and fasten one end firmly, then sew through the fabric using short stitches (following your pencil guide lines). For bolder effects, the stitching can be repeated or used to fill a motif completely in a series of lines.

## BOUND RESISTS

1 Tie soya beans tightly into the fabric using raffia or cotton thread. Dye should not be able to penetrate into the bound areas of the fabric.

2 Wet-out the tied fabric, then slowly lower it into the indigo dye vat. Agitate the cloth for 2–3 minutes, making sure the whole cloth is submerged.

3 Carefully remove the fabric from the vat. Initially the indigo dye will be a greeny-yellow colour, but as the indigo oxidizes the cloth will turn a deep blue.

4 Leave the fabric to oxidize in the air for at least an hour. When it is dry, carefully undo the raffia, or string ties with sharp scissors or a seam ripper.

Above: The star-like patterning on Norma Starszakowna's fabric was created using a tied resist. The fabric was dyed in mineral dyes before being untied.

## STITCHED RESIST

Here, silk fabric is stitched using a polyester thread and running stitches. These are then gathered tightly and firmly secured before dyeing.

## ALTERNATIVE BOUND RESISTS

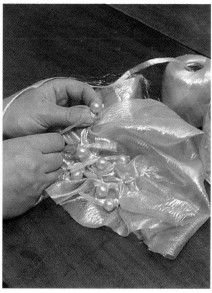

Bound resists need not always use traditional materials. Here, glass marbles are bound into a polyester fabric with polypropylene raffia thread.

Lengths of fabric can be folded into layers and stitched to create a mirror image of the motifs. When the design is complete, all the threads are pulled tight until the cloth is held in closely packed pleats. The threads are then fastened off securely before dyeing. Any cloth in the corrugations of the folds is largely protected from the dye. This enables elaborate designs to be created with a relatively simple technique. Variety in designs is determined by the type of fabric, thickness of threads and the size of the stitches used. By varying these elements the designs can range from simple, bold patterns to intricate, elaborate motifs. Experience will teach you which fabrics and methods are the most appropriate for a planned effect.

An alternative to the running stitch is the whipstitch. This technique is more effective on a single layer of fabric. First the outlines of a design are whipstitched, and then the threads are pulled tight as before. This rolls the fabric into a tight tube

along the line of stitching, protecting the areas of fabric inside it from the dye. This method creates a series of fine diagonal lines on the fabric which can be used as part of the overall patterning effect. Similarly, by over-stitching in opposite directions cross effects can be created. Raffia works extremely well in this technique as it is strong but flat, and covers the fabric well.

Various mechanical methods can be employed for stitched resists. A sewing machine produces a variety of stitched effects. It is important to use a long stitch length and set the tension on a loose setting to enable the fabric to be gathered up after sewing. A machine will give a different patterning effect from hand sewing and is a lot faster. Interesting effects can be achieved by experimenting with different types of stitch.

Small pleating and smocking machines can also be used to produce very fine pleats in a piece of fabric. The machines will stitch through the

fabric at the same time as pleating, enabling the pleats to be gathered up and firmly secured before dyeing. A patterned effect of very fine horizontal lines is produced once the fabric is released from its pleats.

After stitching, the fabric can be dyed. Make sure you choose a dye appropriate to the fabric being dyed. Designs can be built up by layering the stitching and over-dyeing with different colours. After dyeing, the cloth is rinsed thoroughly and dried before removing the stitching with a pair of sharp scissors or a seam ripper. Extra care should be taken to avoid accidentally cutting the fabric when removing the stitches.

### Clamping

Traditionally, fabric is folded into wide pleats to form a strip of cloth which is then folded upon itself to create squares, rectangles or triangles. This bundle of cloth is then placed between two wooden boards or sticks and held firmly in place with string

## CLAMPED RESIST

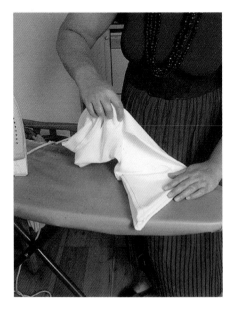

**1 Use an iron to press the fabric into a series of pleats down the length of the cloth. These are then folded upon each other in the form of triangles or squares.**

**2 Place the compact package of cloth between two similarly shaped pieces of wood (either triangles or squares). Firmly clamp it in place using a G-clamp.**

**3 The clamped fabric is now ready to be dyed. We have used an indigo vat dye, but other methods of dyeing are suitable as long as the correct type of dye is used.**

To produce a square lattice design, the cloth is carefully folded into regular-sized squares, dampened and clamped with boards that are the same size as the folded fabric. It is not usually necessary to submerge the whole clamped piece into the dye, only the exposed edges of cloth. The cloth is then rinsed in its clamped state and carefully unclamped and spread out flat to dry. Care should be taken when undoing the cloth to avoid dye marking off onto the white areas of the design. A completely different effect is produced if a similar-shaped pile of cloth is clamped in a diagonal direction using rectangular boards that are slightly larger than the folded square; the two exposed corners are dyed and the process repeated in the opposite direction without disturbing the pile of cloth.

while it is dyed. When dyed, the multiple folds create simple soft-edged geometric patterns. For different effects a variety of materials, such as pieces of metal plate, high-density fibreboard, perspex and acrylic sheet can be cut into shapes and used for the clamping boards. The boards are held firmly in place during dyeing using simple G-clamps or large bulldog clips instead of string. Wooden clothes pegs and bulldog clips, clamped directly onto the cloth, will produce simple but effective patterns.

## CLAMPED RESIST

**4 If using indigo, the clamped parcel must be allowed to oxidize before rinsing the fabric (in its clamped state) to get rid of excess dye. Then remove the clamp.**

**5 Carefully undo the folded fabric. Care must be taken in case there is any dye trapped between the boards which might smudge and ruin the design.**

**6 Finally, hang out the fabric on a washing line, or lay it out flat, to dry. When dry, wash the cloth to get rid of any remaining excess dye.**

By folding the cloth strip into equilateral triangles and clamping with rectangular boards a tortoiseshell effect will be produced. A triangular lattice design will be created if boards the same size and shape as the folded fabric are employed.

Different effects may be obtained by submerging the folded cloth for longer or shorter periods of time into the dye solution, and interesting colour effects can be created by dipping different edges into different coloured dyes. Some dyes will penetrate faster than others producing a halo effect around the shapes. Clamped resist techniques are quick for producing small quantities of cloth and tend to be more successful on thin fine fabrics such as a cotton lawn, poplin or silk as these are less bulky when folded, making the clamping and dyeing process easier.

## Pole-wrapping and Compressing

A variety of diameter, lightweight plastic drainage pipes, obtainable from most building suppliers or DIY shops, are suitable for this technique. Use a length of 1–1.5 metres, which is an easy size to handle. Polish the surface of the cylinder with a small amount of silicone furniture polish which will aid the compressing of the fabric. The fabric can then be fixed to the bottom of the pipe using a piece of masking tape. Slowly turn the pipe to wind the fabric tightly around the pole, keeping it temporarily in place with small pieces of tape. The angle at which the fabric is fixed will affect the direction of patterning on the final dyed cloth. If wrapped with the cloth's selvages aligned down the length of the cylinder, horizontal lines will be created. By wrapping the cloth at a 45º angle to the pole, with the selvages spiralling down the cylinder, a diagonal effect will be produced.

To achieve a random patterning effect, the fabric can then be pushed down the outside of the pipe, while the pipe is twisted in a clockwise direction. This will produce large and unrestricted folds of cloth; it is important at this stage to ensure that the top and the bottom of the fabric

are secured firmly with tape or string before dyeing. A regular pattern can be created by slowly winding thread, evenly spaced, down the cloth as the pipe is turned. The tape can then be removed and the cloth pushed down the pipe into tight, compact folds. By pushing the fabric straight down, an even striped effect can be produced. However, if the cloth is twisted as it is compressed diamond-shaped motifs can be created. It is sometimes difficult to push a large amount of fabric down the pipe in one go. It may be easier to wind and compress the cloth in smaller sections as it moves down the cylinder.

When the fabric has been compressed and fastened to the pipe, the end of the pipe is placed in a dye bath. After dyeing, the fabric is rinsed free of any excess dye and unwound from the pole. Interesting effects can be achieved by repeating the process by twisting the fabric in another direction with the same or different coloured dyes.

**Above: Christine Humphreys used layers of wax resist and dye to give this fabric an interesting textured appearance.**

## MECHANICAL RESISTS

Mechanical resists rely upon the creation of a physical barrier between the colorant and the cloth. This barrier can be a wax, fat, resin, clay, starch or gum, and prevents dye from penetrating to the areas where the resist has been applied. The effect produced is in negative, that is a white pattern on a coloured ground, and is very similar in appearance to a white discharge effect.

### Wax

The process of wax resist is commonly known as 'batik', which is thought to have derived from the Javanese word *ambatik*, the root of which is *tik*, meaning 'to dot or drop'.

Wax resist patterning techniques are relatively easy to use, but may take some time to master fully as the waxes and dyes need careful control. Interesting effects can be created by applying a variety of waxes to a wide range of fabrics with an assortment of tools. The best fabrics to use with this technique are fine cloths made from cellulose or silk, as they will dye easily at the cool temperatures required by the technique.

Various waxes can be used for batik depending upon the final effect desired. Beeswax is expensive, but is very soft and if used alone will not crack or peel off the base cloth. However, it is frequently used in combination with cheaper mineral-based paraffin waxes. Different effects can be created by varying the proportions of the two kinds of wax. The higher the proportion of paraffin wax, the more brittle the resist will become and the more likely it is to crack. If a crackled effect is desired, it is important to find a ratio of the two waxes that will allow the solidified wax to crack without peeling off the fabric. The most common proportion to use

is a ratio 1:1, but trials should be carried out using different thicknesses of wax and base cloths.

Special batik wax is supplied in fine granules or pea-size pieces and can be bought from specialist suppliers. There are other waxes available on the market that are soft like beeswax but make a cheaper alternative. Lump resin is sometimes used in wax mixtures. If this is used during the process the batiks are normally left to set for a day or two before dyeing. The presence of the resin will make it harder to remove the wax once the work is completed.

The base cloth must be stretched taut before applying the wax. A painter's stretcher, old wooden printing screen, picture frame or special handpainting/batik frame can be used. Secure the edges of the fabric firmly to this using drawing pins or silk pins. An outline of the design can be drawn onto the cloth, using a charcoal pencil, and used as a guide for applying the wax.

To apply the wax, it must first be melted; it is essential to use a suitable safe container as this process is dangerous and may cause burns or a fire. The easiest way to melt the wax is to use a *bain-marie* but a clean tin placed in a saucepan of boiling water will do. It is important not to allow the water any higher than halfway up the side of the tin, as any mixing of the hot wax and water will result in the wax spitting dangerously. The wax can then be kept hot on an electric ring or hot-plate. A heater with an open element or flame is not recommended as wax will easily ignite. As a sensible precaution keep a fire blanket close at hand in case of accidents. Double boilers and small electrical frying pans also make suitable melting pots. For an ideal resist, the working temperature of the melted wax should be kept at a constant 120°C (248°F) and it is important to check this at frequent intervals with a thermometer. (Use a specialized jam thermometer which will withstand high

## PREPARING A WAX RESIST

**1 Choose an appropriate type of wax. Place the wax or granules into an electric wax pot or a *bain-marie*. Slowly heat until the wax reaches a molten state.**

**2 The molten wax can now be applied using a variety of tools. A wide brush is used to cover large areas while a tjanting is used for fine lines and details.**

**3 Before applying the wax resist, stretch the fabric over a wooden frame and fix it at the edges with pins or silk tacks to produce a taut, smooth surface.**

temperatures.) If the wax is too hot there will be a danger of fire and the wax, when applied to the cloth, will tend to spread; if too cool, the wax will solidify when it is applied and will not penetrate the cloth sufficiently. It is worth investing in a thermostatically controlled electric wax or glue pot if many batiks are to be made.

Very few tools are required for batik but to achieve fine line work a tjanting is best. This is a special wax pen, consisting of a small copper bowl with a single, or several, capillary spouts depending on the fineness of the lines required. A variety of paint brushes or pieces of polyurethane foam attached to a stick or pencil can also be used to draw or paint the wax onto the cloth. Simple stamps can be made from bent wire and pipe cleaners or small blocks can be employed to print a variety of motifs in a similar way to a tjap (see chapter 9). If using a stamp, tjap or block, a shallow wax container is needed. A heavy-duty roasting tin or an electric frying pan

can also be used if their bases are lined with a piece of fire blanket to make an impregnating pad. Melt just enough wax to saturate the piece of blanket, taking care not to overheat the wax. The blocks or stamps are then coated with wax from the blanket and pressed against the cloth.

With a single-colour design the fabric can be dyed soon after the wax has set. With multi-coloured pieces, the wax is applied in layers and dyeing takes place between each layer, slowly building up the colours in the design. For a multicoloured design, wax over all the white areas in the design before dyeing the fabric in the palest colour. The design is then slowly built up, filling in areas with more wax to protect certain areas of colour, progressing from the palest to the darkest colour. It is possible to scrape off areas of wax after each dyeing to build up other colours in the design but it is quite difficult to remove all the wax at this stage. Ensure the cloth is thoroughly rinsed

and completely dry between each waxing. Some designers find it easier to handpaint colours (using cold water reactive dyes or soluble vat dyes) onto the design rather than submerging the whole fabric into the dye bath.

To achieve a crackled effect, the fabric is crumpled up into a ball, before the last colour is dyed, cracking the surface of the wax and allowing limited penetration of the dye to the fabric beneath. An interesting etched effect can be achieved by covering the fabric totally with wax and then scratching into the wax using a sharp stick or pen; the areas that have been scraped away will allow dye to penetrate to the base cloth.

When dyeing the cloth it is very important to use cold temperature dyes; traditionally, indigo was used but other vat dyes are also suitable, and azoic or napthol dyes are often employed. A wide range of bright colours are readily available in cold water reactive dyes and are suitable for all cellulose and silk fabrics. For

## APPLYING A WAX RESIST

**1 Paint the molten wax onto the surface of the cloth in a pattern. Use a wide brush and make sure the wax is hot enough to penetrate through the cloth.**

**2 Finer details are added using a tjanting. This wax pen feeds the wax down a single, or several, capillary spouts leaving a trail of wax on the cloth.**

**3 The wax is clearly visible as dye is painted over it. When dry, submerge the fabric in a cold water bath, keeping it flat to prevent the resist from cracking.**

**Above: A detail from the batik, 'Edge' (94 x 127 cm), by Noel Dyrenforth, shows the different effects of brushes and a tjanting.**

dyeing methods and recipes, consult chapter 4. It is important to keep a wax resist as flat as possible when dyeing to avoid any unnecessary cracking of the wax. Flat photographic trays make ideal dye baths.

Once the fabric has been dyed, the wax layer must be removed from the fabric. Any excess surface wax can be carefully scraped off with a palette knife. There are several methods of removing the wax and the method chosen depends upon the fastness of the dyes used. A common method is to iron the fabric between layers of absorbent paper to melt the excess wax, but this tends to force the wax further into the structure of the cloth leaving it stiff. Plunging the fabric into boiling water will melt most of the wax and it can be easily removed, but check that the cloth and dyes used are fast; this method is suitable for most cellulose fabrics dyed with reactive, vat or azoic dyes. Do not pour the hot waxy water down the sink, as the wax will solidify and block the drains. Allow the water to cool and lift off the waste wax using sheets of newspaper before throwing it away. Any final residue of wax can then be removed by dry-cleaning.

A cold wax resist developed for ceramics will also work well on thin fabrics, producing a speckled texture. The wax emulsion is painted, stencilled or printed onto the cloth. If a screen printing technique is used to apply the wax to the fabric, the screen must quickly be washed in hot water (which will remove the wax). As soon as the printed wax image is dry, it can be dyed with cold water dyes or covered by painting with solutions of coloured dyes. The thin layer of wax is easily removed by ironing the cloth between two pieces of absorbent paper or dipping into boiling water. It is a good wax for children to use as it does not require heating.

**Starch and Gum Resists**
Resists can be produced using paste recipes. The type of mixture you choose will depend upon the effect required; every fabric base, type of dye and patterning technique produces a completely different result. Most paste resists can be handpainted, stencilled, block or screen printed.

Recipes for various resist pastes are provided in chapter 5. A simple flour and gum arabic paste performs very successfully, if used with block or screen printing techniques. It tends not to crack, but if a crackled effect is required the proportions of gum arabic can be reduced and replaced with extra water. Cassava paste is more glutinous and may be handpainted or stencilled onto the cloth, as it tends to be too sticky to be printed successfully. Japanese rice paste can be stencilled, applied with a fine wooden spatula, or trailed across the fabric's surface through a tube. To stencil with this paste, the cut stencil must to be quite stiff – oiled manila card, a thin plastic or acetate sheet all work well. The rice paste is then pushed through the design with a flexible plastic cooking spatula. This paste can also be applied directly to the fabric by drawing with stiff paintbrushes, pieces of card or thin strips of wood. Syringes or cake icing bags with tubes of different dimensions can also be used to trail the paste over the surface of the cloth.

All the above resists work well on natural fabrics, as their slightly rough surface helps the paste adhere. Natural fabrics also have an affinity for the cold water dyestuffs. Indigo is the traditional dye used to colour these cloths and is still one of the best to use with resist pastes. However, many of the other vat or cold water dyes will give some interesting results – try this technique with mineral, azoic or reactive dyes.

British gum (Dextrin) will also make a very successful resist, and if applied thickly and left to dry, it will produce a crackled effect. Following the recipe in chapter 5, make up the paste for resist patterning. Warming the gum allows it to be painted, block or screen printed onto all types of fabric. The Dextrin is then allowed to dry, and depending upon the speed of drying different textural effects are achieved. If left overnight to dry slowly, a fine crackled effect is produced, but larger crackled patterns are achieved by speeding up the drying process. Once the Dextrin is dry, other dye or print pastes can be painted or blotch printed, with an open screen, on top of the resist (remember to choose the correct type of print paste for the fabric). Any of the print paste recipes in chapters 12 and 14 can be used. Allow the covering pastes to dry before fixing. Any excess dye and Dextrin gum can then be washed out of the cloth. It may be necessary to boil the fabric in hot soapy water to remove the last traces of starch.

## CHEMICAL RESISTS

This technique employs a wide range of chemical compounds, such as alkalis, acids, salts, reducing and oxidizing agents, to prevent the fixation or development of the ground colour.

The choice of resist agent depends upon the dye used – most types of colouring matter can be resisted.

Recently there has been a revival of interest in these resists, using newer dyes and chemicals which create effects that are similar to many discharge processes, but they are easier to print and they do not employ harmful reducing agents. Chemical resists are used mainly on cellulose fabrics but may work on some silks or wools.

The most important chemical resist techniques are pigment-reactive and reactive-reactive (see page 137) resists. Most reactive dyes will fix upon cellulose only in the presence of an alkali. Consequently, the use of a non-volatile organic acid (citric or tartaric acid) or an acid salt (monosodium phosphate), as a resist neutralizes the alkali preventing any of the dye from fixing. The unfixed dye can then be removed during the washing process. Certain reactive dyes are better suited than others for this process; the Remazol system and Levafix P dyes have very little affinity for cellulose fibres and therefore the unfixed dye will wash off easily.

### White Resist for Cellulose and Silk

These resists are produced by the application of non-volatile organic acid onto cellulose fabric before dyeing, or by covering the cloth with a standard reactive print paste. These pastes are handpainted, stencil, block or screen printed onto the fabric. The colourless resist paste is made visible with the addition of a little fugitive dye (C.I. Acid blue 1) which fades with washing.

---

RESIST PASTE
50–80 g citric or tartaric acid
600 g acid resistant thickener (guar or locust bean gum, gum tragacanth, starch or cellulose ether)
350 ml cold water

---

**Below: Melissa Pieterson used a wax resist with indigo dyes. Later, a stripe of red reactive dye was added by handpainting.**

COLOURING SOLUTION
20 g reactive dye
Remazol dyes will give the best results and the following are recommended to wash out to a white if printed on a neutral based fabric:

Golden Yellow G
(*C.I. Reactive Yellow 17*),
Yellow R
Golden Yellow 4G
(*C.I. Reactive Orange 74*),
Brilliant Orange GD
(*C.I. Reactive Orange 15*),
Brilliant Orange 3R
(*C.I. Reactive Orange 16*),
Brilliant Red 5B
(*C.I. Reactive Red 35*),
Brilliant Red GG
(*C.I. Reactive Red 106*),
Brilliant Red GD
(*C.I. Reactive 63*),
Red 3B
(*C.I. Reactive Red 23*),
Brilliant Violet 5R
(*C.I. Reactive Violet 5*),
Brilliant Blue R
(*C.I. Reactive Blue 19*),
Blue 3R
(*C.I. Reactive Blue 28*),
Black B
(*C.I. Reactive Black 5*).

Other types of reactive dye will work but it is generally impossible to obtain a white resist under some turquoise and blue dyes, such as Procion blue P-GR (*C.I. Reactive Blue 5*) and Procion turquoise SP-2G (*C.I. Reactive Blue 63*))

7 g oxidizing agent ( Matexil P-AL)
393 ml hot water
15 g sodium bicarbonate (dissolved in 485 g warm water)
80 g alginate thickener (Manutex F)

For 1000 g of resist paste, mix the thickening agent, acid powder (if the fabric is to be immersed in the colouring solution use 80 g of acid powder) and cold water thoroughly in a suitable container. The paste can then be applied to the fabric using your chosen technique. The resist is then allowed to dry thoroughly, after which the fabric can be quickly immersed in the colouring solution, or painted or screen printed with the dye.

To make up the colouring solution dissolve the reactive dye with the oxidizing agent in hot water and allow to cool to 40°C. Add to this a solution of sodium bicarbonate dissolved in warm

water (which has been allowed to cool) and 80 g of alginate thickener. After dyeing, the fabric is quickly dried and steamed for 10–15 minutes. Then rinse well in cold water, followed by a hot wash to remove all the excess dye and gum. Finally, give the fabric a hot soaping by boiling in a bath containing 1–2 g per litre of non-ionic detergent, before rinsing well and drying.

A standard reactive print paste can then be used to blotch print over the top of the resist (see recipe for reactive printing on cellulose, page 122). Over printing can take place once the resist is dry, but better results are achieved by printing directly on top of the wet paste. The acid in the wet paste reacts with the alginate thickener in the cover print, precipitating in the mesh as alginate acid. This blocks the screen in these areas aiding the resist process. The fabric can then be steamed for 10–15 minutes according to the reactivity of the dye. Baking is not suitable for this technique as tartaric acid requires moisture to release its acidic compounds.

## Coloured Pigment Resists for Cellulose

There are various ways of producing a coloured resist on cellulose fabrics. One of the simplest ways is by the use of an acid resistant pigment as

**Above: The texture of the string is clearly visible in Melissa Pieterson's traditional tied and wax resist fabric.**

an illuminating colour in the resist paste. If possible, the pigment binder employed should be suitable for steam fixation, as this will reduce the amount of processing involved.

The following recipe has been simplified to avoid the need for a specialist emulsion thickener, the production of which is difficult without a high speed mixer.

RESIST PASTE
200 g solvent-based pigment binder
600 g acid resistant thickener
(starch or cellulose ether)
20–50 g pigment colour
50–75 g tartaric or citric acid.
50 g Printogen ES liquid (optional)

For 1000 g of resist print paste, mix together thoroughly the thickening agent, binder, pigment colour, acid and the Printogen ES liquid (if you are using it) in a container. The quantity of pigment added to the solution depends wholly upon the colour that is required. When the paste has been mixed, apply it to the fabric base. The pigment resist is then fixed by dry heat for one minute at 140°C

**Opposite: This unique metal and silk scarf was produced by Kate Wells using a clamp technique and indigo dye.**

followed by atmospheric steaming for 10–15 minutes. Once the dyes are fixed the fabric is washed (as discussed on pages 122–3).

## Coloured Reactive-Reactive Resists on Cellulose

There are two methods (the most up-to-date one is given below) by which reactive dyes can be used as coloured resists under another reactive dye. The basic principle is one of addition and substitution with two different types of reactive dyes being used in each case.

This process sounds simple but to achieve good results many tests need to be carried out. The reactive resist process employs monochlorotriazine dyes (Procion P) for the illuminating colours, and vinyl sulphone reactive dyes (Remazol or Sumifix) as the ground colours. The vinyl sulphone dyes must then be prevented from fixing onto the cloth by the

**Right: Nina Domansky combined both pole-wrapping and screen printing with reactive dyes for her red and yellow scarf.**

addition of a sulphite which will stop the dye bonding with the molecules of the cellulose in the fibres of the cloth. Stabilized sulphite or bisulphate compounds are generally used for this purpose. These chemicals do not affect the fixation of the illuminating monochlorotriazine dyes. These dyes react with the cellulose molecules through a substitution method, and therefore fix onto the fabric.

Using the measurements given in the recipe (left) make up the illuminating resist paste and the cover print paste. Then screen print or paint the well-mixed resist onto the fabric and leave to dry before covering with the print paste.

When the print paste has been blotch screen printed or painted over the illuminating resist, fix the dye onto the fabric. This is done by baking the fabric at a temperature of 120°C for two minutes. Follow this with a steam at atmospheric pressure for 10–15 minutes, and finally rinse the cloth in cold water followed by a hot rinse to remove any excess dye and gum. Finally, give the fabric a hot (boiling) soaping in a bath containing 1–2 g per litre of non-ionic detergent. After this the fabric can be rinsed and dried in the normal manner.

---

### RECIPE

#### ILLUMINATING RESIST PASTE
10-50 g Procion P dye
The following dyes are suitable:
Yellow SP-8G
(*C.I. Reactive Yellow 85*),
Yellow P-3R
(*C.I. Reactive Orange 12*),
Orange P-2R
(*C.I. Reactive Orange 13*),
Scarlet P-2R, Red P-4BN
(*C.I. Reactive Red 3.1*),
Red P-8B
(*C.I. Reactive Red 31*),
Violet P-3R
(*C.I. Reactive Violet 1*),
Blue P-7RX, Blue P-GN, Blue P-5R
(*C.I. Reactive Blue 13*),
Navy P-2R, Turquoise SP-2G,
Olive P-7G, Green P-4BD
(*C.I. Reactive Green 19*),
Brown P-GR, Brown P-2R,
Brown P-4RD
(*C.I. Reactive Brown 17*),
Brown P-5BR
(*C.I. Reactive Brown 9*),
Black P-N
(*C.I. Reactive Black 8*),
but their success varies with
the resist agent chosen)
100 g urea
5 g sodium hexametaphosphate
(Calgon)
250 ml hot water
500 g alginate thickener (Manutex F)
10 g oxidizing agent (Matexil P-AL)
30 g sodium bicarbonate
20 g 'BASF' Reactive Resist Agent.
0-10 g wetting-out agent
(Matexil WA-KBN)
The amount of wetting-out agent
depends upon the type of fabric.

#### GROUND COLOUR
10-50 g Remazol Reactive dye
The following dyes are
suitable:
Golden Yellow G
(*C.I. Reactive Yellow 17*),
Yellow R, Golden Yellow 4G
(*C.I. Reactive Orange 74*),
Brilliant Orange GD
(*C.I. Reactive Orange 15*),
Brilliant Orange 3R
(*C.I. Reactive Orange 16*),
Brilliant Red 5B
(*C.I. Reactive Red 35*),
Brilliant Red GG
(*C.I. Reactive Red 106*),
Brilliant Red GD
(*C.I. Reactive 63*),
Red 3B
(*C.I. Reactive Red 23*),
Brilliant Violet 5R
(*C.I. Reactive Violet 5*),
Brilliant Blue R
(*C.I. Reactive Blue 19*),
Blue 3R
(*C.I. Reactive Blue 28*),
Black B (*C.I. Reactive Black 5*)
0-100 g urea
5 g sodium hexametaphosphate
(Calgon)
275 ml hot water
500 g alginate thickener (Manutex F)
10 g oxidizing agent (Matexil P-AL)
30-80 g Remazol salt FD
0-10 g wetting-out agent
(Matexil WA-KBN)
The amount of wetting-out agent
depends upon the type of fabric.

# 14

# DISCHARGE TECHNIQUES

A discharge technique enables the creation of a negative image – a white or, coloured pattern on a dark background. Using this relatively simple process, intricate designs in light and bright colours can be applied to dark backgrounds without affecting the handle of the cloth, and in comparison to direct printing methods there are fewer registration problems.

Numerous variables can affect the appearance of a discharge print: the strength and choice of reducing agent; the length of time a discharge paste has been left before printing and fixing; the humidity and condition of the steam; the type of dye used for the ground colour; and the fabric upon which the design is printed. Control of these factors requires frequent testing and recording of the effects produced. A perfect discharge print is one in which there is no halo effect around the illuminating colour (also known as the head colour). The halo is caused by the reducing agent spreading into the ground colour. It can be difficult to prevent when using domestic, atmospheric steaming equipment, as the moisture levels of the steam tend to be high. This can be overcome by lowering the amount of reducing and wetting-out agents used in the print paste or by altering steaming times. Print pastes also have poor storage stability. For consistent results the paste should be made, printed and steamed on the same day.

When discharge patterning, you will need to consider several things: the type of dyes needed to colour the ground and the illuminating areas, which discharging agent to use, other auxiliaries and their effect on the final print, and finally the type of thickener required to control the discharge chemicals and dyes.

Discharge patterning techniques will take some time to master, but very effective results can be achieved using a standard white discharge paste. It is advisable to start with this type of paste before progressing onto coloured illuminated effects. All discharge pastes can be applied to fabric in a variety of ways, the most common is via screen printing but block, stencil and handpainting techniques can be employed with equal success. The recipes in this chapter are for natural fibres, as the majority of those for synthetic fibres require specialist equipment and dyes, and good results are difficult to achieve. However, interesting results may be achieved on polyamide using the recipes that follow.

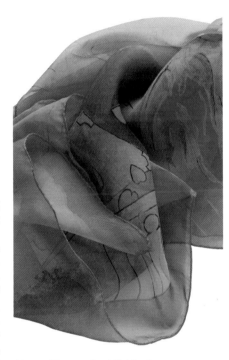

**Above: The work of Robin Greene, screen printed by Belford prints, shows the subtle effects achieved by discharge patterning.**

**Opposite: For this brightly coloured design Tara Sheikh-Kadir used a blue discharge paste on a red/orange ground.**

## DYES
The correct choice of dye used in both the dyeing of the base cloth and as illuminating colours is of fundamental importance. Correct selection is aided by dye manufacturers who will often classify their dyes on a dischargeability scale of 1–5. A dye that has been classified as 5 or 4–5 will discharge to a white; for coloured discharge effects, a dischargeability rating of 3–4 will be needed. Dyes that have a rating of 1 are virtually undis-

chargeable and are therefore suitable as illuminating colours, since they will remain unaffected by the reducing agents. If the fabric is bought pre-dyed, test for dischargeability before starting a large piece.

The following dyes are suitable for ground colours. They are listed by their Colour Index numbers (see page 33) to aid identification. The colours with one asterisk (*) are suitable only for coloured discharge.

### Acid and Metal Complex Dyes:
C.I. Acid Yellow 42, 59, 61;
C.I. Acid Orange 67, 51;
C.I. Acid Red 97, 111, 114, 119, 128, 129, 134, 138, 359;
C.I. Acid Blue 92;
C.I. Acid Brown 282, 355, 357;
C.I. Acid Black 26, 188.

For added brightness a few other dyes can be used but these tend to have extremely poor light-fastness properties, with any white discharge effect being susceptible to darkening with exposure to light:
C.I. Acid Violet 17;
C.I. Acid Blue 83;
C.I. Acid Blue 90;
C.I. Acid Green 9.

### Direct Dyes
The following dyes will discharge to a white and are suitable for dyeing cellulose and some protein fibres:
C.I. Direct Yellow 44, 46, 50;
C.I. Direct Orange 26, 48, 107;
C.I. Direct Red 23, 79, 80;
C.I. Direct Violet 47, 51;
C.I. Direct Blue 1, 2, 25, 71, 76, 78, 76, 78, 80, 199;
C.I. Direct Green 26, 28;
C.I. Direct Brown 2, 95;
C.I. Direct Black 22.

### Reactive Dyes
Most vinyl sulphone dyes (Remazol and Sumifix) are dischargeable and make suitable ground colours for white, pigment and vat discharge techniques on cellulose fabrics. Some of the Procion dyes can also be used for ground colours but it is not as easy to classify those dyes that are suitable for white discharges and those that can only be used in coloured

## COLOURED DISCHARGE

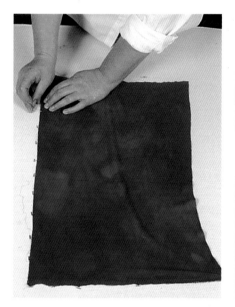

1 Dye your fabric using an appropriate dischargeable dye. Then pin the fabric out onto a backing cloth to ensure that it does not move during patterning.

2 Mix the coloured discharge paste according to the recipe and colour required. For block printing, first brush this paste onto a print pad.

3 Ink up the block from the print pad and then print the block onto the fabric. Repeat this process until you have completed your pattern.

## FIXING AND FINISHING

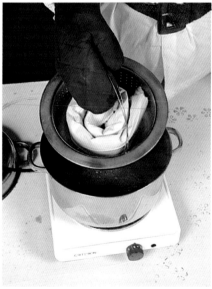

1 Allow the printed fabric to dry. Before steaming, roll the cloth into an intermediate piece of fabric or paper to prevent the print paste from touching itself.

2 Steam the fabric in a steamer (the steaming time for this fine silk was 15 minutes). Then remove the fabric and wash it according to the recipe.

3–4 It is not always easy to see a wet discharge print on a coloured cloth, but once the fabric has been steamed the pattern is clearly revealed.

discharge effects. The following reactive dyes are dischargeable under white, pigment and vat discharges:

C.I. Reactive Yellow 15, 18*, 22*, 84, 85, 135;

C.I. Reactive Orange 12*, 82, 96, 107;

C.I. Reactive Red 21, 174*, 180*,239*;

C.I. Reactive Violet 5*;

C.I. Reactive Blue 28*, 109, 171*;

C.I. Reactive Brown 9*, 16*, 18*, 44*;

C.I. Reactive Green 19;

C.I. Reactive Black 15, 45*.

## REDUCING AGENTS

Nowadays, there are products available that can be used to destroy the background colour in discharge printing. The main ones are listed below, together with the different types of dyestuff and fibres that give the best results with specific reducing agents.

Note that all reducing agents are potentially dangerous and care should be taken when storing and handling them. They should be kept in air-tight containers and kept away from moisture. Always wear protective gloves, clothing and a respirator and steam all discharges in well-ventilated areas.

### C.I. Reducing Agent 2

Sodium formaldehyde sulphoxylate (Formosul and Rongalite C) is a general purpose reducing agent. It is easy to handle and produces a good white on cellulose, cellulose acetate, triacetate and 100% silk fabric. It is rarely used on wool because it may cause fibre damage and shrinkage problems because it functions best in an alkaline pH range. With some finer fabrics the production of a 'halo' effect may cause some problems.

### C.I. Reducing Agent 6

Zinc formaldehyde sulphoxylate (Decrolin, Arostit ZET) is used mainly for the discharging of 100% wool, white discharges on synthetics, and pigment discharges on cellulose. It requires slightly acidic conditions and consequently fibre damage and shrinkage problems are reduced on wool. However, it can cause yellowing with white

**Above: Combining two processes, Sharon Ting first devoréd the viscose pile, and then coloured it with a discharge paste.**

discharge effects. This can be overcome by adding zinc oxide or titanium dioxide to the discharging solution to improve the whiteness.

### C.I Reducing Agent 11

Thiourea dioxide (Manofast) is seldom used now but is employed successfully when discharging nylon. It is chemically inert with many reagents but if heated with an alkali and water an irreversible rearrangement takes place – formamidine sulphinic acid is produced which on decomposition releases sulphoxylic acid, an active reducing agent.

### C.I. Reducing Agent 12

Calcium formaldehyde sulphoxylate is often used in mixtures with C.I. reducing agent 2 to produce the products Rongalit H and Rodanil. These are now manufactured in paste form to overcome previous blockage problems and are often used in silk discharge to provide halo-free prints.

### AUXILIARIES

Various auxiliaries, such as Leukotrope W (BASF), can be added to a discharge paste to improve its overall efficiency. Leukotrope W is required

in the discharging of indigo as it will combine with the reduced indigo dye, in its leuco form, to create a soluble orange alkali that will not re-oxidize, so that the discharged indigo can then be washed away.

Zinc oxide or titanium dioxide are also sometimes added to the print paste; these act as buffers and will ultimately improve the colour of the final discharge by giving it a white pigmented appearance.

There are other moisture attracting and wetting-out agents, such as glycerols, ethylene glycerols and ethoxylated alchohols, that can be included to aid the penetration of the discharge paste on various low absorbency fibre types. Urea can also be included to stabilize and protect some of the illuminating dye pastes.

To avoid excessive halo effects, the fabric can be treated with a resist salt (Matexil PA-L) before printing. This salt acts as a mild oxidizing agent that prevents the spread of unwanted reducing agent.

## THICKENERS

The thickener is important in discharge printing as it controls the illuminating dyes and the reducing agent. The thickener relies upon a high solid content to reduce problems of flushing – the 'halo' effect that often occurs. Traditional thickeners include gum tragacanth, crystal gum, British gum (Dextrin), locust bean gums (Indalca PA/3-R), guar types (Gum 301 Extra) and some starch ethers (Solvitose C5). Refer to chapter 5 for recipes.

## WHITE DISCHARGES

The main problem in discharge printing is visibility. Because the print paste is clear, and the base fabric a dark colour it is difficult to see where the paste has been applied, especially once it is dry. Care must be taken when registering designs to avoid any mark-off onto unprinted areas. A white pigment such as zinc oxide can be added to the paste to aid visibility and also improve the whiteness of the discharged areas. By altering the amounts of discharging agent in the printing paste, different colours and effects can be created. If the amount of reducing agent is halved, the base colour will not fully discharge leaving a residue colour that is often different from the ground colour.

Before starting, it is necessary to colour the base cloth (see chapter 4 for method) using a dye with a dischargeability rating of 5 (see page 139). Suitable dyes are mentioned earlier in this chapter.

---

STANDARD RECIPE
600 g thickener (crystal gum, British gum, guar gum and locust bean gum. For an alkaline discharge use a starch ether or gum tragacanth.)
20–50 g ethoxylated alchohol (Glyezin BC) or glycerine (for synthetic fibres)
200–250 ml cold water or
100–200 g C.I. reducing agent 2, 6

ADDITIONS FOR CELLULOSE
50–100 g Sodium carbonate (optional)
80 g Leukotrope W (optional: needed for indigo dyed cloth but can be added to improve the whiteness.)

ADDITIONS FOR WOOL
20 g wetting-out agent (optional) (Matexil WA-KBN)
50 g whitener e.g. zinc oxide or titanium dioxide (optional)

---

Mix the thickener with the required assistants and any additional chemicals that are needed depending on the type of fabric you are using. An alkaline discharge paste will give better results for cellulose fabrics. When ready to use the print paste, add the reducing agent and mix the paste well. Once the paste has been applied, dry the fabric carefully under a moderate heat before steaming. If you cannot steam immediately, wrap the fabric in polythene and keep it in a cool dark place.

When the print is completely dry it needs to be fixed so that the discharging (reducing agent) bleaches out the background colour. This is done by steaming the fabric for 10–20 minutes at atmospheric pressure, as discussed in chapter 17. After steaming, wash the cloth to remove any chemicals that remain. This should be done by carefully washing first in cold water, followed by a warm soapy wash and a final rinse before drying and pressing.

### White Discharges for Indigo and Manganese Bronze

These discharges can be carried out without steaming equipment on indigo and manganese bronze dyed fabrics. The solutions can be applied by resist dyeing, block, screen or hand-painting techniques.

### Indigo

The oxidizing agent potassium permanganate is used to discharge indigo with the aid of a citric acid solution. Potassium permanganate is a strong oxidizing agent and will damage the cloth if used in high concentrations. The process works best on a medium to lightweight cotton fabric that has been dyed to a mid tone in an indigo bath. The permanganate printing solution is unstable so only a small quantity should be mixed and then used immediately.

### RECIPE
25 g potassium permanganate crystals
125 ml hot water
200 g gum tragacanth

Dissolve the potassium permanganate in the hot water (this takes about 15 minutes), and then strain the solution through a cloth into the thickener and mix well. (If using for a resist dyeing technique replace the gum with extra water.) After mixing with the thickener, print or paint the paste onto the indigo dyed cloth, and allow to dry (the permanganate will have altered the blue indigo to khaki). Then pass the fabric through a bath containing 5–10 g citric acid in 100 g of water. Keep the fabric submerged for a few minutes, until the khaki colour changes to white. If this fails to happen increase the strength of the citric acid bath and repeat the process. Remove the discharged fabric and rinse well. The cloth is then neutralized in a bath containing 5 g of sodium carbonate for every litre of warm water. Then rinse, dry and press.

## Manganese Bronze
The brown colour of manganese bronze (manganous chloride) can be destroyed with an acidic solution that creates a white/cream discharge effect.

### RECIPE
5–10 g citric acid crystals
100 ml warm water
100 g starch ether or gum tragacanth

First, dissolve the citric acid crystals in the warm water, then add this solution to the thickener and mix well. (If using the citric acid bath for a resist dyeing technique replace the gum with extra water.) After mixing, pattern the cloth and allow time for the reaction to take place. The cloth is then rinsed in warm water and then in a neutralizing bath containing 5 g of sodium carbonate for every litre of warm water. Rinse the fabric again, before drying and pressing.

**Below: Anna Vojtisek used an ironed check discharge with steamed discharge lines. Red Expantex adds an accent of colour.**

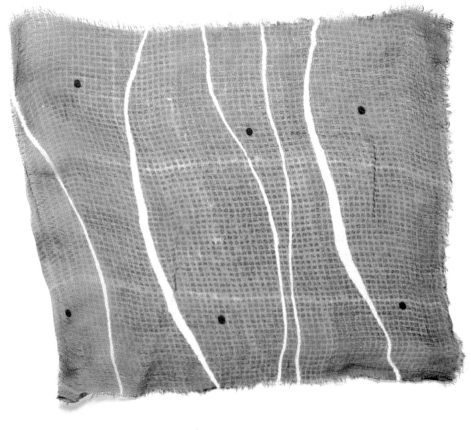

## ILLUMINATING DYES FOR COLOURED DISCHARGE

### Discharge Dyes for Silk, Wool and Polyamide
A limited range of illuminating dyes are suitable for these fabrics. Those with a manufacturer's dischargeability rating of 1 can be used. The most common have the following Colour Index numbers (the asterisk denotes dyes with poor fastness performance):
C.I. Direct Yellow 28*;
C.I. Acid Yellow 236;
C.I. Acid Yellow 7*;
C.I. Acid Red 52*;
C.I. Acid Red 87*;
C.I. Acid Violet 90;
C.I. Direct Blue 106;
C.I. Reactive Blue 198;
C.I. Acid Blue 102;
C.I. Basic Blue 3*;
C.I. Acid Blue 61.1;
C.I. Acid Black 2*.

Other dyes suitable for illuminating colours are produced by Clariant:
Sandocryl Brilliant Yellow B-6GL,
Silk discharge Yellow ON;
Silk discharge Orange RN
  (C.I. Direct Orange 39);
Silk discharge Red G;
Silk discharge Brown BN;
Sandolan Blue N2F.

### Pigment Discharge Dyes
Not all pigment colours make suitable illuminating colours and only those that will resist the reducing agent should be used. The majority of Bricoprint pigment colours and Monaprint E system will work, but avoid using the red pigment range as these are not stable – substitute with Bricoprint Brilliant Pink 3BT and shade with other colours.

### Reactive Discharge Dyes
The following Cibacron dyes are suitable illuminating colours for fabrics where the ground colour has been dyed with direct or reactive dyes:
Brilliant Yellow 3G-P;
Yellow R-A;
Brilliant Red 3B-P;
Violet 2R-P
  (C.I. Reactive Violet 2);

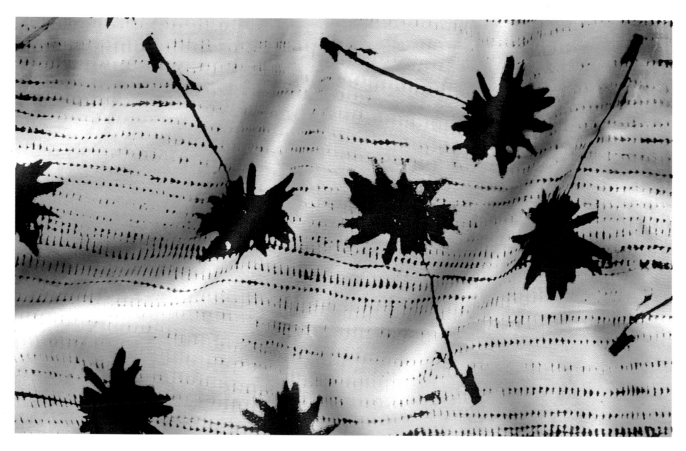

Turquoise Blue GF-P, 4-GP;
Brilliant Green 4G-A;
Brown 6R-P
  (C.I. Reactive Brown 11);
Black BG-A
  (C.I. Reactive Black 1).

## Vat Dyes
The following vat dyes are suitable illuminating colours, but others may work equally well:
  C.I. Vat Yellow 2, 4;
  C.I. Vat Orange 1, 7;
  C.I. Vat Red 1, 14;
  C.I. Vat Violet 1, 3;
  C.I. Vat Blue 4, 5;
  C.I. Vat Green 1, 3;
  C.I. Vat Brown 57;
  Solanthrene Printing Black 2RB (Mix).

Coloured discharge is a more complicated process and there are only a limited range of pigments and dyes available (listed above). These colours are known as illuminating or head colours as they often shine with an extra brilliance from the ground fabric,

especially if it is a dark colour. The type of coloured discharge used depends upon the composition of the base cloth, with various recipes and dyes available for the different types of fibres. For consistent results it is a good idea to test a sample piece first to ensure the right proportions of chemicals and additives are used.

Bleeding, flushing or haloing occurs when too much moisture-attracting agent or reducing agent is used. Although considered a fault in the industry this effect can give the fabric an extra dimension, and with careful selection of base dyes and by altering steaming times, coloured halos can be created. However, these effects are often not repeatable. With so many variables (type of base cloth, dyes and steaming equipment), treat the following recipes as a starting point for further experimentation.

## Coloured Discharge for Cellulose
As with all discharge processes the base fabrics need to be dyed using

**Above: Edmund Taylor's abstract black flowers appear in silhouette upon a silvery white discharged background.**

dischargeable dyes (see page 139). There are three ways of producing a coloured discharge effect on cellulose fabrics: a pigment discharge; vat discharge; and the use of reactive dyes as illuminating dyes. These discharge effects can also be used on silk, but excessive haloing may become a problem. This can be overcome by pre-treating the fabric with a resist salt (a 10% solution of Matexil PA-L) and allowing it to dry before printing with the discharge paste.

## Pigment Discharge
Pigment discharge techniques produce crisp and brilliant coloured patterns on dyed grounds. It is a relatively simple process and ideal for a first attempt. The technique relies upon the use of pigments as illuminating colours; these are simply mixed with

a binder, thickener and discharging agent before being applied to the fabric. The cloth is then steamed, but pigment binders often fix better when baked. The technique can be used on many fabric bases provided that the dyes used for the ground colour are dischargeable. The handle of the cloth is often affected by pigments so it is advisable to use cellulose fabrics on which this is less of a problem.

The following recipe is a simple one that can be reproduced in small workshops with very little equipment. It requires a solvent-based binder such as Bricoprint TW or TS125. If you are unable to obtain such a solvent-based binder, similar results may be obtained by experimenting with pigment systems based upon acrylic binders and synthetic thickeners with a high electrolyte stability.

---

### RECIPE

10–50 g non-dischargeable pigment colour (see page 144)
800 g solvent-based pigment binder
30 g urea
30 ml warm water
100 g discharge resistant thickener
(use an acid resistant gum such as Gum 301 Extra)
100 g C.I. reducing agent 6
4 g ammonium dihydrogen orthophosphate (optional: this makes the print paste slightly acidic)

---

Mix the pigment binder and the colour together to the shade required. The final colour yield will be lower than a standard pigment paste, so do not use less than 10 g per litre. Do not attempt to use a ready-mixed opaque white to lighten the colour, nor metallic pigments. Dissolve the urea in the hot water, allow to cool, and slowly add to the thickener. Add the reducing agent and mix well. When ready to use, combine the two pastes and mix thoroughly. If combined too early the viscosity of the binder may be reduced, resulting in bleeding of the image. Apply to the fabric and then dry carefully under a moderate heat. Steam immediately, or wrap the fabric in polythene and keep in a cool dark place until you can.

The fabric is then steamed for 5–10 minutes at atmospheric pressure (see chapter 17). The steam causes the reducing agent to destroy the ground colour, depositing the illuminating pigment in its place. The time required depends upon the dyes, fabrics and steaming equipment used. The cloth is then baked at 150°C for five minutes, or ironed through clean paper for at least 15 minutes with a hot iron. (You must wear a suitable respirator when ironing discharge prints.)

After fixing, wash the cloth to remove any excess chemicals and gums. Rinse in cold water, followed with a warm soapy wash at 50°C and a final cold rinse, before drying and pressing. This helps to create bright illuminating colours that will not fade.

### Vat Discharge

Vat dyes are very colour fast and produce high quality printed goods through a direct printing method, but because they require a reducing agent they can also be applied as coloured discharge dyes. The reducing agent in this case has two roles: the first is to reduce the dye into its leuco state, and the second is to destroy the colour of the ground. See page 144 for a range of suitable dyes for coloured discharge effects.

Considerable patience is needed to obtain successful discharge effects, with accuracy and consistency required in the mixing of the print pastes. Once the pastes are mixed they must be used on the same day. It is possible to use vat discharges on silk fabrics but halo and bleeding problems may occur and the recipe may have to be adjusted.

---

### RECIPE

1–20 g vat dye
20 g glycerine
100 ml hot water
500–700 g thickener (gum tragacanth, British gum, crystal gum or a starch ether)
100–200 g C.I. reducing agent 2 or 12
50–100 g alkali

---

Mix the illuminating dye with the glycerine and add the hot water,

**Above: Coloured discharge dyes are called illuminating dyes due to their brightness. This can be seen in Saffron Wynne's piece.**

stirring the solution until the dye has dissolved completely. When the dye is cool add it to the thickening agent along with the alkali and the reducing agent. The type of alkali used can vary, potassium carbonate is normally used with vat dyes, but it may cause haloing problems; these problems can be reduced by replacing the potassium carbonate with sodium carbonate. Darker shades in the illuminating colours can often be achieved by using sodium hydroxide solution 38° Bé (72° Tw). Then apply the paste to the fabric and dry carefully under a moderate heat before steaming. Steam immediately or wrap the fabric in polythene and keep in a cool dark place and steam the next day for good results.

sure (see chapter 17). After steaming, the cloth is washed carefully to remove any excess dyes, chemicals and gums. Rinse first in cold water, followed with a hot soapy wash at 90°C and a final cold rinse before drying and pressing.

## Coloured Discharge for Silk and Wool

Dischargeable dyes for silk and wool fabrics are listed on page 144. The following recipe is a starting point, but variations can be made to achieve the result you require.

---

### BASIC RECIPE
0.1–20 g illuminating dye
50 g ethoxylated alchohol (Glyezin BC)
200–250 ml hot water
100–200 g C.I. reducing agent 2, 6 or 12
(all will work, but for the best results on silk use reducing agent 2 or 12 and on wool, reducing agent 6)
500 g thickener (gum tragacanth, British gum, guar gum or crystal gum can all be used)

### ADDITIONS FOR WOOL
5–20g wetting-out agent (optional)
(Matexil WA-KBN)

---

The fabric should then be steamed at atmospheric pressure for 15 minutes in an air-free steamer with a constant flow of saturated steam. The steam causes the reducing agent to destroy the ground colour, at the same time fixing the illuminating dye. The time required varies according to the fabric and steaming equipment (see chapter 17).

After steaming, the fabric is washed carefully to remove excess dyes, chemicals and gum. Then rinse first in cold water, followed by an oxidizing bath containing 2 ml (at 6% strength) of hydrogen peroxide per litre of cold water. Follow this with a hot soaping (90°C) with detergent and sodium carbonate (if necessary) followed by a cold rinse before drying and pressing.

It is also possible to use a small range of reactive dyes as illuminating colours on fabrics the ground colour of which has been dyed with direct or reactive dye.

---

### RECIPE
0.1–20 g illuminating reactive dye
100 g urea
200–250 ml hot water
500 g alginate thickener
(Manutex F or RS)
50g sodium bicarbonate
10 g anthraquinone powder
100–200 g C.I. reducing agent 2

---

Mix the illuminating dye with the urea and add the hot water. Stir the solution until all the dye has dissolved. Allow to cool, and then add the dye slowly to the thickening agent, as well as the other chemicals and mix well. When ready to use, add the reducing agent and mix the paste thoroughly. Apply the paste to the fabric and dry under a moderate heat. Steam immediately or wrap the fabric in polythene and keep in a cool dark place until you can steam it.

The fabric should be steamed for 15–20 minutes at atmospheric pres-

Mix the illuminating dye with the ethoxylated alchohol (Glyezin BC) and add the hot water, stirring until the dye has dissolved. Allow to cool, and then slowly add to the thickening agent along with the wetting-out agent (if using). When you are ready to use, add the reducing agent and mix thoroughly. Apply the paste to the fabric and dry under a moderate heat. Steam immediately or wrap the fabric in polythene and keep in a cool dark place until you are ready to steam.

To fix the illuminating dyes, the fabric is steamed for 15–40 minutes (see chapter 17) at atmospheric pressure. After steaming the cloth is washed carefully and then rinsed in cold water with 2 ml of ammonia solution (at 4% strength) per litre of water. This improves any white areas and prevents re-oxidization of the discharged dyes. Follow with a warm soapy wash at 50°C, a warm rinse and a final cold rinse before drying and pressing.

# GALLERY
# DISCHARGE

Left and Centre
**CLARISSA HULSE**
**These velvet-backed satin scarves have both been patterned with discharge dyes. The purple scarf (left) shows burnt leaves, discharge printed using a photographic technique, while the rainbow effect on the pink scarf (centre) has been produced by discharge dyes in a combination of dip-dyeing, printing and handpainting.**

Right
**ANUJA DOSHI**
**The flower designs on this maroon fabric were created by using a photo-screen printing technique with a coloured discharge paste.**

# THE ROUGH WITH THE SMOOTH

*There is often as much interest in the tactile quality of a piece of fabric as there is in its colour, pattern and design. Fabrics can be made to look like lace, pucker like seersucker, feel like rubber, crinkle like paper, shine like plastic, reflect like metal, or take on three-dimensional qualities. There are a few techniques available that can be employed to produce both textural and relief fabrics without the expense of industrial equipment. In this section, the first chapter looks at techniques which can be used to distort the cloth, creating fabrics with different relief and textural qualities. This leads on to a chapter that describes techniques in which the surface of the cloth is dissolved away to leave delicate, lacy effects.*

**Opposite: Isabel Dodd working in her studio with stretch nylons and latex. Above: Janet Stoyel used the technology of a laser cutter to produce this intricate lace effect.**

# 15

# CREATING TEXTURE

By altering the physical or surface properties of a fabric, many textural, multi-dimensional effects can be created. Some methods use chemicals to distort the surface of the cloth, producing a puckered look; others rely upon the application of glues, rubber solutions and puff binders. Some of these effects will appear rough and others smooth and shiny. Metallic foils and glossy varnishes can be used to produce reflective surfaces, creating contrasting matt and shiny areas on a cloth. The application of heat can permanently set, felt, melt or burn areas of the material, creating further relief and dimensional effects.

Puckering involves the application of a chemical, resin binder or rubber solution to alter and distort the surface of the fabric.

## CHEMICAL CREPON OR CRIMP

This technique is known as *crêpe pelisse* and involves the application of a chemical to the surface of a fabric. The chemical then alters the physical structure of the cloth's fibres causing them to shrink. This shrinkage affects the tension across the cloth creating a cockling and crinkling in the untreated areas. There are two chemical methods that will produce this crimped effect on cloth. The commonest is described here and uses a strong caustic solution that causes localized mercerization (see chapter 4) in cellulose fibres. The second method can be achieved on nylon using a thickened solution of resorcinol, but because this chemical is hazardous this process is unsuitable for small workshops.

## Caustic Crimping

The caustic solutions used for this technique can cause serious burns. It is advisable to wear protective clothing, rubber gloves and eye protection. The best fabric base to use is a fine cotton that has been bleached but not mercerized. The fabric is then treated with a strong caustic soda solution which physically alters the fibres. If the fabric is treated without tension, the areas where the caustic has been applied will shrink causing any untreated areas to pucker and cockle. For good results at least half the fabric should be treated overall. The solution can be screen printed; provided the screens are washed immediately after printing as the caustic solution will destroy any photographic coating. If handpainting the solution,

**Opposite: Sarah Street created this textured fabric by the application of a binder that puffs up when heated.**

**Right: For a three-dimensional effect, Isabel Dodd printed fine lines of neoprene onto a stretch polyamide fabric base.**

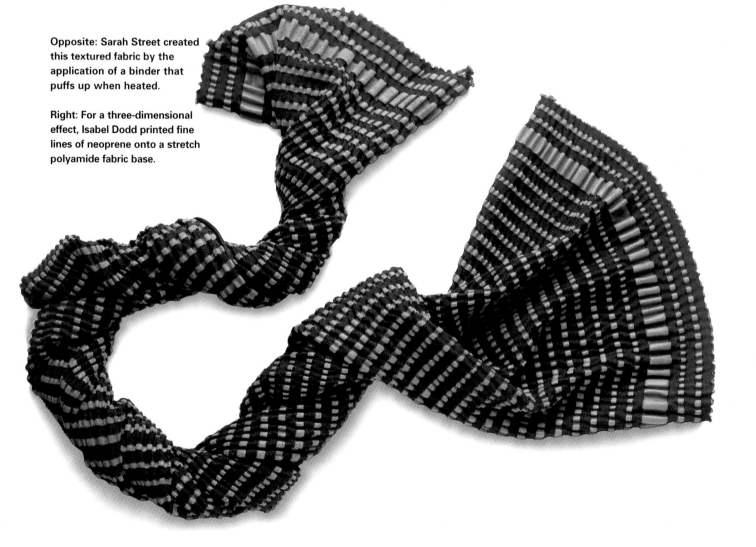

**Above: Sarah Street's embossed fabric involved the printing of a gold pigment and puff binder onto a silk/metal voile.**

use synthetic bristle brushes, as natural hair brushes would be damaged by it. Broad stripe designs resembling woven seersucker fabrics will work very well using this technique.

A colour change will often take place when using strong caustic on top of some dyestuffs. To avoid this dye the cloth after patterning, but remember that the treated areas will often dye to a darker shade. By using dyes in the colouring and patterning of the cloth prior to creping, these effects can often be incorporated into a design. Most reactive dyes will considerably deepen in colour when treated in this way. The following Remazol dyes are suitable for dyeing or printing before creping:

Remazol Brilliant Yellow 7GL;
Golden Yellow G
  (C.I. Reactive Yellow 17);
Golden Orange 4G
  (C.I. Reactive Orange 74);
Red B;

Red 3B
  (C.I. Reactive Red 23);
Bordeaux B;
Navy Blue RR;
Turquoise Blue G
  (C.I. Reactive Blue 21);
Brown GR
  (C.I. Reactive Brown 18);
Brilliant Green GGL;
Grey G;
Printing Black BG.

Crepons may be produced either by direct printing of a strong caustic onto the surface of the cloth or by a resist technique where the areas of the cloth to be cockled are printed with a gum resist or pigment and the cloth passed through a caustic bath.

## Direct Crimping

For direct crimping, apply the caustic solution directly to the surface of the cloth. Flat coloured areas are created by adding a dye to the printing paste. This dyestuff must fix upon the cellulose and remain unaffected by the caustic solution. The following reactive dyes can be used, but other alkali-resistant direct, reactive and vat dyes can also be employed (check with the manufacturers for suitability or carry out a series of tests):

Remazol Brilliant Yellow 7GL;
Golden Yellow G
*(C.I. Reactive Yellow 17)*;
Red B, Red 3B
*(C.I. Reactive Red 23)*;
Bordeaux B, Turquoise Blue B;
Brown 3G
*(C.I. Reactive Brown 16)*;
Brilliant Green GB
*(C.I. Reactive Blue 38)*;
Grey G.

---

CLEAR PRINT PASTE
640 g sodium hydroxide solution
48° Bé (100° Tw)
360 g thickener (crystal gum or starch ether)

---

COLOURED PRINT PASTE
500–650 g sodium hydroxide solution
48° Bé (100° Tw)
300 g thickener (depending on dye)
25 g direct, vat or reactive dye
35 ml boiling water

ADDITIONS FOR VAT DYES
20 g glycerine
50–100 g C.I. reducing agent 2

ADDITIONS FOR REACTIVE DYES
100 g urea

---

Pin out the fabric onto an old backing cloth. Then weigh out the thickener into a non-metallic container and gradually add the sodium hydroxide solution, mixing the two components together slowly but thoroughly for 1000 g of print paste. For coloured

## DIRECT CRIMPING (CLEAR)

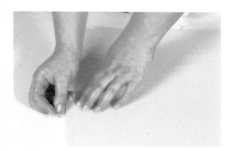

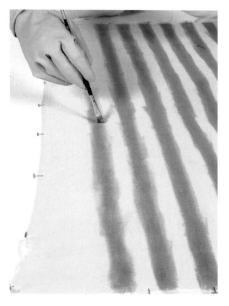

1–2 Pin out a non-mercerized cotton fabric, as taut as possible, onto a backing cloth. Add the caustic solution to the thickening agent and mix thoroughly.

3 Apply the clear paste to the cloth, making sure it penetrates through the fabric. On our fabric the caustic solution has temporarily changed the dye colour.

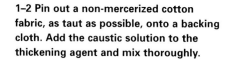

4 Unpin the fabric and allow it to dry, without tension, for up to one hour. When the fabric shrinks, the untreated areas should rise up and cockle.

5 Wash the fabric well to remove all the caustic solution from the fibres. Then neutralize with acetic acid, before allowing the fabric to dry without tension.

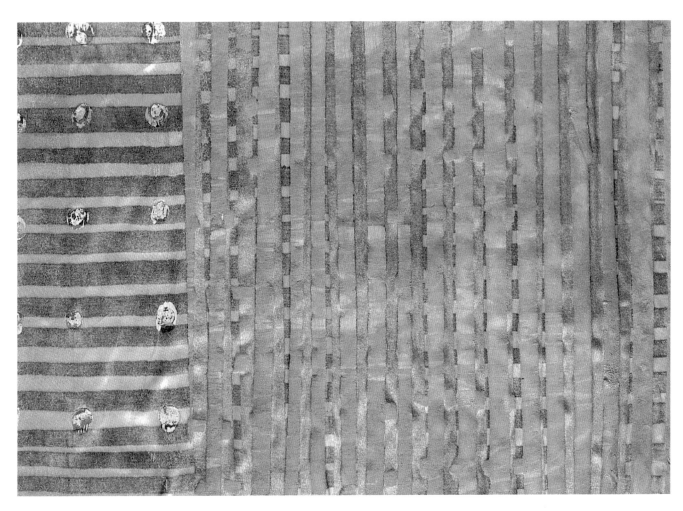

**Above: Elsa O'Hara combined various pigments, foils and binders to create this metallic silver design.**

effects, dissolve a direct, vat or reactive dye in boiling water. If using vat dyes include glycerine and C.I. reducing agent 2 (Formosul), while reactive dyes require urea. Once the dye has been made up, add it to a paste made up of sodium hydroxide solution and thickener. A starch ether (Solvitose C5) or gum tragacanth will be suitable for vat dyes; crystal gum can be used with direct dye; and an alginate gum, such as Manutex, can be used along with reactive dyes.

Screen print or paint this paste onto the fabric, making sure it penetrates thoroughly. Two to four squeegee pulls are normally adequate. Wash the screen, then unpin the cloth imme-diately and wait for the caustic to affect the cotton fibres. The fabric can be left for up to an hour without causing shade loss or damage to the fibres. For coloured crimping, the fabric is then steamed at atmospheric pressure for 15 minutes to fix the dye. Let it dry slightly to avoid mark-off before washing. Rinse the cloth in cold water until all the sodium hydroxide solution is removed. The fabric is then neutral-ized in a 20% solution of acetic acid, i.e. 2 ml. per litre of water. Wash in hot water followed by a final cold rinse before drying without tension to allow the puckering to take place.

**Resist Method of Crimping**
Thick solutions of some gums, such as gum arabic and British gum, resist strong caustic solutions. If a thickened

solution of one of these gums is printed onto a cloth and allowed to dry before being passed through a caustic bath, it will act as a mechanical resist to the caustic solution, while unprotected areas will shrink.

Coloured, puckered effects can be achieved by using a dyestuff in the resist paste, while any areas of cloth unprotected by the thickener will remain white. Multicoloured effects can be created by printing with dyes thickened with a gum that does not resist the caustic solution. Gum tragacanth is the best thickener for this because it does not obstruct the caustic solution when mixed at a standard strength and, therefore, enables flat areas of the cloth to be coloured. If a design is to be printed, it must be taken into account that the image will shrink when treated.

A wide range of colours and dyes can be used with this technique, and these are fixed in the normal manner before crimping. The most suitable colorants are direct and vat dyes, but pigment binders will also resist the effects of caustic. Interesting effects can be achieved by layering colours combined with a discharge technique.

The process is divided into two stages: the application of a white or coloured resist and the fixing of any dyes present; and the crimping of the cloth in a strong caustic solution.

For a white paste mix British gum according to the recipe on page 59–60. While the thickener is still warm use the paste to paint or print a design onto the cloth. For the best results cover less than half the fabric overall. Allow the cloth to dry thoroughly before crimping. A coloured resist can easily be made by substituting British gum for the thickener in any of the direct or vat dyes included in chapter 12 (this will colour the puckered areas of the cloth). An alternative is to use a crepon binder with a pigment printing system. These printing pastes are applied by handpainting or printing, allowed to dry, then fixed.

If a colour or pattern is required in the areas affected by the caustic solution, substitute gum tragacanth for the thickener in any of the direct or vat dyes included in chapter 12. This paste is applied along with the coloured resist, it is then allowed to dry and the dyes fixed.

The fabric is then passed, with care, through a bath of sodium hydroxide solution: 441 g of sodium hydroxide crystals slowly dissolved in one litre of cold water for the correct strength. The resulting chemical reaction will generate heat so allow the solution to cool before using. Allow the fabric to rest for a short while until the cellulose in the non-resisted areas shrinks. Observing the precautions on page 153, carefully squeeze out any excess solution from the fabric and rinse in cold water. Continue rinsing until all the sodium hydroxide solution is removed. The fabric is then neutralized in a 20% solution of acetic acid, i.e. 2 ml per litre of water, and washed in hot water followed by a final cold rinse. Dry the fabric without tension to allow the puckering to take place.

## PUFF PIGMENTS AND RUBBER SOLUTIONS

Puckered and distorted effects may also be created using an expanding pigment or a rubber solution on the surface of a fabric. The success of this technique will often rest with the type of base cloth used and the final effect desired.

**Below: Isabel Dodd's three-dimensional fabric is the result of printing circles of neoprene onto a stretch polyamide fabric.**

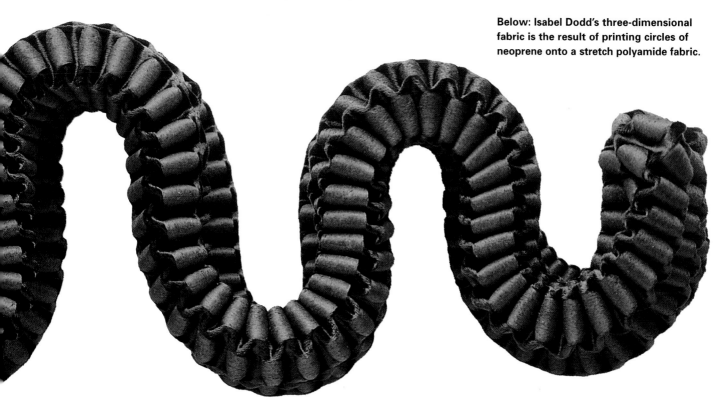

## PUFF BINDER

**1 Puff binders can be purchased in white or as a neutral base. Apply the ready-mixed binder to the taped-out fabric. We have screen printed the paste.**

**2 The fabric is then released and, without applying too much pressure, the puff binder needs to be heat-set by ironing the underside of the cloth.**

**Above: The finished, textured fabric by Edmund Taylor, shows the raised areas of a white puff binder fixed to the blue silk cloth it has been applied to.**

## Puff Pigments

Simple puckered effects can be created by printing on the back of a fabric with a puff pigment binder. For good effects, various factors need to be considered and controlled. First select a suitable base cloth – stretch lycras, velvets and fine organzas will work well, but must be stretched taut during the screen printing operation. Then ensure that the puff binder is applied evenly. Screen printing is used, but fine control is necessary or the technique will not work. Too much binder will create excessive puckering, too little not enough, and an uneven layer will cause irregular results. Simple patterns such as stripes and spots or swirling linear designs are most successful.

The puff binders can be purchased in white or as a neutral base. It may be used in its neutral state as it becomes part of the back of the cloth and is rarely seen. If a translucent fabric is used or the resulting cloth is to be reversible, highly concentrated coloured pigments can be mixed into the base to create the desired shade. (See page 116 for the correct proportions of pigment colour to binder.)

Stretch the fabric over a covered printing surface, securing it firmly in place. Screen print the puff binder onto the cloth and allow to dry. The number of pulls will vary depending upon the design and mesh count of the screen; carry out some tests before embarking upon a large piece. Too much pressure may force the puff binder through the fabric instead of allowing it to sit on the surface of the cloth (this problem is often encountered with fine organzas).

When the binder is dry, release the fabric from the table and fix at a temperature of 160–170°C (see manufacturer's instructions) for five minutes. Under the influence of heat (see chapter 17), the binder will puff up, pulling the fabric inwards and creating ridges and puckers. A hair dryer on its highest heat setting can also be used but requires a considerable period of time to work. Flatter, more rubberized effects can be created by ironing the print with a very hot iron.

## PREPARING A LATEX SCREEN PRINT

1–2 Create a simple pattern by applying a hot wax resist to your screen. Stretch the fabric as taut as possible and pin it in place for printing.

3 As the latex solution is hard to handle, form a trough between your squeegee and one end of the screen. Pour the liquid latex solution into the gap.

### Rubber and Neoprene

As with puff pigments, different rubber solutions can be applied to cloth to produce puckered effects, but the printed areas remain smooth. These solutions do not require heat-setting, but have the disadvantage of being much harder to control. The solutions cannot be coloured very easily so generally remain their natural colour (translucent yellow with latex and black with neoprene). Latex solutions can be used in a variety of ways. If painted or printed onto the cloth they produce a rubberized surface; while others are available that can be used as bonding solutions. It is important to wear a respirator (one designed for ammonia fumes) during this process as Latex is a rubber solution and contains ammonia which evaporates from the fabric as it dries.

With both latex and neoprene solutions it is important to work fast, as they dry very quickly and will rapidly block the screen. This can be prevented to some extent by spraying

## PRINTING LATEX RUBBER

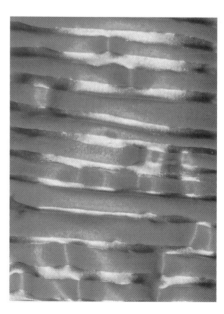

4 Pull the latex solution across the screen with a squeegee, ensuring full penetration of the cloth. You must work fast as latex and neoprene dry very quickly.

5 Allow the latex to dry before unpinning the fabric from the backing cloth. Throughout this process you must wear a suitable respirator as latex contains ammonia.

6 By using a very shiny spandex fabric you can create a wonderful contrast between the matt, rubberized areas and the reflective fabric.

**Above: Sharon Baurley used folding and heat-setting techniques to create silver cubes out of a metalized polyester fabric.**

the mesh with a fine spray of clean water as soon as the fabric has been printed and by washing the screen immediately; any rubber left on the mesh can be rubbed off once it is dry. All rubber solutions coagulate on contact with water, which can cause drainage problems.

The puckering process appears to be most effective when used with stretch lycra-based fabrics. It is the properties of the fibres that help cause the distortion in the cloth.

## Smooth and Shiny Effects
There are a number of industrial finishing processes that produce laminated, plastic-coated fabrics or shiny chintz surfaces, but most of these techniques are unavailable to the

small producer, designer/maker. There are, however, special binders, pigments and resin finishes that produce glossy effects when printed onto various base cloths. Many of these products require heat-setting. Other effects can be created by laminating foils and plastics to the surface of the cloth. Selective use of hologram polyester films and plastic lenses can produce fabrics with a reflective iridescence not normally seen on cloth.

## Flocked Effects
This requires specialist equipment as it usually employs a static field that causes the fibres to stand on end before they set, creating a cloth with a dense even pile. However, similar results can be achieved by shaking the fibres over a glue-covered surface. The main problem is controlling the fibres – they are very fine and will blow around easily so it is important to wear a respirator.

Proprietary flocking adhesives can be screen printed onto fabric in the desired design. The flocking fibres are then scattered over the cloth with a sieve before the glue dries. The fibres will not always settle on end, they tend to create an irregular effect. The fabric is then left to dry undisturbed for several hours, after which time the excess flock can be shaken from the cloth. Most flocked cloths have very poor wash-fastness.

## Relief Effects
Soft relief effects can be produced on wool fibres by utilizing their natural felting properties. These 'sculptured' wools look similar to some of the devoré processes (see chapter 16), but are much more subtle. Some areas of the fabric are protected from the hot soapy solution that causes felting and remain unchanged while unprotected areas shrink and thicken. The resulting fabric contains contrasting milled and unmilled areas. This technique can be divided into two types: one involving the printing of a resist; and the other employing *shibori*, a tie-and-dye technique.

The first process involves the printing of a shrink-resist resin onto an unfinished woollen fabric. The resin is then cured before the cloth goes through a milling process, during which the unprotected areas felt. The resulting cloth will have a design made up of thicker opaque sections surrounded by thinner unaffected areas and can then be coloured using acid levelling dyes. Most woollen fabrics made from worsted or woollen spun yarns are suitable base cloths, with the exception of tightly woven suiting and velour coatings. Some worsted cloths may have a puckered effect after milling which will often complement the design.

RECIPE
300 g alginate thickener (Manutex RS)
15 g sodium bicarbonate
60 g Synthappret BAP (Bayer, 46% solids)
600–625 ml water
25 g wetting-out agent (optional) (Matexil WA-KBN)

Weigh out the thickener into a non-metallic container and add the Synthappret BAP, the sodium bicarbonate and the wetting-out agent. Slowly add the water and mix well, to make 1000 g of print paste. Screen print this solution onto the base cloth; it is important that the solution penetrates through to the back of the fabric. Allow to dry and then bake at 150°C for five minutes. The fabric can then be felted by machine washing in a hot soapy solution. It is then rinsed, dyed if required, and dried.

For *shibori* techniques the basic principle is the same as above but areas of the cloth are protected from the milling process by using any of the methods of tying, stitching or clamping described in chapter 13. This technique will produce more three-dimensionally distorted fabrics.

**Thermal Setting Effects**
All synthetic fibres will melt at a certain temperature, but below this point they will often heat-set into a different form. (To find the melting point of a fabric you will need to carry out experiments on different bases.) This effect can be seen if an acrylic fabric is washed at too high a temperature – any creases that have formed become permanently set in the cloth. By tying, stitching or clamping fabrics into folds before heating, various features can be created. The best fabrics for this effect contain a high proportion of polyester, polypropylene or polyamides. Other natural fabrics can be treated with a thermal resin that will help retain the relief effects.

One of the effects easiest to produce are pleats. These are made by stitching a cloth at set intervals and pulling up the threads as one does with smocking or ruching. The cloth is then heat-set at 190°C for 10 minutes before undoing the threads. Folded papers, or foil, that hold the cloth while it is being pleated can also be employed. Alternatively, some of the *shibori* techniques, (see chapter 13), will produce pointed and rounded effects.

If you do not have access to a baking cabinet, an electric domestic oven will work just as well, but care should be taken to avoid scorching the fabric. A pressure cooker can be used for small pieces.

**Embossing**
The thermal properties of a fibre or resin can also be used to emboss a fabric. This patterning technique is used in the textile industry to produce a wide variety of finishes on fabrics. Simple effects can be produced, without sophisticated equipment, by placing synthetic fabrics over such things as washers, lino cuts and shaped pieces of wood or metal under a heat press for about a minute. Wool treated in a resin solution such as 1% solution of Finish BB will react in a similar manner. Always cover the press table with an old blanket to avoid damaging it when trying this technique. To avoid scorching the cloth protect the top surface with some Teflon paper.

**HEAT-SETTING**

1 Lay some synthetic fabric (above is polyester) onto a piece of foil. Concertina them together in simple pleats held in place by the foil (or paper).

2 When all the cloth is pleated, secure the foil along the edges with a few pegs. Then heat-set the fabric at a temperature below its own melting point.

3 Remove the fabric from the heat source and allow it to cool before removing the foil. The fabric should now be permanently pleated.

# GALLERY
# TEXTURE

Far Right, Above
**KATE WELLS**
A simple binding technique, using glass marbles and a synthetic fabric, has produced a richly coloured and textural, three-dimensional effect. Once the fabric has been heat-set, the marbles are removed.

Right
**ISABEL DODD**
Using latex or neoprene on different stretch fabrics, Isabel Dodd has created a series of three sculptural pieces with a simple spotted motif. The final handle of the cloth remains soft and elastic while adding a new dimension to fashion fabrics.

The devoré (from the French *dévorer*, to devour) technique produces an effect similar to lace. It is often known as burn-out or broderie chimique because of its resemblance to some types of embroidery. The process involves printing a caustic chemical onto cloth which, when heated, will destroy some of the fibres present. This technique is applied to mixed-fibre cloths where one or more of the fibre types are destroyed, leaving both solid and translucent areas.

The devoré technique has experienced something of a resurgence since the 1980s, especially in silk-viscose velvets, and there are now many devoré fabrics available, from lightweight curtaining and blouse fabrics to heavier velvets. A small amount of wool devoré is also finding its way into the field of knitwear and furnishing fabrics.

The success of the technique relies upon the selection of suitable base cloths. For most effects it is important that the different fibres are present in both the warp and weft of the fabric or the cloth might fall apart. A fabric similar to cut work can be created if a cloth with a single fibre type is used; with careful selection of the design, whole shapes can be burned away producing a delicate fretwork effect. By using a cloth in which the devoré resistant fibre is present in only the warp or weft, a floating thread effect can be created; and with cloths that have two resistant fibres multi-layered effects can be produced. By layering different fabrics together – cotton and wool, cotton and polyester or silk and viscose – and then joining them in places by stitching with a polyester thread or using a bonding adhesive, it is possible to burn away areas of the top fabric to reveal the fabric underneath thus creating a multiple cloth. Many exciting results can be produced on fabrics not designed for devoré purposes and it is worth experimenting with unusual fabric combinations.

The most popular devoré technique employs chemicals that liberate an acid when heated to high temperatures; this destroys any cellulose fibres present, but will not damage protein or synthetic fibres. Less common is an alkali devoré that acts by destroying protein and silk fibres, but will not affect polyester, acrylic, cellulose or metal fibres; however, it is often difficult to find suitable base cloths for this technique.

Interesting colour effects can be achieved by dyeing one or more of the fibres in a multi-fibre cloth. For example a polyester-cotton cloth coloured with a disperse dye will have a matt 'chalky' appearance because the cotton present will not take up the dye. When the polyester is exposed, after burning away the cotton, the full shade will be revealed. This effect can be taken further by cross-dyeing the two fibres with contrasting colours. Many complex colour patterns can be created by using various, reactive and resist processes (see chapters 13 and 14) alongside the devoré technique.

To produce successful devoré, extra care needs to be taken to control the amount of paste applied to the fabric's surface and the length of time the fabric is heated. Too much of the reagent, too high a temperature, or too long a heating period will damage other fibres in the cloth, resulting in holes. However, one must also ensure that the chemical reaction works fully and does not leave patches of unaffected fibres.

The process works best if applied via screen printing because, by increasing or decreasing the number of pulls of the squeegee, the quantity of devoré paste applied to the cloth can be carefully controlled. Block printing and handpainting will apply uneven amounts that may cause problems at the burn-out stage. Again, it is important to carry out trials on test pieces.

**Opposite: Vanessa Doyle knitted with a special silk and metal yarn before she devoréd the fabric into delicate flowers.**

**Right: Interesting additional effects can be created by dip-dyeing, as shown in Sally Weatherill's devoréd scarf.**

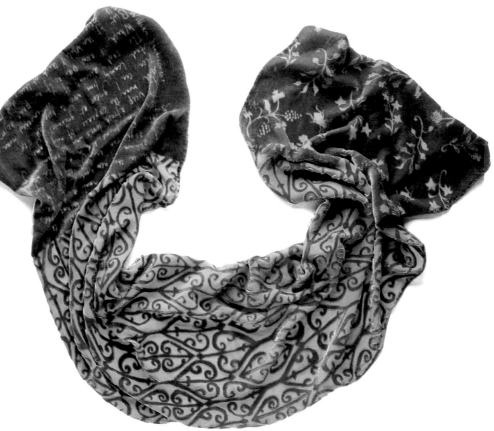

phate to the water. Then weigh out the thickener and add the prepared chemicals. Mix well to make 1000 g of print paste. Screen print this paste onto the fabric, making sure it penetrates thoroughly. When patterning a silk-viscose velvet, you can achieve better results if the design is printed on the silk back rather than the viscose pile of the cloth. However, this will need to be considered when you are preparing the screens or the image may be reversed. The number of pulls needed will depend upon your strength and the type of mesh count used. An average of six pulls is usually adequate for a medium-weight fabric.

The fabric is then dried before being heat-treated. If the cloth is not completely dry at the carbonizing stage the printed areas will not reach a high enough temperature for burning out and the results will be poor. It is often necessary to re-dry fabric that has been stored for any period of time. The fabric is then baked at 170°C for five minutes until the cellulose has carbonized, turning a brown-black colour. This process can be carried out with a hot iron if care is taken not to scorch the unprinted fabric. The carbonized cellulose is removed either by hand or machine washing. However, it is sometimes necessary to rub out the burned cellulose before washing. This should be done in a open area – preferably outside – and it is important to wear a respirator, goggles and gloves for protection. A small hand-held vacuum cleaner will help to suck up any loose fibres. Extra care should be taken not to rub too hard as the fabric will be brittle and holes are easily made. The fabric can then be washed in warm soapy water

away; cotton-polyester and viscose-polyester blends (in light, medium and heavy weights), in which the cellulose is burned away; and cotton furnishing velvet where the surface of the cotton is burned away leaving an embossed effect behind.

---

### RECIPE
400 g locust bean or guar thickener
80 g glycerine
1–10 g urea
150–220 g sodium hydrogen sulphate
or aluminium sulphate
300 ml water

---

Add the urea, glycerine and sodium hydrogen sulphate or aluminium sul-

## Devoré for Cellulose Fibres
This technique relies upon the degradation of cellulose fibres with an acid that leaves the other fibres unaffected. Aluminium sulphate or sodium hydrogen sulphate are commonly used. With the application of heat, these form an acid that carbonizes the cellulose. The most commonly used devoré fabrics are: silk-viscose velvet and silk-viscose satin, in which the viscose is burned

until all the burned-out areas have been removed; then rinse the fabric and press. If a coloured fabric is wanted the cloth can be dyed before or after the burn-out process.

## Coloured Effects on Devoré

Colour and resist effects can also be produced by printing with a alkaline pigment, reactive or vat dye before blotch printing the devoré paste over the design. Then during the baking process the alkali neutralizes the acid, creating a resist with coloured opaque areas and a white burned-out background. Pigment and reactive dyes are particularly suited to this technique as they only require baking to fix the dyes (the recipes included in chapter 12 are suitable for this effect). Alternatively, disperse dyes added to the devoré paste will create both coloured burn-out and white opaque areas if used with a cellulose-polyester fabric.

**Below: Sharon Ting's simple stripe design shows how effective the devoré technique can be without being too complex.**

RECIPE
10–50 g disperse dye
285 ml water
15 g polyester carrier
400 g locust bean or guar thickener
80 g glycerine
150–220 g sodium hydrogen sulphate
or aluminium sulphate

Stir the disperse dye and carrier into the water. Slowly add this to the locust bean thickener and then add the glycerine and sodium hydrogen sulphate (or aluminium sulphate) and mix well. This will make about 1000 g of print paste. Screen print the dye and dry before heat-treating. The disperse dye must now be fixed. This is done by pressure steaming at 21 p.s.i. for 30 minutes or baking at 200°C (see chapter 17). The carbonized cellulose is then removed as described on page 167.

### Devoré for Protein Fibres

This type of devoré relies upon the destruction of protein fibres with a strong alkali. The most common fibre combinations are wool-polyester, wool-acrylic or wool and cellulose. Interesting lace-effect knitwear can be created by knitting two different yarns together, one wool and the other a caustic-proof fibre. To prevent the broken knitted loops of the wool unwinding the fabric is felted slightly before patterning. (To felt, wash the fabric in hot, soapy water and rinse immediately in cold water, see also page 36.) Other effects can be produced from fabric combinations of silk and metal and silk and polyester.

RECIPE
250 g sodium hydroxide solution
48° Bé (100° Tw, 1.5 specific gravity)
500 g starch ether
250 ml water

Slowly mix together the starch ether, sodium hydroxide solution and water. Observe the safety precautions when dealing with caustic solutions as they will burn. Screen print the paste onto the fabric, making sure it penetrates thoroughly (6–10 pulls of the squeegee is usually adequate).

The fabric is then dried before being steamed. If the cloth is not completely dry before steaming the printed areas may bleed and ruin the sharpness of the design. Pressure steam for five minutes at 10 p.s.i. (see chapter 17) until the protein fibres are destroyed and turn a yellow-orange colour. Then wash the fabric in warm soapy water until all the protein fibres are removed – this may take a while, depending upon the structure of the fabric. The alkali in the fabric is then neutralized in a solution of 2 ml of acetic acid (at 20% strength) per litre of water, then rinse and press. If a coloured fabric is required the cloth can be dyed before or after the devoré process.

**Right: Using a wool-cotton base, Gilian Little has devoréd areas of wool to leave transparent cotton diamonds.**

## DEVORÉ

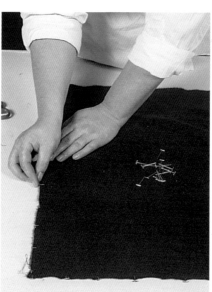

**1 Prepare a screen using masking tape, or by handpainting with a wax resist. Even a simple check pattern (as above) can be effective.**

**2 To prepare for printing, pin out a pre-dyed piece of wool-cotton fabric (wool-side uppermost) onto an old backing cloth.**

**3 Wear protective gloves, glasses and clothing. Carefully pour the caustic print paste onto the screen and screen print it onto the woollen surface of the fabric.**

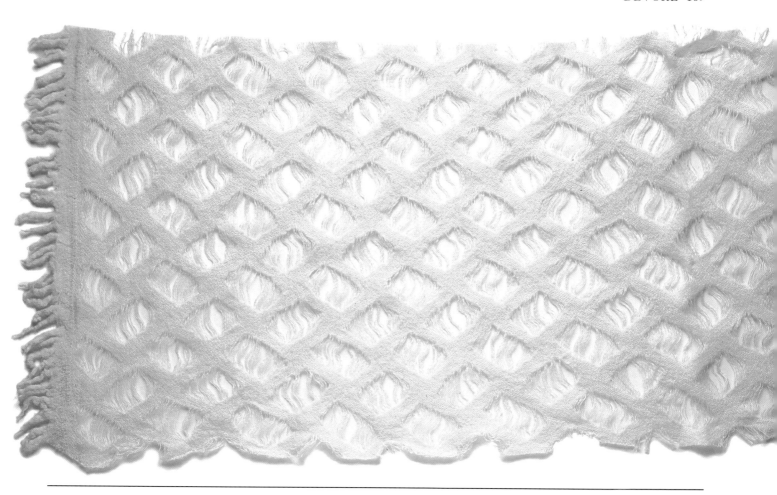

## DEVORÉ

4 About 6–10 pulls of the squeegee may be needed to push the paste through the screen. If printing a repeat, allow the paste to soak in before the next print.

5 Allow the fabric to dry before pressure steaming at 10 p.s.i for five minutes. This will cause the caustic solution to destroy the wool in the printed areas of the fabric.

6 Wash the fabric well to remove the caustic solution and neutralize with a weak acetic acid. The burnt-out areas will now be free of wool fibres.

# GALLERY
# DEVORÉ

Above Left
**SHARON TING**
By over-dyeing an already devoréd fabric
with bold colours, Sharon Ting has created
a bold striped effect.

Centre
**GEORGINA VON ETZDORF**
The subtle colouring and delicate design of
this scarf are ideally suited to the fine qualities
of this devoréd viscose silk-satin.

Far Right
**VANESSA DOYLE**
This original, knitted silk and metal fabric was screen
printed with a caustic paste that burnt away most of
the silk present, leaving behind a lace-like effect.

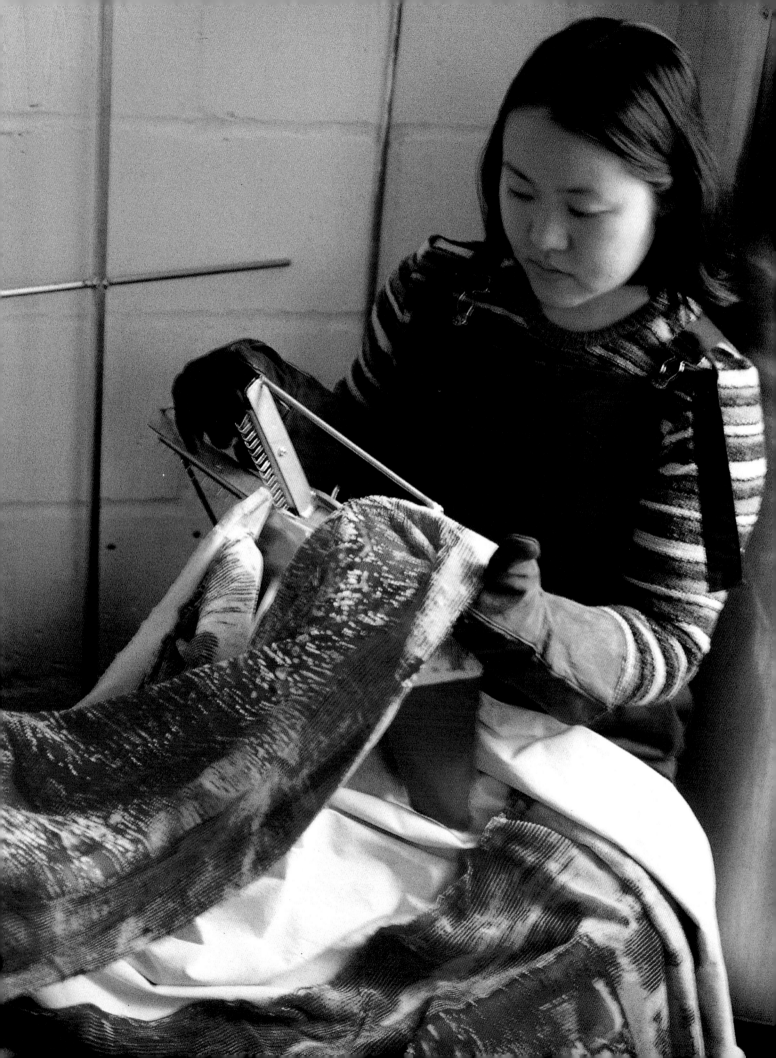

# TOIL AND TROUBLE

*A fabric is not complete until the dyes and colorants that have been applied to its surface are fixed and finished. Many designers look upon this stage of the decorative process as one of 'toil', as there is a lot of physical work and much anticipation in the final stages of patterning cloth. However, it is a process that has as much influence on the final success of a decorated cloth as the patterning technique itself. Adequate time and care should be given to the fixing and finishing of the cloth to avoid mistakes or faults that may ruin the final piece.*

**Opposite: Sharon Ting uses a star steamer to fix discharge dyes onto silk-viscose velvet. Here the fabric and a protective backing cloth are being unloaded from the metal star.**

# 17

# FIXING AND FINISHING

After a fabric has been decorated it must be fixed and finished. Fixation ensures that the dyes are permanently attached to the fabric and finishing is the removal of any excess dye, thickener or printing auxiliaries. Both processes should be carried out with care as faults caused at this stage cannot easily be rectified.

## FIXATION

Most fixation processes require the application of heat to fix the dyestuffs to the fabric fibres. There are various methods available: air fixing, wet processing with chemicals, thermofixation (baking) and steam fixing.

### Air Fixing

Air hanging is one of the easiest methods of fixation. Most resist techniques using vat dyes require air fixing for up to 24 hours to ensure full oxidization. Highly reactive dyes (Procion MX) can be fixed by air hanging, or by wrapping the fabric in polythene and leaving for at least 12 hours in a warm damp place. The results may not be as good as those produced by steaming or thermofixation.

### Wet Development

This method of fixation is used with handpainting and resist techniques such as batik. Some specialist dye systems, obtained in craft shops, use a liquid fixer into which the dyed fabric is immersed, before being washed and dried. Other dyes, like Azoic dyes (see page 45) use one bath to apply a colour salt to the fabric and another to form the dye. Soluble vat dyes are often developed and fixed in a bath of sulphuric or hydrochloric acid.

### Thermofixation

This fixation process relies upon high temperatures (using dry heat) to achieve the fixation of colorants or

**Opposite: Elvira van Vredenburgh finishes off a devoré velvet fabric by vacuuming away the burnt cellulose pile.**

**Right: Zoë Roberts' cloth has been finished correctly; the cellulose has been rubbed away and the residue chemicals removed.**

chemical finishes. It is mainly used for pigments, but some reactive dyes can also be fixed in this manner. Industrial baking cabinets are expensive to buy and run, and are only worth purchasing if large quantities of pigment-printed fabrics are to be produced. Smaller sample machines are available and some infra-red heating units will reach temperatures high enough to fix most reactive and pigment colorants. Small heat-transfer presses can also be used quite successfully.

Thermofixation can also be done by pressing on the wrong side of the cloth with a hot dry iron, set for cotton. This will take at least five minutes for a small sample and the ironing board and patterned fabric should be protected from dye mark-off by a thin piece of paper or cloth (do not use newspaper). When thermofixing synthetic fabrics the temperature can be reduced to prevent melting or scorching the base fabric, but their ironing times must be increased. Larger pieces are fixed by tumble dry-

ing for about 30 minutes at the highest temperature setting or, if fixing reactive or solvent-free pigment systems, a domestic oven can be used. The fabric is folded, wrapped in foil and then baked for at least 10 minutes at a hot setting (do not use this method for solvent-based pigments, as they will give off combustible fumes when heated and may cause an explosion). Gas ovens should never be used for this technique because of potential burning and fire risk.

**Steaming**
Most dye processes need to be fixed by steam. The steam provides both the moisture and the heat required for the successful transfer of dyes from the thickener into the structure of the fibres. The moisture swells the fibres in the cloth so that they readily absorb the dyestuffs, but too much moisture will cause excessive bleeding. The thickener film must also absorb enough water to dissolve the dyes present, but not so much as to cause spreading and bleeding, and enough liquid must be present to allow the dispersed dyes to diffuse into the fibre's structure. A rapid increase in temperature accelerates these processes. In ideal conditions steam will fulfil all these requirements, but the process is often helped by the correct selection of thickener and auxiliaries.

For most dyes and fabric, fixation can be carried out using normal saturated steam but a few fabrics and techniques require the extra heat produced by pressure or superheated steaming operations. Normal saturated steam is water vapour produced at 100°C; this is created by boiling water at atmospheric pressure. The ideal steam for most dye processes should contain no suspended droplets of water.

The steaming times required for complete fixation differ depending upon the type of cloth, dyes and the processes used. The final results are affected by what steaming equipment is employed, as the steam produced varies in quantity and quality from one piece of equipment to another. The recipes listed in chapters 12–16 give standard steaming times, but always carry out test steamings to ensure best results. As a general guide, any designs produced with acid or direct dyes require steaming times of 45–60 minutes, whereas reactives can be fixed in 5–15 minutes, depending upon the reactivity of the dye (steaming times also depend upon the amount of steam being generated). Neither of these dye types are sensitive to the presence of air in the steaming vessel and can normally be steamed using simple equipment.

Vat and discharge processes require the elimination of as much air as possible from the steaming operation. Their success on a small scale depends upon a constant flow of air-free steam of a reasonably high moisture content. A steaming time of 10–20 minutes is normally adequate. Failure in the fixation of vat dyes or the production of unsatisfactory discharges is usually caused by insufficient steam and the presence of too much air during the steaming operation. Any air not displaced at the beginning of the steaming process will rapidly decompose the sulphoxylate formaldehyde present in the print paste, preventing it from fulfilling its role as a reducing, discharging agent.

Disperse dyes and wool devoré processes will give better results if pressure steamed. This generally requires specialist equipment but good results can be achieved on a small scale by using a domestic pressure cooker and altering the steam pressure required.

All the steaming equipment described in this chapter is for batch steaming methods, as no designer/maker will produce enough fabric in a small workshop situation to require continuous steaming processes. Whatever the type of steamer, it is important to protect the decorated cloth and prevent mark-off by interlayering the patterned fabric with paper or a cloth wrapper.

## STEAMING WITH A WOK

1 When you have printed your fabric, roll it up in between layers of paper or cloth to protect the design from mark-off throughout the steaming process.

2 Roll the fabric up and flatten it before winding it into a coil. Then heat a small amount of water in a wok (or a steamer) until it is steaming well.

## Steaming Equipment

Star steamers are vertical industrial steamers and are available in a variety of sizes and depths. They are mainly used for batch production with a fabric capacity of between 10–500 metres of cloth, depending upon its weight. Cloth is loaded onto a series of hooks on a tubular, star-shaped frame that is then hoisted up and suspended in the steaming cylinder, allowing the decorated fabric to hang freely. After steaming, the star is hoisted out and the cloth allowed to dry off slightly before removing.

A dustbin steamer works on a tier principle with racks suspended above the steam supply. The steam is generated by immersion heaters or by a gas ring at the base of a metal dustbin-like container. It then passes through the fabrics which have been previously wrapped and folded like parcels and placed on racks in the bin. The disadvantages of this type of steamer (the time it takes for the steam to penetrate through the fabric parcels and the inclusion of air when loading and unloading) make it unsuitable for vat or discharge techniques.

A bullet steamer is ideal for the small-scale designer as it has a capacity of 1–10 metres of medium-weight cloth. It usually consists of a double-walled stainless-steel tube that rests on top of a container of water. This may have an enclosed immersion heater, or it may need to be placed on top of an electric hotplate or gas ring. The fabric is either rolled in paper, or a fine cloth around a tube. A solid cardboard tube can be used but does not last very long – a lightweight metal alloy tube is better. It is important to leave a margin of at least 5 cm of backing cloth at each side of the fabric to ensure that they do not touch each other. Seal both ends of the roll, fixing securely to the support tube before placing in the centre of the steamer. Make sure the tube does not touch the sides of the steamer, then replace the lid and steam for the required period of time.

Box steamers are similar to bullet steamers, but fabrics are wrapped, folded into a parcel or coil and placed on a rack in a long stainless-steel box like a fish-steaming kettle. It does not have its own heat supply. Take care not to overfill the water reservoir or rings and watermarks may form on the cloth.

Small samples and fine fabrics of lengths up to 3 metres can often be steamed quite successfully in domestic food steamers, preserving kettles, woks and pressure cookers. (Never cook food in pots used for steaming dyed fabrics.) Wrap the decorated fabric into a roll with sheets of newsprint or lining paper, ensuring that none of the samples touch and the ends are sealed securely, then flatten and roll it into a coil. Fill the bottom of the pan with water to a depth of 2 cm and place a trivet or rack in it to act as a shelf above the water level. Heat the pan until steam is produced. The fabric package can be placed in a basket and covered with a piece of paper to prevent the roll becoming too wet from condensation. Place it on the rack and cover the whole fabric parcel with a sheet of aluminium foil to prevent water droplets, from the lid of the container, falling onto the cloth during the steaming. Firmly secure the lid and steam the fabric for the requisite period of time.

A domestic pressure cooker, with the correct weights applied to its top, can also be used to produce steam under pressure. However, you should refer to the manufacturer's instructions for the correct usage and make sure that all the pressure is reduced before opening the lid.

### Avoiding Faults

Inadequate fixing will cause dyes to run and fade in the finishing process. It is also important to prevent any drops of water touching the fabric during steaming, as isolated areas of the design could bleed and run where any water comes in contact with the fabric before fixation is completed. It is essential that the appropriate fixing chemical is included in the patterning

**3 Once the steam has forced all the air out of the wok, place the rolled up fabric on a rack above the level of the boiling water and replace the lid.**

**4 After steaming for the requisite period of time, remove the fabric parcel and carefully unwrap. Allow the fabric to dry before washing and pressing.**

paste. Designs will be ruined if one element of the patterning paste recipe is forgotten or if the fixing or discharging agent is left at the bottom of the dye pot because the paste was not thoroughly stirred. Extra care should be taken to wash-off the fabrics with plenty of clean water to avoid any mark-off.

The iron and pressing surface must be free of dyes. Use the correct heat setting for the fabric; wool will easily scorch and polyester fibres melt if the temperature of the iron is too high.

**Finishing**

Finishing can be divided into a wet process in which the fixed cloth is washed, and the final drying and pressing process. Some dyestuffs will require an intermediate process to re-oxidize any dyes that may have become reduced during the fixation process. The finishing of a piece of fabric is as important as its fixation because any excess dyes, chemicals and thickeners are removed during

this time, returning it to its original state. Most of the decorative processes described in this book require a wash-off procedure. If a fabric has been decorated with pale colours, complete fixation of the dyestuffs is possible but the gums and thickeners used to control the colorants will still need to be removed from the fabric. The only exceptions are some pigment systems where the cloth requires no finishing at all, but a gentle wash will still improve the handle of the fabric. It is not absolutely necessary to finish a cloth immediately after the fixing process, but once the operation has been started it must be completed or staining and mark-off will result.

The thickener held on the fabric surface can be removed by vigorous washing at low temperatures, but removal of the excess dyes needs to be done at higher temperatures. The main problem encountered during the wash-off operation is the staining of unpatterned areas by dyes in the

**Right: Karen Johnstone's striking acid dyed, silk mono-print was fixed by steaming the fabric in a wok.**

wash liquor, it is therefore important not to allow unfixed dye to accumulate. Various dyes and processes require different wash-off procedures and these are described along with the relevant dye.

In a small workshop washing-off should take place in as large a container as possible. A large kitchen sink will be adequate for one metre samples and individual scarves, but a bath is much better for longer lengths. Domestic or industrial washing machines can sometimes be used for this process but avoid overloading the machine and long soaking times on the washing cycles, or mark-off may occur. After a fabric has been washed it can then be dried. It is often better to press the cloth in a damp condition as this will help remove any stubborn creases.

## USING A BULLET STEAMER

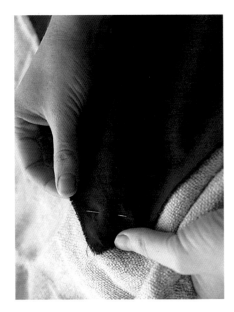

**1** Pin the printed fabric onto a fine open-weave backing cloth. Make sure you leave plenty of space between the fabric and the top and bottom of the backing cloth.

**2** Once all the fabric is pinned out, roll it with the backing cloth onto a cardboard or metal alloy tube. Secure at both ends to prevent the fabric touching the water.

**3** Carefully place the rolled up tube into a pre-heated bullet steamer. Replace the lid and allow to steam for the requisite period of time before removing.

# 18

# SETTING UP A WORKSPACE

The aim of this book has been to introduce as wide a range of patterning techniques as possible. The amount of equipment needed depends upon the quantity and size of the fabric to be patterned, and long lengths of cloth may require specialist textile equipment normally found in art colleges, university textile departments and workshops. Most effects can, however, be achieved by modifying domestic equipment and adapting the available space. An ideal set-up is a fully equipped, self-contained workshop, but this is often not available so areas of the house must be used (provided that all the safety precautions are observed).

The first consideration in setting-up a workshop is to decide what techniques you wish to use. The amount of equipment required to start can be quite small, but the greater the number of techniques used and the larger the pieces undertaken the greater the amount of equipment needed. When setting-up a work area some general points should be considered. Space

should be carefully planned to include a clean, wet and dry area, a printing and patterning area, a dyeing, drying and finishing area and safe storage for cloths, dyes, thickeners, chemicals and finished fabrics. The smaller the space the greater the care needed in planning and organizing to ensure maximum efficiency, production and safety. A good work area must be well lit, preferably with natural light, for accuracy in colour selection and the matching of dyestuffs. If this is not possible try to use daylight bulbs.

The work area should be well ventilated. An extractor fan offers the best solution, but if this is not practicable open as many windows as possible whilst working. A supply of hot and cold water, with safe disposal of spent dyebaths and wash-off water is essential, as is a stove – a portable camping stove or electric hotplate is adequate. There must also be a number of electrical points to avoid overloading the circuit (an overhead track system avoids any trailing cords). Outlets for a kettle, mixer, iron, fan heater or hair dryer are needed, and sockets should be situated away from wet areas to avoid the risk of electric shocks. In addition, a solid working surface, storage areas and a clean laundry area are needed.

Safe storage of dyes, colorants and chemicals is essential as most chemicals are irritants, with a few being

toxic or even poisonous. These must be kept away from foodstuffs and out of reach of small children and animals. Ideally, the mixing area for dyes and patterning pastes should be kept well away from any clean printing areas as fine-powdered dyestuffs easily become air-borne and settle on any clean or wet cloth that is lying around. If this is not possible it is important to cover all clean areas when weighing and mixing dyes. There should also be a wash area where screens, blocks and brushes can be cleaned, and a clean finishing area to wash and press the final cloth.

## Measurement
Accurate measurement of powders, liquids and temperature is essential. Scales that can measure both large amounts of gum and small quantities of chemicals and dyes are needed. A kitchen scale is adequate for most purposes, as most are capable of weighing amounts from 1 g to 1000 g, but their accuracy in weighing smaller amounts may not be good. Letter scales are more accurate, but it may be worth investing in a laboratory scale. These are available with different degrees of accuracy – those that weigh from 0.1 g to 1000 g are suitable for most dyes. A tare facility is also useful as it allows one chemical to be accurately weighed after another in the same container.

**Opposite: Dissolving dyes in a small pan, Brian Whitewick is shown working in a studio with plenty of potential ventilation.**

**Below: This skilfully handpainted design, by Sally Greaves-Lord, shows what can be achieved with much practise.**

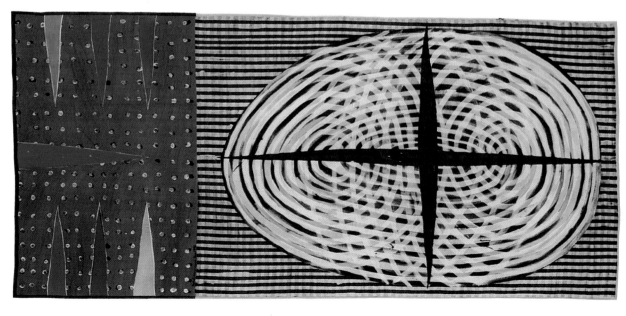

A range of measuring cylinders are needed for the measurement of liquids; glass cylinders will not stain and are easy to clean. Some suppliers of laboratory equipment sell plastic bottles that have a small measuring cylinder in their top. These are useful for storing and measuring liquids.

A good thermometer that can measure temperatures from 0–100°C, is needed for dyeing. A hydrometer capable of measuring Baumé or Twaddle is necessary for measuring the viscosity of some liquids; and a waterproof pH meter, or pH indicator papers, are used to measure the alkalinity or acidity of solutions.

### Mixing

Some gums such as alginate or cellulose ether gums are easily dispersed in cold water. Others require mechanical mixing; for small amounts use a hand-held mixer or whisk, but larger amounts require a large domestic mixer (solely for studio use).

### Storage

A large variety of containers are needed. Large glass or plastic jars are ideal for salts, gums and chemicals that are supplied in a loose state. Empty sweet jars can be used for the storage of chemicals such as urea and sodium carbonate, but make sure they are clean and dry before using, and label each container clearly. A wide range of heavy-duty wide-neck plastic bottles can also be purchased from equipment suppliers. Smaller glass jars are adequate for dyes and print pastes, but many are narrow-necked and difficult to use for mixing. Plastic pots with lids make ideal paste containers in which most dye and patterning pastes can be safely stored for several weeks. Many art shops and dye suppliers sell suitable cheap containers but Tupperware makes a good alternative. For the small amounts of dye solution used in handpainting techniques, plastic disposable beakers make a cheap alternative, but do not use these with any solvent-based products as they may melt. Most products are supplied in suitable

plastic bottles labelled with the relevant safety information; do not transfer these chemicals to other containers unless you clearly label the new bottle with this information. Hazard labels can be obtained from chemical and equipment suppliers.

All dyes and chemicals should be stored safely on shelves or in cupboards. Strong acids should be locked away in a suitable box or cupboard and only diluted solutions should be left in the studio area.

### Dyeing and Finishing Equipment

A heat-proof jug is essential for dissolving dyes. This can be glass or stainless-steel, but should be able to hold one litre of liquid and be easily cleaned. Stainless-steel buckets and pots make good dyeing containers as they are easily cleaned and will not stain or affect any of the colours. Old enamel buckets, bowls and pans are adequate provided that the enamel is not chipped (these areas may rust and cause iron marks on the cloth). Plastic buckets, troughs and storage containers make useful dyeing and finishing containers for many of the cold water dyeing methods provided that they are solidly built.

Long lengths of cloth will require winch dyeing; this machinery can be bought from specialist equipment suppliers but tea urns or nappy boilers work well if the cloth is agitated frequently during dyeing. They can also be adapted to use as steamers. Twin-tub washing machines or old mangle machines can fulfil a dual role for both finishing and dyeing but they must be cleaned out well between processes.

It is important to have a clean area to wash, dry and press any completed pieces (suitable equipment and methods are discussed in chapter 16). A double sink unit is useful for the washing-off of small patterned pieces, but for larger lengths a bath is better.

### Brushes, Blocks, Frames and Screens

For many of the patterning processes the colouring paste is applied using handpainting techniques. A wide variety of brushes, paint pads,

sponges and rollers are recommended (see chapter 7). Similarly the three sorts of printing block available (wooden, metal and lino) are discussed in detail in chapter 9.

Simple frames are required for stretching fabric above the work surface in many of the handpainting, batik and marbling techniques. A simple fixed frame can be constructed out of four pieces of softwood, and glued or nailed together using butt or mitre joints. Specialist frames and stretchers can be purchased from art and craft shops. One example is a 'slot and sliding' frame (which uses screws and wingnuts), which allows fine adjustments to be made to the tension of the fabric. For smaller pieces an embroidery hoop can be used.

Screens of all sizes, materials and mesh types can be purchased from craft shops and specialist suppliers, but simple wooden screens can be constructed from softwood. It is essential that a well-seasoned, non-warping wood such as sycamore,

---

### MATERIALS FOR A SCREEN

**You will need a rectangular, flat wooden frame, a staple gun and a pair of sharp scissors to cut a piece of silk-screen mesh larger than the frame.**

beech, birch, cedar, redwood, pine or spruce is used. Teak and mahogany can be used for small screens but they tend to be heavy if used for larger sizes. It is important that the wood is straight, free of knots and dry. For small screens, a 40 x 60 mm cross-section will be strong enough, but the bigger the screen the larger the cross-section required to provide enough strength and prevent warping. A 60 x 100 cm screen requires a cross-section of 50 x 50 mm, and a 77 x 115 cm screen requires a cross-section of 50 x 80 mm. Several joints can be used in a wooden frame, the weakest being a mitred joint which would require reinforcing with metal angles; dowelled, dovetail or half-lapped joints are stronger. If constructing a frame, make sure it is perfectly square and that it sits flat on a table.

The wooden frame must be covered with a taut nylon or polyester mono-filament mesh. This mesh can be stretched by hand for small screens, but the larger the frame the harder it is to apply enough tension to the mesh. Although a canvas stretcher may help with larger frames, the best results require a specialized screen stretching unit. A variety of meshes are available in a range of gauges or counts, the best for a small general-purpose screen is 39–43 TT (10–12 XX). I do not recommend stretching your own screens with fine mesh counts such as a 60–72 TT (14 XX), as the fabric is stiffer and it is difficult to apply enough tension on the mesh to produce the fineness of work this size of mesh is intended for.

There are several methods available for attaching the mesh to a screen; stretching machines use a waterproof glue but the easiest method for a beginner is a staple gun. The objective is to produce a surface that is tight like a drum skin and free from any soft spots or ridges.

Place the mesh over the frame with the selvage running down one side and secure the mesh to a corner with several staples. It is often better to use an over-large piece of mesh so that extra tension can be applied when stretching, and smaller pieces will provide little fabric to hold onto. Pull the mesh taut and straight along the selvage edge and attach at the next corner with more staples. This side is then fastened to the screen with a series of diagonally placed staples, about 3 cms apart. The fabric is then stretched to the third and fourth corner and secured in the same way. A second row of staples are staggered between the first, but sloping in the opposite direction. This holds the mesh more securely and there is less chance of it splitting. Any excess mesh can now be trimmed away, and staples that are not flush with the wood should be hammered down.

The mesh must be cleaned to remove any dirt, grease or size. This is done by scouring the mesh with proprietary screen cleaner; a cheaper alternative is a domestic scouring powder or a cream kitchen cleaner. Rinse the screen well to remove all

## MAKING A SCREEN

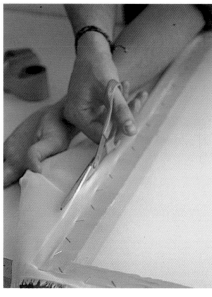

**1 Staple the mesh at one corner, pull the selvage taut to the next corner and fix. Staple along this side, then stretch the mesh to the next corner and repeat.**

**2 The staples should be placed diagonally down the sides of the frame. Trim off the excess screen mesh and hammer down any protruding staples.**

**3 Finish the screen with parcel tape on both the inside and outside edges to prevent any dye paste seeping out between the frame's edge and the mesh.**

## A PRINTING TABLE

**A simple screen or block printing table can be made from a table covered with block or chipboard. Staple an old blanket in place for a padded surface.**

## A WATERPROOF TABLE

**A cheap and easy waterproof printing surface can be achieved by covering the padded surface of a table with a heavy-weight polythene sheet.**

the detergent and allow to dry. All screens are taped on the outside and inside edges to stop any printing paste leaking out between the mesh and the frame. Brown paper parcel tape is used to tape the insides. Place the screen on a flat surface and tape each of the four corners with a square of tape. Each square is folded in half, in both directions, and one of the creases cut up to the centre. Wet and fold one square neatly into each corner of the screen. The side pieces are then cut slightly shorter than the length of each side, folded in half length-wise, wet and glued along the inner edges of the screen forming a protective seal. Extra strips are then placed on the mesh to form an area for the printing paste. The screen is turned over and strips of tape are placed over the frame and the mesh to the same point as the tape inside. Wipe off excess water and allow to dry, if possible, in a flat position as excess gum in the tape might run down the face of the screen, blocking the mesh. When the tape is dry it can be waterproofed with polyurethane varnish to completely seal the edges. If cleaned and stored correctly a silk screen will last for many years before needing to be repaired or replaced.

### Tables
A solid table is also essential. For small handpainting, mono-printing, batik or tie-and-dye work, a large, stable, smooth, light-coloured surface is ideal. A large melamine-coated board, placed on trestle legs makes a good alternative and can be folded away when not in use. The tables required for block printing and screen printing are slightly different. They need to be wider than the maximum width and longer than the length of fabric to be printed. It is almost impossible to achieve accurate registration if a cloth has to be printed in areas and then moved to allow other areas to be patterned. A block printing table has to be very strong to take the pounding that is needed to print a block cleanly and evenly. Commercially-made screen printing tables are expensive, but if you are considering

producing precise screen printed fabrics it is worth investing in a level table with an accurate straight registration bar. Small screen printing tables are about 3 metres long and 1.5 metres wide. Commercial tables are longer but require a large workshop space to accommodate them.

A wooden table can be constructed but add extra support to the underneath if it is to be used for block printing. To build a table with an accurate registration bar is a more complicated and costly operation.

### Wash-off Area
Small screens can be cleaned in a bath or shower with the aid of a hand-held shower or hose. Larger screens are more difficult to clean in a home studio, but it may be possible to clean them outside using a hose. In a larger workshop, a specialized wash-off bath can be bought or constructed. A small pressure-hose system is useful for blasting away stubborn pigment colours or old photographic coating.

### Miscellaneous
Basic design tools such as brushes, pencils, pens, rulers, rollers, set squares, scalpels, scissors (both for paper and material), sponges and tailor's chalk are also needed. Other pieces of equipment and material are: backing cloths and steaming wrappers to protect the table surfaces and cloth during fixation, T-pins, silk push-pins and dressmaker's pins to attach the fabric to the backing cloth and frames. Fan heaters and hair dryers may be used to speed up the drying times. It is advisable to keep two irons: a steam iron which remains perfectly clean for pressing finished cloth, and another for ironing down backing cloths and colour sampling. Electrical wax pots or hotplates are needed for batik and wax resist work. The list may seem endless but many things can be acquired gradually as the different techniques are tried.

**Opposite: For this satin-silk, Georgina von Etzdorf has used brightly coloured acid dyes and a discharge technique.**

**Acid Dyes** – These are **anionic** dyes that are categorized by their **substantivity** for protein, polyamide or other fibres containing basic groups. They are normally applied in an acidic or neutral state.

**Adire** – The name of a Nigerian resist patterned fabric, traditionally dyed with indigo.

**Anionic dyes** – Dyes that dissociate in an aqueous solution to give negatively charged coloured ions.

**Auxiliary/Auxiliary product** – A chemical or formulated chemical product that is used in dyeing, printing or finishing – or if a given effect is desired – and enables these processes to be carried out more effectively.

**Azoic dyes/Ice colours** – Insoluble dyes that are produced in the fibre directly by the interaction of two separate components, an azoic diazo component and an azoic coupling component. They were known as Ice colours because of the necessity to use ice to lower the temperature of this reaction and avoid premature breakdown of the diazo compound.

**Bake** – See **thermofixation**.

**Basic dyes** – These **cationic** dyes have a **substantivity** for acrylic, modacrylic, dyeable polyester fibres and some protein fibres. They cannot dye cellulose directly and to do so, they need to be deposited on the fibre in an insoluble form, and require the addition of tannic acid.

**Batik** – Derived from a Javanese word, and describing a resist process using molten wax.

**° Be** – Abbreviation for the Baumé scale of specific gravity of liquids.

**Bleeding** – The loss of **colorant** from a coloured fabric in contact with moisture. This often leads to the coloration of other materials or adjacent areas of the same cloth.

**Blotch Printing** – A process in which an open screen is used, and where the dyestuff covers the entire surface of the fabric.

**Carrier** – An **auxiliary product** that is a type of accelarant commonly used in the printing of **hydrophobic** fibres with **disperse dyes**.

**Cationic dyes** – Dyes that dissociate in an aqueous solution to give positively charged coloured ions.

**Causticize** – The treatment of cellulose fabrics with a sodium hydroxide solution under such conditions that a full **mercerizing** effect is not obtained, but the colour yield in dyeing and printing is significantly enhanced.

**Colour Index (C.I.)** – See pages 32–3.

**Colorant** – A colouring matter, dye or **pigment**.

**Colour fastness** – The resistance of a cloth's colour to various situations, for example washing, light or rubbing. These are measured on standard scales of 1–5, where 5 signifies no visible change and 1 substantial change. For light, grades are used where 8 represents the highest fastness.

**Covalent bond** – A chemical bond involving the sharing of electrons between atoms in a molecule.

**Crêpe** – A fabric that is categorized by having a crinkled or puckered surface. The effect is produced in a number of ways, for example weaving with yarns of different twists, or by the application of a chemical or heat.

**Crepon** – A heavier fabric similar to **crêpe**.

**Crimp** – The waviness of a fabric.

**De-size** – The removal of the gelatinous solution or dispersion that is normally applied to **warps** and sometimes **wefts** before weaving to protect them from abrasion, and strengthen and lubricate the yarns during weaving.

**Devoré** – Sometimes known as the burn-out style. This is the production of a pattern on a fabric by printing with a substance that will destroy one or more of the fibres present.

**Direct dyes** – An **anionic dye** that has a **substantivity** for cellulose and some protein fibres. It is normally applied from a dye bath containing an **electrolyte**.

**Direct style** – A style of patterning in which one or several colours are applied to the surface of a fabric and are usually fixed by **thermofixation** or steaming. The fabric base is usually white but may have been previously dyed. This method was rarely used until the advent of synthetic dyestuffs.

**Discharge** – The chemical destruction of a dye or **mordant**, already present on a fabric, to leave a white or differently coloured pattern behind. The process is normally achieved through a printing technique.

**Disperse dyes** – These dyes are insoluble in water but have a **substantivity** for most **hydrophobic** fibres, such as polyester and cellulose acetate. They are often applied from a fine aqueous dispersion under pressure or with the aid of a **carrier**.

**Dyed style** – A method of patterning in which a **mordant** is applied to a fabric before dyeing. Only the mordanted areas permanently fix the dye. Different mordants can produce different colours with the same dye upon the a piece of fabric.

**Electrolyte** – A substance used in dyeing to aid the absorption of dyes into the fabric.

**Emulsifier** – An **auxiliary** that aids the conversion of a substance into an **emulsion**.

**Emulsion** – Often used as a thickener, it is a milky liquid with oily or resinous particles suspended in it. Half emulsions are made when an equal proportion of an emulsion is mixed with an alginate or guar thickener.

**Exhaust dyeing** – Using water, additives and sometimes heat, the fibres of the cloth are able to take up the dye. This continues until all the dye has been absorbed into the cloth leaving an 'exhausted' dye bath.

**Exhaustion** – The degree to which a fibre or fabric absorbs a dyestuff or chemical, at any stage of a process, in relation to the amount that was originally available.

**Felted** – The matting together of a material's fibres to create a fabric that is characterized by the entangled condition of many of its component fibres. (See also **milling**.)

**Flushing** – The production of blurred edges and loss of fine detail around a white **discharge** printing. (See also **haloing**.)

**Fugitive** – Describes a dyestuff that will quickly fade through washing or exposure to light.

**Full-drop/Square-drop** – A common form of **repeat** used in textile printing in which the design unit, when repeated, is placed next to the last in the form of a grid system, exactly horizontal and vertical to the last unit.

**Grey scale** – A series of pairs of neutrally coloured chips, showing increasing contrast between the pairs. These are used to assess contrasts between other pairs of colours.

**Half-drop** – A common form of **repeat** used in textile printing in which the design unit is stepped down half its original length.

**Haloing** – A white ring that resembles a 'halo' around a coloured **discharge** print. This is caused by migration of the soluble **reducing agent** around the printed design.

**Handle** – The tactile quality of a fabric or yarn base – for example, roughness, smoothness, thickness, pliability, stretchability.

**Hue** – An attribute of a colour whereby it is recognized as being predominantly yellow, orange, red, purple, blue, green, brown, etc.

**Hydrophobic** – A tendency to repel water.

**Hygroscopic** – [of a substance] Tending to attract and absorb water from the air.

**Lake** – An insoluble **pigment** that is created by precipitating natural and artificial colouring matters onto a suitable **substrate** in the presence of another chemical or metal salt. This is the main principle applied in **mordant** dyeing and the **dyed style** of patterning.

**Leuco** – Used to describe a reduced **vat dye**.

**Mercerizing** – The treatment of a cellulose yarn or fabric with a strong caustic alkali, commonly sodium hydroxide solution, where the fibres are swollen and the strength, **handle** and dye affinity of the material is increased or modified.

**Milling/Fulling** – A finishing process that involves the consolidation or compacting of fabrics that are usually made from wool or other animal fibres.

**Mordant** – A chemical substance, usually a metal salt, that will form an insoluble complex with a dyestuff when applied to a fibre. This often has greater affinity for the **substrate** than the dyestuff itself.

**Nap** – The fibrous surface on a fabric created by brushing, teazing or rubbing – lifting fibres from the basic structure. This term is often wrongly confused with the term **pile**.

**Oxidize** – This describes the addition of an oxygen molecule to a reduced dyestuff to ensure that the dye colour is fully restored and permanently fixed within the cloth's fibre.

**PH value** – measure of hydrogen ion concentration.

**Pigments** – These are insoluble coloured substances that have no **substantivity** for materials, but can be applied to their surfaces by means of another medium which creates a bond between them and the fibres of the cloth.

**Pile** – A surface effect on fabric that has been formed by tufts or loops of yarn that stand up from the main body of the cloth.

**Plissé** – Often applied to fabrics with a puckered or crinkled effect. It is a French term meaning pleated. (See also **seersucker**.)

**P.s.i** – The abbreviated form of pounds per square inch. A unit of measurement used in pressure steaming.

**Reactive dye** – A dye that is capable of reacting with the **substrate** to create a covalent bond between the dye and the material under suitable conditions.

**Reducing agent** – A chemical substance that is capable of removing oxygen from another chemical. The resulting effect in the case of dyestuffs is the removal of its colour.

**Registration** – The accurate fitting together of all the patterning elements of a design.

**Repeat** – The exact reproduction of any element of a design placed in a geometric relationship with itself and other elements. Various repeating patterns are given names, for example, **full-drop** and **half-drop**.

**Resist** – A substance that prevents the uptake or fixation of dye on a **substrate** in the areas where the resist has been applied. Resists can be mechanical or chemical barriers.

**Resist style** – A patterning style in which fabric is treated with **resist** whereby on dyeing or developing, a white or coloured pattern is obtained on a coloured ground.

**Saponification** – Alkaline finish given to cellulose acetate that is often known as S-finish. The alkali causes hydrolysis of chemical groups within the fibres allowing the fabric to be dyed with dyes intended for cellulose.

**Scouring/Washing** – The removal of impurities such as natural waxes, fats and dirt from a fabric by means of washing with a detergent, and the addition of other assistants, or a solvent. (The process will vary with the type of fibre.)

**Seersucker** – A fabric categorized by the presence of both puckered and relatively flat striped areas, but may also be found in the form of checks. Normally produced by weaving methods or printing cellulose fabrics with a strong sodium hydroxide solution.

**Sericin** – Often known as silk gum, this consists of a gelatinous protein that cements the two fibroin (tough elastic protein) filaments together and often forms 20–30% of the total mass of raw silk. It is removed after processing to improve the **handle** of the cloth.

**Size** – See **de-size**.

**Slubby** – A fabric that contains slubs in the yarn that has been used to produce it. A slub is an abnormally thick area in a yarn.

**Strike-off** – The production of a sample print to prove the accuracy of a printed design and **registration** of screens or rollers.

**Sublime** – The ability of a substance to change from a solid state to a vapour state in the presence of heat. On cooling, the substance returns to its solid state.

**Substantivity** – The attraction between a **substrate** and a dye or other substance in which the latter is selectively extracted from the application medium by the substrate.

**Substrate** – A material or fabric to which dyes and chemicals may be applied.

**Swimming tub** – A wooden tub or box used to ink up printing blocks. It is half filled with old gum or printing paste to give a resilience, over which is stretched a waterproof membrane upon which rests a sieve. This is known as a tiering tray and consists of a frame that has been stretched with a woollen cloth. Print paste is spread upon the sieve and the block pressed against it before printing.

**Thermofixation** – The fixation of some colorants, commonly **pigments**, and chemical finishes with dry heat (often known as baking).

**Tint** – The production of a paler colour by the addition of white.

**Tjanting** – A tool that is used to apply wax in **batik** processes. It consists of a small copper bowl, having one or more spouts, attached to a wooden or bamboo handle.

**Tjap** – This is a printing block that has been made entirely from strips of metal. It is used to stamp molten wax onto a cloth, producing an effect similar to hand-drawn **batik**.

**Tone** – Used in the description of colours to describe the degree of luminosity of a **hue**.

**º Tw** – The abbreviation for measurements taken with the Twaddell scale. A scale used for expressing specific gravity of liquids.

**Vat** – A vessel or a tank, or a liquor containing a reduced (**leuco**) **vat dye**.

**Vat dyes** – Insoluble dyes that are applied to the **substrate** in an alkaline solution of the dye in a reduced (**leuco**) form. This is then fixed within the fibres of the **substrate** by **oxidizing** it back to its insoluble form.

**Vatting** – To dissolve a **vat dye** by the combined action of an alkali and a **reducing agent**.

**Warp** – Threads that run lengthways in a woven fabric.

**Weft** – Threads that run widthways in a woven fabric.

**Wetting-out** – The full penetration of a solution into a fibre in order that dyeing or printing will take place evenly.

# SUPPLIERS

## GREAT BRITAIN

**Adelphi Engineering and Sheet metal Co.**
Steeple Street
 ıcclesfield
 ıeshire SK10 2QR
 ıl: 01625 425946
 Screen printing tables and registration bars)

**Amaleen Products Ltd.**
Dewsbury Road
Elland
West Yorkshire HX5 9BG
Tel: 01422 379729
(Gum 301 Extra)

**Ashill Colour Studio**
Jenny Dean
Boundary Cottage
172 Clifton Road
Shefford
Bedfordshire, SC17 5AH
Tel: 01462 812001
(Natural dyes, mordants and books)

**BASF Plc.**
P.O.Box 4
Earl Road
Cheadle Hulme
Cheshire SK8 6QG
Tel: 0161 485 6222
(Dyes and auxiliaries)

**Bayer Plc.**
Bayer House
Strawberry Hill
Newbury
Berkshire BD18 1BD
Tel: 01635 563000
(Dyes and auxiliaries)

**Candle Makers Supplies**
28 Blythe Road
London W14 0HA
Tel: 0171 602 4031
(Batik equipment, reactive dyes, fabric
inks and paints, steaming equipment)

**Ciba-Geigy**
Hulley Road
Macclesfield
Cheshire SK10 2NX
Tel: 01625 421933
(dyes and auxiliaries)

**Clariant (previously Sandoz)**
Calverley Lane
Horsforth
Leeds LS18 4RD
Tel: 0113 258 4646
(Dyes and auxiliaries)

**Dylon International Ltd.**
Worsley Bridge Road
London SE26 5BE
Tel: 0181 663 4801
(Reactive and multi-purpose dyes)

**Fibrecrafts**
Style Cottage
Lower Eashing
Godalming
Surrey GU7 2QD
Tel: 01483 421853
(Natural dyes, mordants, acid dyes,
dyeing equipment and textile books)

**George Weil and Sons Ltd.**
18 Hanson Street
London W1P 7DB
Tel: 0171 580 3763
(Fabrics, batik materials, dyes and inks,
screen printing equipment, textile books)

**Kemtex Services Ltd.**
Tameside Business Centre
Windmill Lane
Denton
Manchester M34 3QS
Tel: 0161 320 6505
(Dyes and textile auxiliaries)

**Macculloch & Wallis Ltd.**
25 Dering Street
London W1R OBH
Tel: 0171 409 0725
(Cottons and silks)

**Magna Colours Ltd.**
Oodworth Business Park
Upper Cliffe Road
Dosworth
Barnsley
South Yorkshire S75 3SP
Tel: 01226 731751
(Pigments and screen printing binders)

**M & R Dyes**
Station Road
Wickham Bishops
Essex CM8 3JB
Tel: 01621 891405
(Acid, reactive, basic and
natural dyes, textile chemicals)

**Merck Ltd.**
Merck House
Poole
Dorset BH15 1TD
Tel: 01202 664487
(Chemicals, pearl and metallic pigments)

**Quality Colour London Ltd.**
30b Evelina Road
Nunhead
London SE15 2DX
Tel: 0171 635 0718
(Dyes and auxiliaries)

**R.A. Smart (Holdings) Ltd.**
Clough Bank
Grimshaw Lane
Bollington
Macclesfield
Cheshire SK10 5NZ
Tel: 01625 576255
(Screen printing equipment and steamers)

**Scientific & Chemical Supplies Ltd.**
Unit 13, Chestom Road
Bilston
West Midlands WV14 0RO
Tel: 01902 402402
(Chemicals, safety equipment, measures)

**Sericol Group Ltd.**
Unit 2, Britannia Business Park
Brittania Road
Waltham Cross
Herts EN8 7TU
Tel: 01992 782600
(Screen printing supplies)

**Tiranti**
27 Warren Street
London W1P 5DG
Tel: 0171 636 8565
(Latex, carving tools, measuring bottles)

**Whaleys (Bradford) Ltd.**
Harris Court
Great Horton
Bradford
West Yorkshire BD7 4EQ
Tel: 01274 576718
(Specialist fabric supplier)

**Wolfin Textiles Ltd.**
64 Great Titchfield Street
London W1P 7AE
Tel: 0171 636 4949
(Basic cotton fabrics)

**Zeneca Colours (previously ICI Colours)**
P.O.Box 42
Blackley
Manchester M9 82S
Tel: 0161 740 1460
(Dyes and auxillaries)

## AUSTRALIA

**Art Stretchers Pty Ltd.**
28 Orr Street
Carlton
Victoria 3053
Tel: 03 663 8624
(Textile inks and printing equipment)

**Batik Oetoro**
203 Avoca Street
Randwick
NSW 2031
Tel: 02 398 6201
(Dyes, inks and auxiliaries)

**Calico House**
521 Chapel Street
South Yarra
Victoria 3141
Tel: 03 826 9957
*(Natural cotton fabrics for printing)*

**Commission Dyers Pty Ltd.**
7 Pinn Street
St Marys
South Australia 5042
Tel: 08 276 2844
*(Dyes and printing auxiliaries)*

**Creative Hot Shop**
96 Beaufort Street
Perth
West Australia 6000
Tel: 09 328 5437
*(Printing equipment, dyes,
inks, art and design material)*

**Days Screen Printing Supplies**
119 Camberwell Road
Hawthorn East
Victoria 3123
Tel: 03 813 1511
*(Screens, mesh, printing equipment
and inks, drafting film, opaque media
and photographic screen emulsion)*

**Edman Wilson Co. Pty Ltd.**
18–20 Whiting Street
P.O. Box 290
Artarmon
NSW 2064
Tel: 02 436 0371
*(Screens, mesh, printing equipment and inks)*

**Harlequin Inks**
45 Peel Street
South Brisbane
Queensland 4101
Tel: 07 846 5211
*(Screen stretching, inks and auxiliaries)*
*and*
52–62 Amcliffe Street
Amcliffe
NSW 2205
Tel: 02 597 6366
*(Textile inks and screen cleaning chemicals)*

**Kraft Kolour Pty Ltd.**
Factory 11
72 Chifley Drive
Preston
Victoria 3072
Tel: 03 484 4303
*Australia-wide mail order service.*
*(Dyes, inks and auxiliaries, screens,
mesh, film, opaque media and
photographic emulsion)*

**Marie France**
92 Currie Street
Adelaide

South Australia 5000
Tel: 08 231 4138
*Also in Victoria.*
*(Silk and dyes for handpainting)*

**Oxford Art Supplies Pty Ltd.**
221–223 Oxford Street
Darlinghurst
NSW 2010
Tel: 02 360 4066
*(Art materials, screen printing equipment,
textile inks and photographic emulsions)*

**The Paper Merchant**
316 Rokeby Road
Subiaco
West Australia
Tel: 09 381 6489
*(Textile inks, screen printing
equipment and wood blocks)*

**Toyo Screen**
28 Boyland Avenue
Coopers Plains
Queensland 4108
Tel: 07 274 1300
*Also in Victoria and South Australia.*
*(Photographic screen emulsion, cleaning
agents and screen strippers)*

**Walch's Art and Graphic Supplies**
130 Macquarie Street
Hobart
Tasmania 7000
Tel: 002 233 444
*(Art and design materials, textile
inks and screen printing equipment)*

**Zart Art**
4–41 Lexton Road
Box Hill
Victoria 3128
Tel: 03 890 1867
*(Art materials, screen printing equipment,
inks, dyes and printing auxiliaries)*

## NEW ZEALAND

**Art Stretchers Pty Ltd.**
Allied Colour NZ Ltd.
28 Poland Road
Glenfield
Auckland
Tel: 09 444 1755

**Tillia Dyes and Fabrics**
5/6 Polaris Place
East Tamaki
Auckland
*and*
P.O.Box 58536
Greenmount
Auckland
Tel: 09 273 9517
*Tollfree nationwide – 0800 884 554.*

**Universal Screen Supplies**
81 Orbell Street
Sydenham
Christchurch
Tel: 03 366 3877
*and*
44 Andromeda Crescent
Carlton
East Tamaki
Tel: 09 274 3831

## SOUTH AFRICA

**Chemag SA (PTY) Ltd.**
101 Misa Centre
15 Catherine Avenue
North Cliff
Johannesburg
Tel: 011 476 2206

**Chemosol**
22 Trump Street
Selby
Johannesburg
Tel: 011 493 0164

**Central Graphic Supplies (PTY) Ltd.**
60 Eloff Street
Village Deep
Johannesburg
Tel: 011 493 9360

**Jancke Combrinck Studio & Art School**
11 Olifant Street
Brackendowns
Alberton
Tel: 011 868 1408

**Pro Touch Dyes**
18A Rietfontein Street
Primrose
Tel: 011 873 6692

**Rolfes Ltd. (Head Office)**
12 Jet Park Road
Jet Park
Elandsfontein
Tel: 011 826 3511

**Savannah Chemicals (PTY) Ltd.**
Bedford Centre
Smith Street
Bedfordview
Tel: 011 616 1210

**SA Arts & Crafts CC**
78A High Road
Eastleigh
Edenvale
Tel: 011 452 0005

**Tri-Chem SA**
Bryan Park Shopping Centre
Grosvenor Street
Bryanston
Tel: 011 463 7045

# PRODUCT MANUFACTURERS

## DYES

| PRODUCT NAME | MANUFACTURER |
| --- | --- |

### ACID DYES

**Acid Levelling Dyes**

| | |
| --- | --- |
| Amacid | American Colour Chemical |
| Erio | Ciba-Geigy |
| Lissamine | Zeneca |
| Sandolan E | Clariant |
| Suprecen | Bayer |

**Acid Half-milling Dyes**

| | |
| --- | --- |
| Sandolan P | Clariant |
| Supramin GW | Bayer |

**Acid Milling**

| | |
| --- | --- |
| Coomassie | Zeneca |
| Eriosin | Ciba-Geigy |
| Polar | Ciba-Geigy |
| Sandolan N | Clariant |
| Supranol | Bayer |

**Acid Super Milling**

| | |
| --- | --- |
| Carbolan | Zeneca |
| Irganol | Ciba-Geigy |

**Metal Complex**

| | |
| --- | --- |
| Irgalan | Ciba-Geigy |
| Isolan K | Bayer |
| Lanasyn | Clariant |
| Lanasan | Clariant |
| Orlatan | BASF |

### AZOIC DYES

| | |
| --- | --- |
| Azanil | Hoechst |
| Variamin | Hoechst |
| Intramin | Hoechst |
| Azoic | Bayer |
| Naphthol | Bayer |
| Brentamine | Zeneca |
| Brentol | Zeneca |
| Ciba naphthol | Ciba-Geigy |
| Irga naphthol | Ciba-Geigy |

***Acid Dyes for Handpainting***

| | |
| --- | --- |
| Dupont colours (silk & wool) | Dupont |
| Jacquard | Rupert, Gibbon & Spider Inc. |

### BASIC DYES (MODIFIED)

| | |
| --- | --- |
| Astrazone | Bayer |
| Maxilon | Ciba-Geigy |
| Synacril | Zeneca |
| Sandocryl | Clariant |

***Basic Dyes for Handpainting***

| | |
| --- | --- |
| Orient Express | Pebeo |

### DIRECT DYES

| | |
| --- | --- |
| Diazol | Zeneca |
| Sirus | Bayer |
| Solar | Clariant |
| Solophenyl | Ciba-Geigy |

### DISPERSE DYES

| | |
| --- | --- |
| Dispersol | Zeneca |
| Foron | Clariant |
| Terasil | Ciba-Geigy |

***Disperse Dyes for Handpainting***

| | |
| --- | --- |
| Crayola Transfer Crayons | Crayola |
| Deka Iron-on Paints | Deka Textil-farben GmbH |

### MULTI-PURPOSE, DOMESTIC OR UNION DYES

| | |
| --- | --- |
| Dylon | Dylon International Ltd. |
| Deka L | Deka Textil-farben GmbH |
| Putman | Putman |

### PIGMENTS

| | |
| --- | --- |
| Acramin | Bayer |
| Bricoprint | BASF |
| Imperon | Hoechst |
| Monaprin | Zeneca |
| Printofix | Clariant |

***Pigments for Handpainting***

| | |
| --- | --- |
| Creatoutiss Non Fusant Paints | Creatoutiss |
| Deka Permanent Colour Paints | Deka Textil-farben GmbH |
| Javana Fabric Paint | C.Kreul GmbH |
| Setacolour opaque | Pebeo |

### REACTIVE DYES

| | |
| --- | --- |
| Cibacron | Ciba-Geigy |
| Drimarene | Clariant |
| Hostatan | Hoechst |
| Lanasol | Ciba-Geigy |
| Levafix | Bayer |
| Procilan E | Zeneca |
| Procion MX, H, HE, P | Zeneca |
| Remazol | Hoechst |
| Verafix | Bayer |

***Reactive Dyes for Handpainting***

| | |
| --- | --- |
| Deka Silk Painting Dye | Deka Textil-farben GmbH |
| Setacolour Transparent | Pebeo |

### SOLUBLE VAT DYES

| | |
| --- | --- |
| Anthrasol | Bayer |
| Indigosol | Clariant |
| Inkodye | Screen Process Manufacturing |

### VAT DYES

| | |
| --- | --- |
| Caladon | Zeneca |
| Cibanone | Ciba-Geigy |
| Dumndone | Zeneca |
| Indanthren | Bayer |
| Sandothrene | Clariant |

***Vat Dyes for Handpainting***

| | |
| --- | --- |
| Inko (solubilized) | Screen Process Manufacturing |

## TRANSFER PAPERS AND PASTES

| PRODUCT NAME | MANUFACTURER |
| --- | --- |
| Magic Touch | Magic Touch |
| Paracopy | Target Associates |
| Image Maker | Dylon |
| Metran | Sericol |

## GUMS

| PRODUCT NAME | MANUFACTURER |
| --- | --- |
| Celacol | Courtaulds |
| Guaranate | Societe Francaise des Colloides |
| Indalca PA/3-R | Cesalpinia |
| Manutex | Kelco |
| Solvitose C5 | Avebe |
| 301 Extra | Grünau |

## AUXILIARIES

| PRODUCT NAME | MANUFACTURER |
| --- | --- |
| BASF Reactive Resist Agent | BASF |
| Decrolin (C.I. reducing agent 6) | BASF |
| Finish BB | Breaks Brothers |
| Glyezin BC | BASF |
| Leukotrope OV | BASF |
| Luprintan PFD | BASF |
| Lycol BC | Clariant |
| Remazol salt FD | Hoechst |

## DYE CARRIERS, FIXERS AND ASSISTANTS

| PRODUCT NAME | MANUFACTURER |
| --- | --- |
| Albegal B | Ciba-Geigy |
| Fixagene | ICI Surfactants |
| Levafix | Bayer |
| Lyogen FN | Clariant |

## DETERGENTS

| PRODUCT NAME | MANUFACTURER |
| --- | --- |
| Alcopol GSO | Allied Colloids |
| Metapex | Hayes |
| Scourbrite (handwash) | Domestic |
| Stergene (handwash) | Domestic |
| Woolite (handwash) | Domestic |

WITHDRAWN

# INDEX

Page numbers in **bold** refer to the illustrations

# BIBLIOGRAPHY

*Hand Block Printing and Resist Dyeing* – Susan Bosence
David and Charles, London 1985 (reprinted 1991)

*Indigo Textiles: Technique and History* – Gösta Sandberg
A & C Black, London, 1989

*An Introduction to Textile Printing: A Practical Manual for use in Laboratories, Colleges and Schools of Art* – W. Clarke
Butterworth, 4th Edition 1974

*Natural Dyes, Fast or Fugitive* – Gill Dalby
Ashill Publications, 1992

*Shibori: The Inventive Art of Japanese Shaped Resist Dyeing* – Wada, Rice and Barton
Kodanski International

*The Technique of Batik* – Noel Dyrenforth
Batsford, London, 1988

*Textile Printing* – Edited by Leslie W.C. Miles
Society of Dyers and Colourists, 1994

*The Thames and Hudson Manual of Dyes and Fabrics* – Joyce Storey
Thames and Hudson Ltd., London, 1978 (reprinted 1992)

*The Thames and Hudson Manual of Textile Printing* – Joyce Storey
Thames and Hudson Ltd., London, 1974 (reprinted 1992)

# ACKNOWLEDGEMENTS

This book would not have been written without the support of the Royal College of Art. I wish to thank all the staff, students and graduates for the help and patience they extended to me over the eighteen months it took to write, photograph and pull this book together.

It was the questions from students in the field of Textile Design and Fashion and enquires from people interested in decorating fabrics that created a need for this book. I cannot thank every designer, graduate and student who has helped in the lending of fabrics to be photographed and who has given their time for free to allow photography to take place in their studios and workshops. Special thanks go to the Surrey Institute of Art and Design, Farnham campus (contributors include Nina Domansky, Emma Louise Fathers, Jackie Hayes, Melissa Pieterson, James Ward and Caroline Whelan); Belford Prints and the students who were successful in their bursary scheme; Pamela Cummins who, from a layman's point of view, had the patience to read, punctuate and query a large volume of unedited text; Martin Cummins and Dale Russell for their encouragement and support from the beginning when I felt that the task of producing this publication was too much to achieve on top of all the other commitments I had undertaken; Professor John Miles for both his contribution in writing the introduction and the support he has given me during this endeavour; and Peter Kinnear for his patience in taking photographs to illustrate the many processes involved in each technique described in this book.

p.8, above, Latin Stock/Ace Photo Library; p.8, below left, The Ancient Art & Architecture Collection; p.8, below right, Dugast/Panos Pictures; p.9, Pictor International; p.10, above right, Finlayson/Colorific; p.10, below left, Hulton Getty; pp.11–12, Courtesy of the Trustees of the Victoria & Albert Museum; p.13, below right, McCartney/ Colorific; p.13, above left, Singh/Colorific; p.47, Joël Degen; pp.79 & 181 FXP.